MARCO
POLO

MARCO POLO

Journey to the End of the Earth

Robin Brown

Foreword by Jeremy Catto

SUTTON PUBLISHING

First published in the United Kingdom in 2005 by
Sutton Publishing Limited · Phoenix Mill
Thrupp · Stroud · Gloucestershire · GL5 2BU

Paperback edition first published in 2007

British Library Cataloguing in Publication Data
A catalogue record for this book is available from the British
Library.

ISBN 978-0-7509-3421-3

Typeset in 10.5/13pt Goudy.
Typesetting and origination by
Sutton Publishing Limited.
Printed and bound in England by
J.H. Haynes & Co. Ltd, Sparkford.

Contents

Note on Illustrations

The colour images are from MS Bodleian 264, Part III. Marco Polo, *Li Livres du Graunt Caam*: miniatures (not whole pages), including the famous view of Venice, made in England by the illuminator Johannes and his school, *c.* 1400. Roll161C (38 frames). These illustrations are interesting for a number of reasons, not least the way that the manuscript was already being sanitised by its translators a century or so ofter its conception. The Grand Khan's court appears much more western than it was, soldiers battle in suits of armour western style, Asian religious figures are often grotesque and the Christians saintly. Only the drawing of the Polos leaving Venice in their little boat bears any relation to reality.

The black and white images are from the collection of Carolyn Horton.

Foreword

After two centuries of strenuous exploration and a landing on the moon, we are all familiar with incredible journeys. Even in the remote past, the capacity of humans to accomplish immense distances by land or sea never fails to surprise. In the century of Marco Polo the Mongols, nomads of the northern steppes, exemplified this in a dramatic though not unprecedented manner by sweeping through the settled lands to the south of them in large numbers, and demonstrating that they could reach from China at one end of the Eurasian landmass to Central Europe almost at the other in the course of a single season. In comparison the snail-like progress of the Polo family from Venice to the Mongol capital of Khan-Balik (Beijing), taking years to get there, seems much less impressive. But in another sense their journeys (for taken together there were several) can properly be described as incredible. For one thing, not everybody believed them. They were written up by an author of romances, Rustichello of Pisa, who claimed to have been told the story in a Genoese prison, and they circulated as an item in the well-known genre of the prose romance, like the entirely fictional *Travels* of Sir John Mandeville. Rustichello certainly gave the book its entrancing quality as a story, and it may owe some of the literally unbelievable details to his literary invention. Contemporaries treated it as a story, at best suspending their disbelief. Many later and more literal-minded critics have dismissed the whole of it as a literary forgery on much less substantial grounds, for instance for such negative reasons as the lack of any reference to the Great Wall of China; they have forgotten that in the Mongol Empire of Kublai Khan the Wall was a meaningless internal border and was probably ruinous for long stretches. The *Travels* of Marco Polo were not a guidebook to China, but a literary confection, an artful story. They can only be appreciated as a masterpiece of Rustichello's marvellous story-telling genius.

Nevertheless, there is overwhelming evidence from independent Chinese and other sources that (and this is the other, more popular sense in which the journeys are incredible) both the main structure of Marco Polo's travels and a surprising amount of the detail are authentic. The court of the Khan, the organisation of the Mongol Empire, the important role within it of indigenous Christian priests of the Nestorian church and many other features of the Central Asian world as he described them are confirmed by the reports of the Christian missionaries and envoys (Marco himself, in a sense, among them) sent by the Roman curia to the terrifying but hope-engendering new rulers of the East. He was neither the first nor the last of the series of travellers, from Giovanni di Piano Carpini between 1245 and 1248 to Guillaume du Pré in 1365, who sought to use the Mongol power to defend and enhance Latin Christendom. But the confirmatory evidence from China is even more impressive. Marco's description of the Imperial Palace at Khan-Balik is authenticated by the lineaments of the surviving Forbidden City. His account of the cities of Kinsai (Hangzhou) and Zaiton (perhaps Quanzhou) with its abundant commerce on the China Sea accord with contemporary Chinese descriptions. There is so much detail of trading and manufacturing activity, both in China and in Central Asia, that we must suspect Rustichello of using some lost *relazione* or commercial report written by Marco for the use of Venetian merchants – in which case the statement that he heard the story from Marco's own lips in a Genoese prison must be a literary device.

One of the notable features of the *Travels* is its account of exotic animals and plants unknown in Europe. Marco Polo was careful to record them both as sources of wealth and objects of trade, and as dangerous beasts of prey – the horses, falcons and sheep of Central Asia, the white horses of Mongolia, the Mongols' sables and other furs, the musk deer of Tibet, the snakes of Kara-jang, the featherless and furry hens of Kien-ning-fu, the rhinoceros (or 'unicorns') of Sumatra, the tarantulas of south India, the elephants and unique birds of Madagascar and many others. Previous accounts of the travels have not given them much attention; now, at last, Robin Brown, a noted naturalist and maker of nature films, has taken proper account of Marco's observations. This is a very welcome addition to the considerable but patchy literature devoted to the *Travels* of Marco Polo.

Jeremy Catto
Oriel College, Oxford

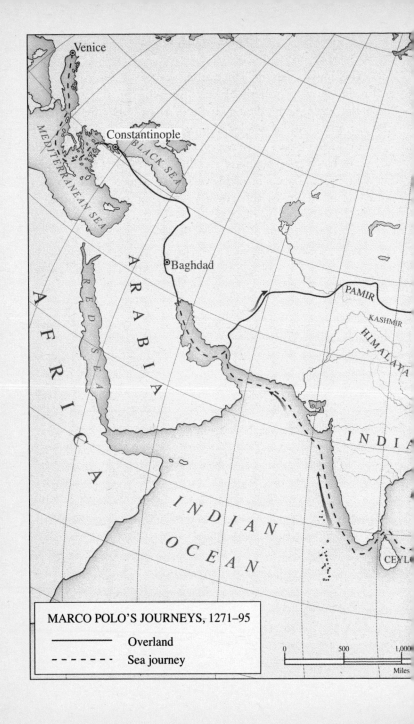

MARCO POLO'S JOURNEYS, 1271–95

——————	Overland
- - - - - -	Sea journey

0   500   1,000
Miles

Marco Millione

The truly incredible story of Marco Polo's journey to the ends of the earth, the book that earned him the title 'the Father of Geography', has for the last seven hundred years been bedevilled by doubts as to its authenticity. How much of his tale is a factual record, how much hearsay, and how much the best that Marco, bored with incarceration in a Genoan gaol, could recollect or indeed imagine? Did this intrepid Venetian actually trek across Asia Minor, explore the length and breadth of China as the roving ambassador of Kublai Khan, the most ruthless dictator in history? Did he really make his escape from almost certain death at the hands of Kublai's successors by directing the construction of fourteen huge wooden ships in which he delivered Kublai's relative, a beautiful princess, as bride to the Caliph of Baghdad after a voyage halfway round the world and so fraught with danger that it resulted in the death of 600 members of his crew?

Marco claims to have survived Mongol wars, hostile Tartar tribes, insurrections, blizzards, floods, the freezing cold of the world's highest mountain plateaux and the scorching heat of its most arid deserts. Indubitably it was he who wrote the very first descriptions of real 'dragons' (Indian crocodiles) and huge, striped 'lions' (tigers) that swam into rivers to prey on men in boats, horned, armoured 'monsters' (rhinoceros), armies of elephants with castles of archers on their backs, of a bird with feathers nine feet long (the great auk); of the salamander; and of cloth that would not burn (asbestos) and black rocks that burned like wood

1

(coal). For good measure he claimed that the currency used in this mysterious Orient – where the cities were larger than any in the West and a rich trade was to be had in glorious silks, cloth of gold, pearls, silver, gold, Arabian horses, ceramics, spices and exotic woods – was paper! And in passing he introduced his native Italians to ice cream (frozen creams) and, yes, pasta (noodles) from his observations of Chinese cuisine.

Such wonders are supported by a wealth of minor detail: regional histories, descriptions of cities, inhabitants, races, languages and government, people's different lifestyles, diets, styles of dress, marriage customs, rituals and religions. There are accounts of trading practices, crafts, manufactured products, plants, animals, minerals and terrain. And all this from a teenager who went to China aged seventeen!

Understandably for a red-blooded young Italian, he waxes lyrical about the beautiful Arabian and oriental girls, especially those who are obliged to sleep with travellers before they can expect to marry!

It is Marco Polo who furnishes Samuel Taylor Coleridge's fevered brain with the images that produced the immortal lines 'in Xanadu did Kublai Khan / A stately pleasure-dome decree . . .', and it is Marco who supplies the erotic detail about what went on in such domes and of the damsels, practised in the art of 'dalliance and seduction', ensconced in love-pavilions admin-istering what we now call recreational drugs to an early cult of Middle Eastern suicide-bombers.

His adventures read like a medieval soap opera and indeed they turn out to have been written, or at least ghosted, by a writer of them, the romance-writer Rustichello of Pisa, who shared Marco's prison. Small wonder that initially these seemingly tall tales were greeted with open incredulity and derision. Who was there to confirm one word of it? No one! And that was to hold true for almost five hundred years. Ethnocentric Europeans simply refused to entertain the notion that a civilisation larger and more advanced than their own existed in the East. Europe was undoubtedly the centre of civilisation, as everyone knew. Europeans had visited the fringes of the Orient and ventured into North Africa, and the people they had seen were observably backward and primitive. Marco Polo's accounts of a massive empire employing advanced financial systems, such as the use of paper currency, were staunchly and universally rejected as romantic fiction.

He became known by the derisory title 'Marco Millione' ('Marco of the Millions'), the teller of a million tall tales. After his death he was lampooned at Venetian carnivals by a comic figure dressed as a ruffian clown whose act consisted of outlandish and exaggerated gestures and expressions.

Sadly this reputation prevailed throughout his lifetime. Indeed, right up until the twenty-first century, to tell 'a Marco Polo' was to be guilty of exaggeration verging on the untrue. The priest who attended Marco Polo on his deathbed in 1324 felt impelled to ask him whether he wished to recant any of his story. Marco replied curtly: 'I have not written down the half of the things I saw.'

Now, the passage of time and the travels, mostly in the twentieth century, of others have largely vindicated Marco Polo. His route map is somewhat eccentric and he is not always very objective about hearsay information (if it is spicy he, or Rustichello, prefers to keep it that way), but he usually warns the reader when he is quoting questionable sources. It should also be remembered that the account was written down from memory supported (it is thought) by notes brought from Venice to his prison cell.

Admittedly, contemporary doubters of Marco Polo have emerged in recent times, their work based largely on what are seen as significant omissions from his description of China, in particular his failure to describe the Great Wall or to note that Chinese women bound their feet. Indeed, a case for his never having visited China has been built on his missing structures as large (or feet as small) as this.

But again Marco Polo's account has won through. The academic consensus is that the Great Wall of China did not reach its current all-embracing form until the Ming dynasty, in about 1500. If the story had mentioned the wall it would certainly be fictional.

Marco Polo is now confirmed as the first traveller to describe a journey across the entire continent of Asia and to name the countries and provinces in the proper consecutive order. A growing awareness that the man could be relied upon also encouraged further exploration of the world: a well-thumbed copy of Marco Polo's book was taken by Christopher Columbus on his voyages to the New World.

Even his erotic 'gossip' has been shown to have an essential veracity, a good example of which is the story of the 'Old Man of the Mountains'. Admitting that the story is hearsay and probably ancient history he nonetheless includes it, and with all the titillating detail he can bring to it.

The Old Man of the Mountains lived in a beautiful mountain between two lofty peaks and there built a luxurious garden boasting every fragrant shrub and delicious fruit from far afield. Streams (conduits) flowed with milk, honey and wine, and damsels skilled in the arts of singing, the playing of musical instruments and love (to which Marco Polo refers delicately) lived in a series of luxurious pavilions; the whole guarded by an impenetrable fortress through which the only access was via a secret tunnel.

At first glance this has all the hallmarks of a licentious fairy story, good tabloid stuff, at which Rustichello, remember, was an expert.

The Old Man of the Mountains made a selection from among the young men of the mountains who were renowned for their daring and bravery and were well versed in the martial arts. Every day he described to these young acolytes the 'Paradise' which the Prophet Mohammed had promised the Faithful and eventually he revealed to them that he too possessed the key to Paradise. They were then drugged with opium and hashish, carried unconscious through the secret tunnel and handed over to the obliging damsels in whose company they spent four or five days enjoying the singing, playing, delicate food, wines or milk and honey, and, says Marco Polo, 'exquisite caresses'.

Drugged back into unconsciousness at the end of this experience they were carried out with happy smiles on their faces and awoke to a promise from the Old Man of the Mountains that they could return any time to Paradise if they swore fealty to him. Moreover, this would almost certainly be their fate as he was recruiting them to a cult of political assassins who would wreak suicidal mayhem across the Levant. Marco Polo records: 'They had absolutely no regard for their own lives in the execution of their master's will and their tyranny became the subject of dread in all the surrounding countries.'

Many of Marco Polo's debunkers say this type of reporting is driven either by Rustichello's imagination or the licentious thoughts of a young man in his early twenties. His book is certainly illuminated by his obvious attraction to Oriental women; for instance, he describes the Northern Persians as 'a handsome race especially the women, who, in my opinion, are the most beautiful in the world'. Of a region further east, he says that its women 'are in truth, very handsome, very sensual'. And everywhere there is a fascination for sexual mores, as in his description of the women who are not allowed to marry if they are virgins and whose parents get round this problem by leaving them beside busy roads for the enjoyment of travellers.

But contemporary research, including a very descriptive work by the war correspondent and travel-writer Martha Gellhorn, has confirmed the truth of Marco Polo's seemingly fantastical tale.

The Old Man of the Mountains was in fact Alo-eddin (Aladin?), a dissident Sunni rebel of the early Muslim faith who, after falling out with the Caliph of Cairo, fled east where, with his fanatical followers, he captured the mountain fortress of Alamut and established a sect which must surely be regarded as the prototype of today's suicide squads. Hassan lived at Alamut for four decades, reportedly never leaving the place other than occasionally to walk the battlements, and came to be known as Sheik-al-Jabal, the 'Old Man of the Mountains'. He did indeed raise an elite corps of assassins, in fact the word owes its origins to the 'hassashin', as these killers were said to be 'crazed' by hashish when they carried out their murders. They almost invariably gave their own lives in these attacks (mostly carried out for maximum terror effect, in public view and in broad daylight) in the belief that they would go directly to Paradise.

Nor was the sect just a passing phenomenon. The Old Man of the Mountains and his successors held sway for more than two centuries over vast areas of the Middle East and Asia Minor, from Kurdistan to Egypt, where they eventually kept formal embassies and occupied dozens of castles. Elements of the sect still exist today (thoroughly peacefully) as part of the Aga Khan's Sunni Muslim following.

Marco travels through mountains one of which, he claims, has Noah's Ark on its summit. As he was in the location of Mount Ararat this represents the first actual identification of the site. He also describes a substance which has all the characteristics of crude oil and, given that today this region is a major oil producer, here we have another first. In what is now modern Iran he describes the tomb of the Three Wise Men and recounts the 'Christmas' tales associated with them.

He also gives the first potted history of the legendary Prester John credited at this time by the West with ruling over a 'lost faith' of Christians (Nestorians) deep inside Asia who, if only they could be contacted, might mount an attack on Islam's flank to assist the Crusaders. Marco admits, however, that his information on Prester John is hearsay and historically questionable. Nowadays the consensus is that Prester John was probably a powerful Tartar prince, a khan in his own right, but the possibility of a Christian kingdom lost in the soft underbelly of Asia obviously fascinated Marco Polo and he refers to Prester John (calling him George in one reference) on several occasions.

Similarly, serious doubts as to Marco's veracity were aroused by the many 'magical' objects which Marco Polo saw and described. His reports of black rocks that burned and a mineral wool that when roasted in fire 'echoed the Salamander' in becoming fire resistant were greeted with disdain by his original readership. Of course, we now know that he was describing coal and asbestos, both then unknown in Europe.

When he lectured on how he had climbed to the 'Roof of the World' and described the wonder of water being slow to boil, people shouted 'Marco Millione' at him. Hundreds of years later, in the high latitudes of Afghanistan, more or less where Marco said it was, the Pamir Plateau was discovered and named, and we all know now that a lack of oxygen makes it difficult for climbers to boil their tea there. Indeed, parts of the 'Roof of the World' have not been explored to this day. It is also an exceptionally tough climb even for those dressed in the latest weatherproofs, using modern mountaineering equipment and assisted by oxygen cylinders.

Marco's story also seems particularly 'incredible' when you realise that he is describing a trek made without maps 700 years ago. The fact that he survived at all is little short of miraculous. Literally nothing in the way of extreme travel equipment existed then, indeed the very concept of travel on the scale undertaken by Marco Polo did not exist. He walked or rode through half a dozen wars, through lands where the plague, leprosy, typhoid, smallpox and malaria (to mention but a few) were endemic. He climbed in areas where there would have been an ever-present danger of falling, frostbite and other accidents, all of which would almost certainly have proved fatal in his time. He spent days, nay weeks, in awful, waterless deserts like the Gobi and the Lot. In virtually all of the countries he traversed a traveller positively expected to be attacked, robbed and murdered and, given his colour, hair type and language, he must have appeared frighteningly alien to all he met.

And yet he survived all this for twenty-five years in a place and in an age when there was only the most primitive of surgery, medicine based on superstition, the odd efficacious plant, and certainly no hospitals. There were times when he was obviously seriously ill – he describes having to go up into the mountains for almost a year to recover his health on his way out to Kublai's court in China. But these difficulties are always marginalised and it is clear that essentially he was inspired by and loved every minute of his incredible journey.

I am not at all surprised that nobody believed him. He was a traveller from time, someone who had visited the future and, incredibly, come back to tell the tale.

Admittedly, Marco and his family were almost the first Westerners to exploit a very narrow window of opportunity to go East. Europe was awakening from the Dark Ages. Western trade promoted by the Crusades was rapidly expanding. In China an ancient insular civilisation had succumbed to the Tartars whose ruthless chief, Kublai Khan, was in the process of building one of the largest empires ever to exist. When that empire crumbled the doors to China swung closed again, barring Western entrepreneurs like the Polos for centuries to come.

As a trading nation, Venice had benefited enormously from the construction of ships for the Crusades, even agreeing to fund one such endeavour as a smokescreen for the invasion and conquest of Constantinople. Its own empire was not insubstantial, boasting possessions as far away as the Greek mainland.

But up until this time (1250) only fables existed of the faraway land of China, mostly legends dating from the time of the great Greek incursions of Alexander the Great. Between Europe and China stood a singularly unfriendly Muslim Middle East which regarded all Europeans as aggressive infidels practising a heretical religion and bent on the conquest of their most holy sites. And in part they were right. For hundreds of years the holy rule of Allah had been to keep out these apostates at all costs. A virtually identical view existed on the European side.

While a meagre exchange of trade was sustained by a clan of itinerant merchants, this did not entail an exchange of cultures and ideas, or even of much basic information. There had always been a 'Silk Road' between Europe and Eastern Asia since the time of the Roman Empire but little accurate information had travelled down it. Europeans thought, for example, that silk was a vegetable product made from a bark, rather than from the cocoons of silkworms.

While Europe was coordinating its financial muscle, and trading states like Venice and Genoa were casting speculative eyes eastwards, China, largely unknown to the West, was beginning to collapse. The culture was decaying of old age and the 'barbarians' from the north, as the Tartars were known, had started to make serious inroads into the Chinese lands.

This unlikely dominance of the most advanced and sophisticated race on earth by a rabble of mounted raiders from the northern steppes had been initiated about fifty years earlier by Genghis Khan who was just thirteen when he inherited the chiefdom of a small Mongolian tribe. Genghis lived to see the Mongol 'horde' dominate more land than any other race on earth and drive the Europeans back to the banks of the Dnieper.

In 1206 Genghis (or Chinghiz) had been elected leader of the Mongols by a great confederacy of these nomad people, gathered at Karakoran, a plain they regarded as holy, and there, as Marco Polo avows, they made up their minds to conquer the whole world.

Similar forces were rallying in the West. A year before the accession of Genghis, the gateway to the East, Constantinople, had been invaded and conquered by mercenaries led by Baldwin of Flanders, with the direct and moral support of the Pope in Rome and the material support of the merchants of Venice. They were rewarded by the lion's share of the trade in the Levant, which Marco Polo describes as stretching from eastern Persia to the Mediterranean.

Genghis Khan spent the next twenty-seven years of his life uniting the Mongol tribes, by a combination of savage retribution and shrewd diplomacy. That achieved, he turned his attention to a Tartar invasion of northern China, orchestrated under three huge armies commanded by three of his sons and four of his brothers. He himself commanded the largest army, assisted by his youngest son, Tule, father of Kublai Khan, who would become Marco Polo's mentor and master.

All three armies were successful and seemingly would have been content to rest in the conquered north had it not been for an unfortunate incident involving the Shah (or Khan) of Persia.

Genghis sent word to Persia offering, according to Marco Polo, 'Greetings. I know thy power and the vast extent of thy empire; I regard thee as my most cherished son. Thou must know that for my part I have conquered China and all the Turkish nations north of it. Thou knowest that my country is a hall of warriors, a mine of silver, and I have no need of other lands. I take it that we have an equal interest in encouraging trade between out subjects.'

This offer appeared to have been received favourably, but the first Mongol traders were put to death and when, through an ambassador, Genghis demanded the surrender of the governor responsible, the ambassador was summarily beheaded and the rest of the delegation returned to Genghis, ignobly shaved of their beards.

The war that followed earned Genghis Khan a permanent place in history as a barbaric slaughterer; it was a reputation not undeserved. He marched his armies across the continent and over the mountains of Tibet. Tashkent surrendered, Bokhara fell and Shah Mohammed of Persia was harried from two sides by separate Mongol forces. Cities were sacked and burned and their inhabitants slaughtered. After a siege of six months, the city of Herat was taken by a Mongol army said to be eighty thousand strong. The entire population of more than 1.5 million men, women and children was massacred.

Meanwhile the flying columns harrying the Shah were sweeping on into Europe, driving the Turkish resistance before them. In 1222 the Mongols advanced into Georgia and, after yet another set of envoys had been put to death by the Russians, Genghis Khan swung his troops into Greater Bulgaria in an orgy of slaughter, rape and pillage which was to render his name synonymous with unbridled savagery for all time. Europe was only saved from further Mongol incursion by the death of Genghis Khan and of his son, who died suddenly when the Mongol armies were already occupying Hungary, Poland and Kiev and were encamped on the east bank of the Dnieper.

It was into the very heart of this mighty Tartar advance that Marco Polo, his father Nicolo, and his uncle, Maffeo, opportunistic merchant adventurers from Venice, marched when Marco was just seventeen.

In 1255 they had set out for Constantinople to set up a trading post dealing in goods from the Orient, the earlier barriers to trade between Europe and Asia having been broken down by Mongolian expansion. Nicolo left behind his wife, fully expecting to return home within a year or so. But on one of their trading expeditions they found their way home blocked by a war for the Caucasus region between two of Genghis Khan's grandsons. They were obliged to deviate dramatically to the east, ending up in Bokhara, a city to the north of Afghanistan and one then as now famed for its carpets. There they met an ambassador of Kublai Khan who inferred that the only way they could get home was to obtain a firman from the Grand Khan himself, and with this in mind they decided to accompany Kublai Khan's ambassador to the court in China. Circumstances had caused them unwittingly to travel further east than any traders before them.

It was also the first time Kublai Khan came into extended contact with sophisticated Westerners; he had just begun to settle into the rule of a vast kingdom with all the problems that such a task entailed. Moreover, the Polo brothers were astonished to discover that he did not act like the mass murderer of European legend, but instead apparently wanted his people to convert to Christianity.

Kublai gave the two Venetians an epistle to the Pope requesting that he send him a hundred 'learned men', which the Polos took to mean priests (historians have suggested that what Kublai really wanted was more foreign advisers to help him administer his disparate kingdom). One cannot escape the thought that the world would have been a very different place had the Polos been able to deliver this religious manpower.

To confirm his Christian leanings, Kublai Khan also asked the Polos to bring him some of the holy oil from the lamp that was kept burning over the Holy Sepulchre in Jerusalem. Kublai Khan had a taste for such curios: later he would send to India for a beggar's bowl said to have belonged to Buddha and to Madagascar for feathers of the great auk.

The Polos did other favours for the Grand Khan and convinced him of the value of foreign advisers. His uncles, Marco claims, later helped bring the war in southern China to a close by showing Kublai Khan's generals how to make siege engines and were rewarded with a golden tablet from the Grand Khan guaranteeing their safe passage out of China. This is generally regarded as a rather dubious claim.

Their return journey took four years. Overcoming huge risks at the hands of the various belligerent Tartar tribes and the usual problems with extremes of climate they finally reached the Venetian colony at Acre, where the papal legate informed them that Pope Clement IV had died and that no one had yet been elected to replace him. The brothers decided it was time they went home, where Nicolo discovered that his wife had died but that he was the father of a son, Marco, now aged fifteen.

The papal election hit an impasse and many months passed. The brothers, fearful that their absence might fatally compromise the unique trading links they had managed to forge with the Grand Khan, decided to proceed with their commission as best they could. With Marco, they travelled to Jerusalem and picked up the holy oil. The Papal Legate, Tebaldo, would only commit himself to two priests, but when the Polos ran into a Tartar rebellion in the eastern Mediterranean these friars got cold feet and went home – a momentous decision if you consider the impact even a hundred Catholic priests might have had on Kublai's world.

Nicolo, Maffeo and the young Marco were struggling on alone when they were called back. News reached them that Tebaldo had been elected Pope, taking the name Gregory X, and that if they could return to Laius, in Southern Albania, they would find letters waiting for them which had been sent by fast ship from the new Pope to be taken to Kublai Khan. They picked up the letters, they were in possession of the holy oil and, in a sense, the young Marco Polo, a devout Catholic in a time of fervour for the Crusades, replaced the hundred learned priests!

Ahead of them stretched another four years of gruelling travel. After almost a year the intrepid trio found themselves in the Persian Gulf where they had planned to board a local ship to sail from Hormuz to China. Expert ship-builders themselves, they were appalled by the apparently flimsy construction of these craft. Marco notes with contempt how the ships 'were sewn together', detail which has added the stamp of authenticity to his report. We now know that Arabian and Indian dhows have been constructed in this way since time immemorial, but the Polos were so concerned they elected to take on the even more hazardous overland journey.

Marco contracted a fever (probably malaria) from which he nearly died; he was saved, he says, by 'the magical quality' of the high air of the mountains of Afghanistan. (The late, great explorer, Wilfred Thesiger, with whom I made a documentary film, lived among the Marsh Arabs of lower Iraq for seven years, and routinely escaped the clouds of mosquitoes which are the plague of the marshes in summer by going climbing in these same mountains.)

Marco convalesced for a year before tackling the Pamir Plateau between Afghanistan and Tibet, in itself an incredible achievement and one of which a modern climber boasting a supply of oxygen and all the modern climbing gear would be proud. Known now as 'The Roof of the World' as a result of Marco's enthusiastic description, its height inadvertently revealed with Marco's observation that water took longer to boil.

The Polos stayed to trade among the Tibetan Buddhists in Campichu for about a year, moved into Turkistan, crossing the then unexplored and terrifying Gobi Desert on foot until finally they reached an unknown eastern coast which turned out to be that of China. They had crossed virtually the whole of Asia and had started to despair of ever finding Kublai Khan and his court – when the court came to them!

Cautious and cunning as ever, Kublai had been watching their progress for a long time from afar.

When the Polos' by now decrepit expedition was still forty days' march from his capital, Kublai Khan sent escorts to accompany them in style to the city of Shangtu about 180 miles west of Peking. It was 1275 and Marco was now a man of twenty-one years. He was adept in the Tartar languages thanks to lessons from his father and his uncle, and obviously he knew the country well.

The young Marco Polo immediately revealed himself as an observant raconteur with an interest in the unusual and the erotic and, as time went by, it seems that gift for telling tales was exactly what Kublai wanted (no derisory Marco Millione here). For their part Kublai's own high officials, kow-towing constantly as tradition dictated, and terrified of the Khan's savage rages which could lead to lethal injunctions, preferred to confine themselves to carefully phrased and censored diplomatic reports.

Kublai Khan seems to have spotted Marco's latent talents and taken the young man under his wing. While Nicolo and Maffeo were left in peace to trade (and are hardly mentioned in Marco Polo's book hereafter) Marco was groomed, as he describes it, as the Grand Khan's roving ambassador. Twenty-seven years now pass, years of extraordinary travel, adventure, political intrigue and military campaigns as Marco Polo matures into the role of 'ambassador at large' to his lord and master Kublai Khan.

These stories are told in three 'Books' that cover the initial journey out to China and the Kublai Khan's very mobile court, Marco's travels and adventures in the employ of the Great Khan, and finally the trials and tribulations of getting home. There are a confusion of Introductions and Prologues, sometimes called the Invocation.

Over the years the story has appeared under various titles such as *The Travels of Marco Polo*, *A Description of the World*, *Della Navigazioni e Viaggi*. It is generally agreed that the lost original was written in bad French. The book is still one of the great works of travel, arguably the greatest because of its vast range. Even now after the lapse of seven centuries it remains the authority for certain parts of Central Asia and of the vast Chinese Empire.

Dates remain slightly vague as we do not know Marco Polo's exact birth date. His father Nicolo had gone, in 1260, with his brother, Maffeo, on an initial pioneering journey trading in the lands of the Tartars. The generally accepted date for Marco's birth is 1254 with the brothers returning to Venice with a commission from Kublai in 1269 when Marco was about fifteen. They set out to return to the Great Khan's court in 1271 when Marco was probably in his seventeenth year, and the three of them remained in Kublai's court for a further seventeen or so years, returning to Venice in 1295. The journeys back and forth themselves took years. Marco, now a rich Venice merchant in his early forties, becomes embroiled in a war with Genoa, which the Venetians lost, and our hero ends up in jail where, sometime in the next eighteen months, with Rustichello, he writes a book which few believe. Indeed, how little Marco was credited may be judged from the fact that the map of Asia was not modified by his discoveries until fifty years after his death in 1324.

Manuscript Versions and Recensions

Let us return to Marco in prison, possibly stuck there for life. The sea battle he took part in was supposed to have been conclusive, with the richest of the Venetian merchants pooling their funds to build a fleet of sixty fighting craft each rowed by dozens of oarsmen and designed to smash and crush the upstart Genoans.

Genoa had approximately the same number of ships, and the Genoans won. Moreover, they won convincingly, dragging all the Venetian ships back into harbour with their masts and pennants trailing in the water as a mark of disrespect. The humiliated commander of the Venetian fleet was so cast down that he dashed his head on a stone of the jetty and killed himself. All the 'Gentlemen Captains' of the Venetian fleet, most of them rich merchants, were gaoled, not too uncomfortably, and within the year most of them had returned home after the payment of substantial ransoms.

Not so Marco Polo. No one knows whether the Genoans wanted to keep him or whether his family failed to put up the money. He was in the second year of his confinement when he met Rustichello, a minor writer of romantic fiction. It is not known whether they fortuitously ended up in the same cell together or whether Marco Polo, bored and thinking he might fill his time by setting down the story of his travels, sent for Rustichello.

Crucially, whether or not Marco Polo could call on notes has never been satisfactorily established. Ramusio, the first editor of a printed version of Marco Polo's travels, claims that Marco Polo did send to Venice for his notebook and papers, but we have no confirmation of them ever arriving in Genoa.

Most introductions to a Marco Polo manuscript make a point of mentioning that he always made detailed notes to satisfy the Grand Khan's love of minutiae and gossip. But this observation appears to have been emphasised later when the authenticity of the account was under heavy attack. I believe that Marco Polo did in fact have access to his notes; there is simply too much detail for the author to have remembered it all more than two years after his return to Venice.

Giovanni Battista Ramusio's edition (c. 1553) is believed to be one of the earliest printed editions of a Marco Polo translation, if not the earliest. In it he describes how Marco languished in his prison in Genoa. Venice was actually at war with Genoa and the rich Polo family was called upon to equip a fighting galley. Marco sailed as the 'merchant captain' of this ship as part of an armada of some sixty vessels commanded by the fighting cleric Andrea Dandolo and fought in the battle of Curzola on 6 September 1298, which proved a diaster for Venice. Marco was carried as a prisoner to Genoa and accounts vary as to how long he was interred and why he was not exchanged for ransom money. Be it one year or three, captivity was wearisome and he talked a lot, finally attracting the attention of one Rustichello of Pisa, a romance writer who quickly 'saw a book' in Marco's ramblings.

Some accounts have Rustichello as a fellow-prisoner in the Genoan gaol, but I consider it more likely that Rustichello was called in to ghost-write Marco's book. The luck involved in finding a famous romance writer languishing in the same prison stretches credibility (even though by now credibility had already begun to stretch in several directions). The book which eventually came to be written is a product of Marco's recollections of journeys undertaken anything from five to thirty years previously, and of Rustichello's creative writing abilities, of which there is considerable evidence. Not for nothing was Marco later to be called 'Marco Millione' for what the public mostly regarded as innumerable tall stories. That said, his manuscript has in the main stood up remarkably well to seven hundred years of intense scholarly nit-picking, indeed as China has been explored new findings and details have, if anything, tended to corroborate his story.

As for his co-author, we learn that Rustichello was not an obscure Pisan gaolbird but a fairly eminent writer of his day who had enjoyed the patronage of Edward the Confessor and accompanied him on a Crusade to Palestine where he may even have met the Polos. He wrote a romanticised history of Arthur of Round Table fame, another on the battle of Troy and a biography of Alexander the Great, paying as much attention to the romance as to the history.

Polian scholars, in particular the *éminence grise*, Italian Professor L.F. Benedetto, have demonstrated that Marco's invocation in his introduction to 'Emperors and Kings, Dukes and Marquises' to read the book is taken verbatim from Rustichello's Arthurian romance. But this is no more than window-dressing. There was just one man and one alone who, in 1298, had been where no European had ever been before – and that man was Marco Polo.

The poet John Masefield, who was also a Polian scholar and wrote the fine introduction to the little 1908 Everyman edition entitled prosaically *Travels: Marco Polo*, speaks of Marco's achievements as follows:

When Marco Polo went to the East, the whole of Central Asia, so full of splendour and magnificence, so noisy with nations and kings, was like a dream in men's minds. Marco Polo saw her in all her wonder, more fully than any man has seen her since. His picture of the East is the picture which we all make in our minds when we repeat to ourselves those two strange words 'the East' and give ourselves up to the image which that symbol evokes. It makes us proud and reverent of the poetic gift to reflect that this king (Kublai), 'the lord of lords', ruler of so many cities, so many gardens, so many fishpools, would be but a name, an image covered by the sands, had he not welcomed two dusty travellers, who came to him one morning from out of the unknown.

With the arrival of the printing press we would do better to think of Marco Polo's story as a wondrous exotic plant, changing colour, changing shape, growing new leaves, petals, twigs and branches; suffering light and heavy pruning and in some cases, bonsai.

The original manuscript is gone, lost irrevocably. There is no trace of the original handwritten document which Rustichello penned in rough French in their prison cell. And I would argue that the plant was growing even then. Can you not hear Rustichello, with his leanings towards romantic fiction, suggesting that the story would read better if this point was emphasised or that made a little more weighty? Then he must have taken it out of the prison, this great jumble of dictation, and edited it, probably in a great hurry and without much consultation with the author. The book was apparently ready in three months.

From the very beginning the seeds of change were planted – and how they have flourished!

In 1928 Professor Benedetto published a long and learned quantification, which included a validating count, of the various Marco Polo translations. An earlier count had been attempted by the famous English scholar Henry Yule, who listed a startling seventy-eight different versions. But the Benedetto count (which the author rather ironically published under the title *Marco Polo: Il Millione*) took the total up to 138. Of these 138 translations (the figure is certainly higher now) no two are the same. In addition there are literally hundreds of associated works, explaining, exploring, supporting and debunking that original manuscript. A manuscript, remember, which no longer exists.

Plotting Polo has become a science (and sometimes a black art) in itself and it is arguable whether these acres of scholarly examination have helped the true story emerge. The wheat of this incredible tale has become blurred in a veritable cloud of academic chaff. With the best of good intentions, everyone who has ever picked up a Marco Polo manuscript has found reason to change it, or changed it without reason simply as a result of the application of nuances of common usage of the time. And this process has been happening in at least five major languages which in turn were translated into other languages and so on, and on. The very ancient (Alexandrian) Greeks were reported to have had a method for accurately copying handwritten manuscripts such as the early Christian writings known as the Kabra Negast. They would count the words of the original manuscript and find the middle word. Then they did the same with the copy and considered its middle word. If this word differed from the middle word of the original manuscript, you sharpened a new feather and started again from the beginning!

This level of precision has rarely, if ever, been applied to a Marco Polo manuscript other than perhaps with the very early ones of 700 years ago. And added to all the above is the effect of the phenomenon known as 'Chinese whispers'. Statistically it has been shown that it is all but impossible to pass a whispered message accurately down a line of ten people. Taking that into account, it is nothing short of a miracle that after seven centuries of academic 'whispering' the Marco Polo texts we possess, while individually different (sometimes markedly different: the Ramusio, for example, is a third longer than the earliest translations), are all recognisable as the same work. Looked at positively we now have a rich kaleidoscope of interpretations each displaying its time's seminal influences, mores, styles, accents and innuendos, yet all still sharing a common thread.

But there is no unravelling this cat's cradle. The original reference work has vanished into the maw of time along with the knowledge of who made the first translation. Scholars have long since given up the search for this Holy Grail, consoling themselves with a very rough approximation of which early translation led to another.

But what of the essential story? Thankfully, the driving force of a very dramatic narrative has kept that essentially pristine. So far as I am aware, every version has Marco fighting his way through the desert of 'Lop' which takes thirty days to cross at its narrowest point and you should, too, be prepared to eat your pack animals and resist the blandishments of the 'evil spirits . . . which amuse travellers to their destruction with the most extraordinary illusions'. Depending on which text you are reading, that may, for example, come out as: 'Euill fpirites, that make thefe foundes, amd alfo do call diuerfe of the trauellers by their names, and make them leave their company, fo that youfhall paffe this defert with great daunger' (John Frampton, 1597). Or, some four hundred years later: 'Spirits talking in such a way that they seem to be his companions . . . often these voices make him stray from his path so that he never finds it again' (Ronald Latham, 1958).

Today scholars debate not so much the genesis of the text as the academic issues it raises, such as where Lop really was. With the help of modern explorers, they have long since decided it was the notorious Gobi; crossing it is every bit as hazardous today as it was in Marco Polo's time, although global positioning satellites have largely exorcised the evil spirits.

A word in passing about the Frampton translation which I have referred to above and which has been one of my prime references. I decided early on that Marco Polo's story was essentially a gutsy travelogue enlivened by the imagination of a very young man with all that entails. A lot of this flavour – juice, if you like – would have fallen foul of the religious probity of the early translators, who were all monks. But Frampton was an Elizabethan who suffered from no such inhibitions. In addition his translation, first published in the age of Shakespeare and the first in English, was taken from the Santaella, a manuscript of the Venetian recension or family and revealed by subsequent researchers such as Professor Benedetto to be one of the most important of the Polian books.

Overall there are five loose groups, called recensions, into which academia has gathered the classic translations of Marco Polo. They are essentially language groupings created by scholars, primarily Professor Benedetto, to bring some order to the chaos of the various manuscripts and their provenances.

The first recension, the Geographic Text, consists of just one volume – a French handwritten manuscript first published in 1824 by the French Geographical Society. It is extremely old, thought to come from the library of the French kings at Blois, and is widely regarded by the experts as the closest to the original that we have. As a result the experts, again led by Professor Benedetto, have subjected the manuscript to particularly close scrutiny to see if there are any clues to its age and authenticity. Specifically, he compared the other writing of Rustichello to the French manuscript. Some of Rustichello's other writings, romances based on French Arthurian legends, have survived. Since Benedetto's painstaking research revealed practically identical phrases and idioms in the two works, he concluded that the same care and diligence that produced the romances had also produced the Geographic Text. And he makes an even more dramatic claim, that Rustichello did not copy down at Marco Polo's dictation but produced the Geographic Text (or maybe a version, of which that manuscript is a descendant) after a prolonged and detailed study of all the notes that Marco Polo supplied to him. Professor Benedeto argued:

> *Compito espresso de Rustichello dev' essere stato quello di stendere in una lingua letteraria acceptabile quelle note che Marco, vissuto cosi' a lungo in oriente, non si sensitive di formulare con esattezza in nessuna parlata occidentale. Abbiamo intravisto abbastanza com' egli, assovendo un tal compito, si rimasto fedele allo stile ed alla visuale dei romanzi d'avventura. Ma non possiamo dire nulla di piu.*

Or, in other words, Marco Polo was not a trained writer and after being so long away in the East he did not trust his ability to tell his story in a style acceptable to Western readers. He had been provided with a professional storyteller: it made sense to supply Rustichello with all the information and leave him to write up the story.

But this hypothesis widened rather than narrowed the academic debate. Other scholars (Sir Henry Yule among them) compared the texts and decided that the Geographic Text was much cruder, more inaccurate and more Italianised than Rustichello's romances. They noted that the narration had a halting style, which supported the theory that it had been dictated. Moreover, the man who enjoys the reputation of being Marco Polo's first print-editor, Giovanni Battista Ramusio, does not support this theory. He produced three volumes of travellers' tales, published between 1556 and 1559, and covers Marco Polo's journey in the last of these. In his introduction, Ramusio does not specify that Rustichello was Pisan, or that he took the account down as dictation; he simply says that Marco Polo was assisted by a Genoese gentleman 'who used to spend many hours daily in prison with him'. Which rather suggests that Professor Benedetto may be half-right in his claim that Marco Polo lacked confidence in his skills as a writer and called in a professional. I personally doubt the claim that Rustichello was given notes and went away to write up the story on his own. We have no firm evidence that Marco Polo worked from notes, and even if he did they would not have covered the story's wealth of detail. Marco Polo must have recounted, or dictated, a lot of his material from memory. Some of the stories, like that of the Old Man of the Mountains, sound as if they were remembered rather than transcribed from detailed notes. On the other hand, there are many who think that the tale of the Old Man of the Mountains was pure contrivance on Rustichello's part, thinking the book needed a bit of sex at this point.

So about the best that can be said of the Geographic Text is that it is one of the earliest manuscripts, perhaps the earliest extant manuscript but probably not copied from the original. Unfortunately, it is also famously awkward and tautologous and as such has never been the manuscript of choice for subsequent translators.

Next in the list of recensions is the famous Gregoire Version. For a time this was thought to be simply a translation of the Geographic Text, but when examined word by word, some of the lacunae (the gaps) were markedly different. The version is now thought to be a translation of a 'brother' version of the Geographic Text, long since lost. The Gregoire bred fifteen versions of its own. And remember, no two translations are entirely the same!

At the beginning of the fourteenth century a Franco-Italian translation gave rise to what is known as the Tuscan Recension. There are five copies still in existence, of which the most famous is housed in the Biblioteca Nazionale in Florence where it is much adored as the Codex della Crusca. The group also contains a Latin translation by one Pipino, which corrupts the Tuscan translation but is largely responsible for Marco Polo's name being known worldwide. Fra Pipino wrote the first best-seller based on Marco Polo's story. In itself it became the subject of several translations and what might be termed the first modern editions of Marco Polo's incredible journey; the basis of H. Murray's well-known English translation of 1844, and a translation by the French Geographical Society in 1824.

Sadly, Marco Polo's story has become fragmented in the various translations of the Tuscan Recension and even when taken together they still lack some historico-military chapters. Students use the Tuscan Recension manuscripts to correct corruptions in the Geographical Text.

The fourth on the list, the Venetian Recension, is widely regarded as the most important grouping and contains over eighty manuscripts, of which the Santaella is one. Most important of them is the Casanatense 'Fragment', which is believed to be directly descended from the prototype manuscript. As the name implies, it falls short of a complete telling of the tale but has an important pedigree because it served as the source of Fra Pipino's famous version. Pipino's inference that he worked from the actual Marco Polo prototype spawned innumerable copies of his work; some fifty classic editions in French, Irish, Bohemian, Portuguese and German, and five 'popular' ones or, as one commentator described them, 'in the vulgar tongue'.

The Santaella represents a side road off the Tuscan Recension, probably a brother to the five original volumes which are the most important in this group. Two brothers in fact. There is a Venetian version housed at Lucca of seventy-five pages, which has a last page stating that it was completed on 12 March 1465 by one Daniel da Verona, and a Spanish (Castilian) version, Frampton's Santaella, of seventy-eight unpaginated folios, which has a very interesting history.

This manuscript lived at Seville's Biblioteca del Colegio Mayor de Santa Maria de Jesus until 1791 when the college and the university were split. The manuscript vanished without trace and was feared lost. Years later it was discovered in the garret of an old building belonging to the college and found its present home at the Biblioteca del Seminario, in Seville. It is a very complete version of one hundred and thirty-five chapters published on 20 August 1493, some two hundred years after Marco Polo's death, which makes it among the oldest of the printed classical Marco Polo manuscripts. All the Santaella editions are of extreme rarity but there is one, printed in 1529 and housed at the British Museum, which some believe is the actual copy used by John Frampton when he made the first translation into Elizabethan English some forty years later.

Frampton's manuscript is almost as rare as its prototype with just three copies in existence. Frampton himself is as intriguing a character as the strange sequence of events that caused him to turn to a Spanish prototype when he decided to introduce Marco Polo to the Elizabethans. It has been suggested that he might even have been a commercial spy for Britain.

That Frampton spoke and read excellent Spanish is confirmed by comparing his translation with the Santaella. It is very accurate. The Santaella itself is also regarded as a sophisticated translation from the early Venetian Recension so Frampton made a good choice of source material. Between 1577 and 1581 he produced six long works, all translations from Spanish manuscripts – and all of a particular genre. They concerned themselves exclusively with the fruits of the vast Spanish trading empire, for which England at that time was virtually at war.

Contrary to popular belief it was not John Lane and Francis Drake who introduced the British to the joys of tobacco but John Frampton in the book that preceded his Marco Polo translation called *Joyfull Newes*. The joyful news contained in these pages was a description of all the medicinal plants the Spanish had found in the New World as well as 'the rare and fingular virtues of diverfe and sundrie hearbes, trees, oyles, plantes and ftones, with their applications, af well for phificke as chirugerie'.

Frampton got his hands on a copy of a letter from Jean Nicot (nicotine) when the latter was the French Ambassador to Lisbon for Catherine de' Medici of France, in which Nicot describes smoking tobacco and claims to have sent seeds to the queen. 'The smoke of this Hearbe, the whiche thei receive at the mouth through certain coffins [paper cones], fuche as the Grocers do ufe to put in their spices.'

Most translations begin with a foreword but you will not be

surprised to hear that every one is different both in length and content. This is one of the shorter versions:

> All you Emperors, Kings, Dukes, Marquises, Knights; everyone in fact who would like to know of the diversity of the races of mankind and of the many kingdoms, provinces and regions of the mysterious Orient should read this book.
>
> You'll find in it many a marvellous description of the people of these places, especially of Armenia, Persia, India and Tartary, as they are severally related in the present work by Marco Polo, a wise and learned citizen of Venice, who states distinctly what things he saw and what things he heard from others. For this book will be a truthful one. It must be known then, that from the creation of Adam to the present day, no man, whether Pagan or Saracen, or Christian or whatever progeny or generation he may have been, ever saw or enquired into so many and such great things as Marco Polo above mentioned. Who, wishing in his secret thoughts that the things he had seen and heard should be made public by the present work, for the benefit of those who could not see them with their own eyes, he himself being in the Year of our Lord, 1295 in prison in Genoa, caused the things which are contained in the present work to be written down by master Rustichello, citizen of Pisa, who was with him in the same prison at Genoa; and he divided it into three parts.

The whole Prologue has been omitted from quite a few of the translations including the famous Marsden, the version most often used by English translators. It exists, however, in an old Latin translation published by the French Geographical Society and also in an early French version, which dates from 1298 published by the same society. That said, it was almost certainly not written by Marco Polo. The industrious Professor Benedetto has shown that Rustichello lifted verbatim the Prologue's opening invocation to 'Emperors, Kings, Dukes and Marquises' from his Arthurian romance.

Finally a note on my 'translation', and here I have to confess to difficulties. In the sense that it is a modern version of an old story it is technically a translation, but that was not my original purpose. I had, as I said, been obliged to study Marco Polo as a reference source for another book and had found that very hard going. Apart from the several languages (including arcane versions of those languages), all the English editions are very 'reverent'. Marco Polo and his book have become academic icons, the stuff of historical scholarship.

Throughout my readings, however, I felt the presence of this vital, lively young chap fighting to get out from the pages of volumes that had been edited and embellished by monks, censored by the Establishment and finally worshipped by academics (there is a vast school of Polian studies). Where was the nitty gritty? Where was Marco the teenage tearaway, the lusty lad, the court jester, Kublai's gossip merchant? It was like peering at a 700-year-old picture which you knew was highly coloured but would only reveal itself after a good clean, and thankfully this proved to be the case. Once I had got rid of all the 'by the Grace of Gods' and 'in the Year of our Lords' etc. the story began to romp along.

Like most translators before me I have abandoned Marco's original chaptering. It has no logic, is sometimes just a paragraph or two long and it slows the story down.

This then is the intimate memoir of a teenager who exceeds his wildest dreams by becoming courtier and confidant to the most powerful ruler on earth, the Grand Khan, Kublai, and a traveller *extraordinaire*, outrageously rich and famous.

The Prologue

When Baldwin II was Emperor of Constantinople and the city was administered by a magistrate appointed by the Doge of Venice, Marco Polo's father, Nicolo, and his uncle, Maffeo, decided to set up business in that city. They fitted out a ship of their own loaded with a rich and varied cargo of merchandise and, in the year 1250, reached Constantinople safely.

They made an appraisal of trading conditions and decided that the best profits were to be made in the Euxine or Black Sea area. They bought a lot of good jewel stones and took their ship to the port of Soldaia where they set up a small caravanserai and then set off on horseback for the court of a powerful chief of the Western Tartars named Barka who ruled the cities of Bolgara and Assara. Barka, it should be said, had the reputation of being one of the most civilised and liberal of the Tartar princes.

On arrival they carefully observed his reaction to the jewels they had brought with them, noting his satisfaction at their beauty – then gave them to him!

This astute gesture paid off. Barka, unwilling to be bettered by foreigners, directed that double the value of the jewels should be presented to the Polo brothers and in addition he gave them several rich presents. It should also be said that Barka was actually very pleased to be in contact with Venetian traders and he treated them with considerable distinction.

The Polos remained with Barka for a year then decided the time had come to go home, but they were impeded by the sudden outbreak of a war between Barka and the chief of the Eastern Tartars, Alau. The roads being completely unsafe for travellers, they were advised to strike out to the east by a little-used route around the edge of Barka's territory. They followed this advice and made their way to Oukaka on the very edge of the Western Tartar lands. It turned out that the conflict dictated that they continue to the east.

They crossed the Tigris (one of the four rivers of Paradise) and found themselves confronted by a desert (the Karak). A terrible journey of seventeen days during which they found not a single town, castle, or even a substantial building, just whole stretches of barren plain that was home to Tartar bands living in tents, brought them eventually to Bokhara in a province of the same name and in the dominion of Persia, governed by a Prince Barak.

Exhausted, they rested in this noble city for three long years but were fortunate enough to make the acquaintance of an extremely talented person of considerable importance, an ambassador from the court of the aforementioned Alau to the Grand Khan, Kublai.

Kublai's court, they were told, was at the extreme end of the continent, between north-east and east. The ambassador had never met Italians before and the brothers, who by now were fluent in the Tartar languages, impressed him with their manners and conversation in the several days that they spent together, which resulted in an invitation to accompany him to the Grand Khan.

The ambassador assured the brothers that they would be made welcome at Kublai's court, which had hitherto not been visited by any Italians, and would be given many gifts in recompense for undertaking the long and hazardous journey.

Convinced that to try to make their way home would be an extremely risky business, the brothers accepted the invitation, put themselves in the hands of the Almighty and, accompanied by several Christian servants they had brought with them from Venice, and as part of the ambassador's entourage, set out on their epic journey to the far north-east.

An entire year was to stretch ahead of them before they reached the imperial residence. They fought their way through several blizzards and swollen rivers, the latter often causing long delays. But they also saw many wondrous things in the course of this journey (which will be dealt with later) and when they finally reached court Kublai was very respectful, affable and friendly; characteristics which they were later to learn were typical of the man.

When it was established that they were indeed the first Latins to be seen at the court, feasts were held in their honour and they were treated with great distinction. The Grand Khan turned out to be intrigued by the western parts of the world, by the Emperor of the Romans who reigned in Constantinople and by other Christian kings and princes. He asked about their relative status, the extent of their lands, the manner in which justice was administered, how they waged war. Above all he was intrigued by the Pope, the affairs of the Church, and the religious belief and doctrines of Christians.

The Polos, being men of experience, answered these questions with some care, but thanks to their command of the language they soon gained Kublai's confidence and had many meetings with him. When he had absorbed all the information they had to offer he expressed himself well satisfied and, after consultations with his cabinet, he appointed them to be his ambassadors to the Pope.

One of his most senior officers, Khogotal, was appointed to go with them. The party carried a request to the Pope to send a hundred learned men to the Khan's court. Kublai wanted men thoroughly acquainted with the 'seven arts' and able to argue the case for Christianity and support the claim that it was more truthful than the other religions, that the idols worshipped by the Tartars were no more than evil spirits and that the people of the East in general were wrong to worship them as divinities.

The Grand Khan also instructed the party to bring him from Jerusalem some of the oil from the lamp of the Holy Sepulchre, Kublai having assured them that he venerated the Lord Jesus Christ as the One True God.

The Polos eagerly accepted the commission, promising to do their best for the Grand Khan who gave them letters bearing his name addressed to the 'Pope of Rome' and a special tablet made of pure gold, a *Tichikovei* embossed with the royal cipher which guaranteed them safe passage. Provincial governors were instructed to assist the party from station to station and every city, castle, town and village to supply them with generous provisions and secure accommodation.

Less than twenty days into this return journey, however, Kublai's representative, Khogotal, fell dangerously ill and with his agreement the decision was taken that the brothers should press on alone in the hope that the golden tablet would see them through. It worked perfectly. They had escorts everywhere they went and all their needs and expenses were fully covered.

They were less fortunate with the weather. Extreme cold, snow, ice and flooded rivers so slowed their progress that three years elapsed before they reached Laiassus, a port in Lesser Armenia. Taking passage by sea they finally reached the port of Acre, a maritime city in Palestine, in April 1269, where they received the disturbing news that Pope Clement IV had passed away the year before. A legate from the papal see, Tebaldo de Vesconti di Piacenza, was then resident in Acre and the Polos attempted to hand over to him the letters and requests from Kublai Khan.

Tebaldo demurred, insisting that the completion of their business would have to await the election of the new Pope. As this was likely to be some considerable time the brothers decided to go home.

They sailed for Venice and there Nicolo received the sad news that his wife had died after giving birth to a son, Marco, who was now fifteen, the self-same Marco who would, twenty-five years hence, write the remarkable story of their travels entitled 'A Description of the World'.

The Polos languished in Venice while attempts went on to find a new Pope, and they grew ever more concerned that Kublai would be mightily displeased at the delay. When almost two years had passed the brothers decided they could at least go to Jerusalem and they set out on that journey taking the young Marco Polo with them. They successfully obtained some oil from the Holy Sepulchre and were also able to persuade the friendly legate to provide them with a letter to Kublai explaining the papal election delays. Armed with these they set out on the long journey back to the Grand Khan's court in China.

While still in Armenia, however, they received word from Rome that Tebaldo had actually been appointed Pope, taking the name Gregory X. Gregory had immediately sent letters to King Leon of Armenia requesting that, if the Polos were still in his territory, they be asked to return home as Tebaldo, in his new role, was ready and willing to satisfy the wishes of the Grand Khan. The Polos were found and happily accepted Leon's offer of a fast, armed galley to take them back to Acre.

His Holiness greeted them as old and distinguished friends and soon sent them on their way again with proper Papal Letters. But the most he could manage in the way of wise men were two senior theologians, Fra Nicolo da Vincenza and Fra Guielmo da Tripoli who were, however, licensed to ordain priests, to consecrate bishops and to grant Absolution. The party also carried several fine crystal vessels, personal gifts from the Pope to Kublai.

Again they set sail for Lower Armenia, only to learn that a war was being fought across their proposed route. The Sultan of Babylon, Bundokdari, had marched into Armenia at the head of a great army and had largely overrun and laid the country to waste. This proved altogether too much for the scholarly friars who refused to journey on. They handed over the Pope's letters and presents to the Polos, and placed themselves under the protection of a troop of Crusaders of the Order of Knights Templar, who took them home.

The Polos, who had faced these kind of problems before, pressed on looking for a way round the troubled areas. Their ensuing wanderings finally resulted in an epic trek which lasted more than three and a half years. They crossed several deserts and endured again the rigours of two bitter winters. They skirted innumerable mountains and deep valleys until word reached them that the Grand Khan was in residence in the large and magnificent city of

Taiyuenfu, in the western part of his domains. Kublai heard of their approach and while they were still some forty days distant sent out a party to meet them. He gave orders that they should be made comfortable at every place through which they passed and with this help, and through the Blessing of God, they were conveyed in safety to the royal court.

The full assembly of the Grand Khan and his principal officers greeted the Polos, who prostrated themselves on the floor before him. Kublai Khan ordered them immediately to rise and to tell the story of their intrepid journey and all that had occurred with the Pope. The Polos took great care with their story and the Grand Khan listened in attentive silence.

The letters and presents from Gregory were laid before Kublai Khan who had them read. The Polos were much commended for their fidelity, zeal and diligence. The oil from the lamp of the Holy Sepulchre was received with due reverence and the Grand Khan gave orders that it be preserved as a holy relic. Then Kublai Khan noticed and asked to be introduced to Marco.

'This is your servant and my son,' Nicolo said.

'He is welcome and pleases me much,' Kublai replied, directing that the young man be enrolled among his attendants of honour.

A great feast with much rejoicing was held to mark the Polos' return and for the rest of their time they were treated as courtiers. Marco was held in particular esteem. He quickly adopted the manners of the Tartars and was soon proficient in four of their languages, both in reading and writing.

Recognising these accomplishments, Kublai elected to put his talents in business to the test and sent him on an important matter of state to Khorasan which, together with Persia, was ruled by Ahmed Khan, a close relative of Kublai; it was six months' journey away from the imperial residence. Marco completed the Khan's business with such wisdom and prudence that his diplomatic skills, in spite of his age, became highly valued.

Marco also noticed that Kublai liked to hear all the gossip and detail of the manners and customs of faraway places and he made a point of compiling extensive notes of everything he saw and heard to gratify his master's curiosity. In short, during the seventeen years he spent in the service of the Grand Khan, Marco made himself so useful he was sent on confidential missions across the length and breadth of the empire and its dominions.

Sometimes he went on long trips of his own, although these were always sanctioned by Kublai. He had soon acquired a unique knowledge of what to Europeans were still the secrets of the East. All this he regularly committed to writing as will be revealed in the sequel to this Prologue.

But it also has to be said that he acquired so many honours from the Khan that he made a lot of people jealous.

So, our Venetians, having lived at the imperial court for many years and accumulated a great fortune in gold and valuable jewels, developed a strong desire to go home; in fact it became an obsession. They also reflected on Kublai's extreme old age (he was approaching eighty) and feared that his death would deprive them of the protection and help they would need to overcome the innumerable hazards they would face on a return journey.

Nicolo chose a day when Kublai appeared particularly cheerful, prostrated himself before him and begged to be allowed, with his family, to go home.

He was flatly refused! What possible motive could they have for wanting to expose themselves to the obvious hazards of such a journey, hazards that would probably cost them their lives? Was it money, Kublai asked? If so he was prepared to double their fortunes and to grant them as many honours as their hearts desired. But, he said, out of the regard he bore them, he must positively refuse their petition.

Fate then came to the aid of the Polos. In faraway Persia, Queen Bolgana, wife of King Argon, died leaving a written request that no one should succeed to her place on the throne (or the affections of the King) unless they were a descendant of her own family from Cathay in the north of China.

With extreme reluctance, which was evident on his face, Kublai accepted that the only people at his court with the experience to deliver the Princess of his choice to remote Persia were the Polos. Eventually, with good grace, he sent for them, demanding a promise that when they had spent some time with their family they would return to him.

They were furnished with another gold tablet guaranteeing safe conduct and ample provisions in every part of the Empire and Kublai appointed them to be his official ambassadors to the Pope, the Kings of France and Spain and other Christian princes.

Extraordinary preparations dictated by the need to ensure the safety of the Princess were then made for the journey, which the Polos decided could only be made by sea. Fourteen large ships were fitted out. The ships were specially rigged with four masts and nine sails and four or five of them had between two hundred and fifty and two hundred and sixty crewmen each. They provisioned the ships for two years. Aboard were the Princess, a number of ambassadors, the two brothers and Marco. Before taking leave of them the Grand Khan presented the Venetians with many rubies and other handsome jewels of great value.

The initial stage of the voyage, to Java, took about three months. The Polos witnessed much of great interest, which will be revealed in Marco's text to follow. A further eighteen months were spent upon Indian seas where they also observed many amazing things, which will soon be described.

But the voyage was so demanding some six hundred crewmen were lost. Of the ambassadors on board only one survived. Fortunately only one of the Princess's ladies-in-waiting and female attendants was lost. Moreover, when finally this severely depleted expedition reached the port of Ormuz in the Persian Gulf they learnt that King Argon had died the year before. The government of the country was being administered on behalf of Argon's young son by a regent, Ki-akato. What to do with the Princess?

Ki-akato said that they should present the lady to Prince Karsan, another of Argon's sons, who was then resident in

Khorasan on the borders of Persia near a famous impregnable mountain pass known as the Arbor Secco where an army of sixty thousand men was billeted to deter foreign incursions.

The Polos delivered the Princess as instructed then returned to the residence of Ki-akato which was on their route home. When they took their leave of the Regent he gave them four gold tablets each a cubit in length and weighing between 20 and 30 ounces. They bore an inscription which invoked the blessing of the Almighty on the Grand Khan (showing that Ki-akato still recognised the sovereignty of Kublai) and guaranteed the Polos safe passage, escorts and all necessary provisions – on pain of death!

This proved very necessary, and through many places the Polos were often escorted by as many as two hundred men. Ki-akato, so it turned out, was very unpopular in the country and the people committed outrages and were openly insulting of him, which they would never have dared do under their proper sovereign.

And it turned out that the brothers had left China in the nick of time. Kublai Khan died in 1294, aged eighty, while they were still making their way home.

Over the next several months, the Polos worked their way up to the city of Trebizond on the Euxine, then Constantinople, then Negropont and finally, in 1295, to Venice. They were exhausted but in good health – and enormously rich! They offered up their thanks to God for seeing them safely home.

The purpose of this chapter has been to make the reader familiar with the opportunities and the circumstances in which the Polos acquired the knowledge of the things Marco Polo will now describe.

BOOK ONE

The Journey Out

I began my journey in Asia, in Lesser Armenia (Armenia is divided into Lesser and Greater.) The King here lives in Sebastos and is noted for his fairness and justice. Towns, forts and castles are numerous and there is an abundance of the luxuries of life as well as the necessities. Game, both birds and beasts, is numerous. But the air of this country is not particularly healthy and while in former times the people were regarded as good soldiers today they are, frankly, worthless.

On the coast is the busy port of Laiassus, frequented by merchants from Venice, Genoa and many other places. The trade here is in spices and medicinal plants of various sorts and they manufacture silk, wool and other quality cloths. People who intend to travel into the interior usually go via Laiassus.

Lesser Armenia is bordered to the south by what is called the 'Land of Promise' (now occupied by the Saracens), to the north by Karamania, a territory of Turkomans, and to the northeast by Kaisariah, Sevasta and a number of other cities all subjects of the Tartars. On the western side is the sea, all the way back to Christendom.

The inhabitants of Turkomania fall into three classes: Turkomans who worship Mahomet and are rather primitive and dull, dwelling in mountain places difficult to get to where there is good pasture for the cattle upon which they are dependent. There is an excellent breed of horse here, called Turki, and fine mules which are highly valued. Then you have the Greeks and

Armenians who reside in the cities and fortified towns and earn their livings by manufacturing and commerce. Cities like Kogni, Kaisariah and Sevasta (where the late St Blaise achieved his martyrdom) make the best and most handsome carpets in the world, also silks of crimson and other exotic colours.

All pay homage to the Grand Khan, Kublai, Emperor of the Oriental Tartars who rules here through governors. I now want to move on to Greater Armenia, also known as Armenia Major, an extensive province entered via the city of Arzigan where they make a very fine cloth called bombazine and other curious fabrics. It is also the seat of an archbishop. Arzigan has the most excellent thermal baths to be found anywhere hereabouts. The other cities of any consequence are Argiron and Draziz.

The country is under the domination of the Tartars and in summer on account of the good cattle pasture, part of the army of the Eastern Tartars is billeted here. Then in winter, when the snow is too deep for horses to graze, the whole garrison decamps south.

There is a rich silver mine guarded by a castle called Paipurth on the road from Tresibond to Touris.

In the heart of Armenia stands an exceptionally large, high mountain upon which Noah's Ark is said to have finally rested and so is named 'The Mountain of the Ark'. It takes two days to walk round the base of the mountain and it is unscaleable as the snow leading to the summit never melts, indeed increases with each successive fall.

In the valleys, however, melting snow waters the ground and produces such lush grass that cattle from all around find rich grazing here.

Bordering on Armenia Major to the south are the districts of Mosul and Maredin, of which more later. To the north you have Zorzania bordering the Caspian where there is a fountain of oil that gushes so prolifically as to provide loads for many camels. It is used to treat skin conditions both in humans and animals rather than as a food and it is also good for burning. People come from miles around for the oil and everyone uses it in their lamps.

Zorzania (Georgia) is ruled by a king called David Melik which in our language means David the King. One part of the country is subject to the Tartars, the other, thanks to strong fortresses, has remained in the possession of local princes. It is located between two seas, the Euxine and, to the east, the Abaku (Caspian.) The Abaku, 2,800 miles in circumference, is landlocked. The sea boasts several islands graced with handsome towns and castles some of which are inhabited by refugees from the conquests of the Grand Tartar when he laid waste Persia. Others are not even cultivated. There are also refugees sheltering in the mountains.

The Abaku produces an abundance of fish, particularly salmon and sturgeon at the mouths of rivers as well as other large fish. The wood hereabouts is box.

I was told that in ancient times the kings of this country were born with the mark of the eagle on their right shoulder, suggesting perhaps that they were a branch of the imperial family of Constantinople who have the Roman eagle among their insignia.

The people are sturdy, bold sailors, expert archers and make fairly good soldiers. They are Christians, followers of the Greek Church and they wear their hair short like Western priests.

There is a famous narrow pass here which is said to have put paid to Alexander the Great's northern advances. Along the full 4 miles of its length it is washed by the sea on one side and flanked by high mountains and forests on the other. Just a few men could defend it against the whole world. Angered by his failure, Alexander built a great wall at the entrance to the pass and fortified it with towers to prevent people on the other side from molesting him. So strong is this fortification that the pass is known as the Gate of Iron, and it is commonly held that Alexander was thus able to enclose the Tartars between two mountains. This is incorrect. There were no Tartars here then, just a race called the Cumani who came later under Tartar dominance, and a mixture of other tribes.

In this province today there are many towns and castles and the people live well. The country produces great quantities of silk and they also manufacture silk cloth interwoven with gold.

There are huge vultures here of a species called *avigi*.

In the main the people here earn their living by trade and working on the land and the mountainous nature of the country with its narrow, strong valleys has prevented the Tartars from conquering it completely.

A miraculous event is said to occur annually at the convent of monks dedicated to St Lunardo. On the border where the church is situated there is a large salt water lake, Lake Geluchalat, where the fish never make an appearance until the first day of Lent! From then until Easter eve they swarm in great abundance whereupon they disappear completely for the rest of the year.

Into the aforementioned Sea of Abaku, which is surrounded by mountains, four great rivers, the Herdil, the Geimon, the Kur and the Araz as well as many others discharge. Genoese merchants have recently begun to navigate the Abaku, bringing out with them a handsome kind of silk called *ghellie*.

Zorzania has a fine, well-fortified city, Teflis, home to both Armenians and Christians as well as a few Mahometans and Jews. The manufacture of silks and many other articles goes on here. I have described only a few of the principal cities in this part of the world, indeed only those where something special goes on. There are many more, but I want to move on to the less well-known countries of the south and east.

The large province of Mosul, on the western banks of the River Tigris is home to Mahometans who are called Arabians and Nestorian, Jacobite and Armenian Christians. They have their own patriarch, Jacolit, who consecrates his own archbishops, bishops and abbots. Nestorian missionaries are sent from here to India, Cairo, Baghdad, and to all the haunts of Christianity in the same way as the Pope of the Church of Rome spreads his faith.

Cloths of gold and silk called *muslin* are produced in Mosul and the merchants are called 'Mossuline'. They also trade large quantities of spices and medicinal herbs from here to other countries.

In the mountain areas there is a race of people called Kurds some of whom are Mahometans others Nestorian and Jacobite Christians. They are an unprincipled people who make a living robbing merchants. Cotton is grown in great abundance in the towns of Mus and Maredin from which they prepare a cloth called *boccasini* as well as many other fabrics. Everyone here is subject to the rule of the Tartars.

Baghdad [Baldach] is a huge place formerly the residence of the Caliph of all the Saracens, just as the Pope is to the Christians. A great river, the Tigris, runs through it and is used by the merchants to transport goods inland from the Sea of India also known as the Persian Gulf. The voyage can take up to seventeen days, the river being so windy.

Ships bound from Baghdad to the port of Kisi, from where they go to sea, pass the city of Basrah on the south-east side of the Shat al Arab about halfway between the point where the Tigris and the Euphrates rivers converge at the Persian Gulf.

They grow the best dates in the world around here.

Baghdad is famous for its silks wrought with gold, damask, and carpets ornamented with the figures of birds and beasts. Almost all the pearls we get in Europe are first brought here for the process of boring. It's also a centre for the study of Islamic law, magic, physics, astronomy, geomancy and physiognomy.

Baghdad is certainly the largest and noblest city in this part of the world.

The Caliph of Baghdad, who is rumoured to have stored away greater treasures than any other king, came to a very sticky and miserable end.

This was the time when the Tartar princes were starting to push outwards from their Mongol homelands. Four brothers, of whom the eldest, Mangu, reigned, were competing in this territorial expansion.

First they subdued Cathay and the districts around it, but this nowhere near satisfied them, indeed they dreamed of a universal empire – of dividing the world between the four of them!

It was agreed that one of the brothers, Ulua, should go south, another east and that the other two would take on anyone remaining.

Ulua assembled a huge army that swept all before it until, in 1255, it fell upon Baghdad. Baghdad was, however, a strong city with a prodigious population and Ulua elected to take the place by cunning strategy rather than by siege.

His army consisted of one hundred thousand Tartar horsemen as well as infantry, but to deceive the enemy Ulua split them, posting one division behind Baghdad, the other in a wood while he advanced boldly with the third to within a short distance of the city gates.

The strategy worked. The Caliph made light of the force he saw ranged before him and, trusting in what he thought was Islamic superiority, marched out of the city with his guard, convinced he could destroy the enemy.

Ulua pretended to retreat drawing the Caliph's forces into the wood where his second division was concealed. The third division then closed from the rear. The army of the Caliph was surrounded and broken, he himself made prisoner, and the city surrendered.

Ulua entered the city where, to his amazement he found a tower brim full of gold. He called the Caliph before him, accused him of avarice and of jeopardising Baghdad by not spending the gold on an effective army, and locked him up in the tower. But he was given nothing to eat or drink. And so, surrounded by his gold, the Caliph's miserable existence was soon over.

Which was little more than this Caliph deserved. Since his accession in 1225 he had worked tirelessly and brutally to convert the Christians in his territory to Islam, killing those who refused to disavow their faith. He continually mocked the Christian scriptures until one day his learned men pointed out a claim they had found in these gospels, the one which says 'If ye have faith as a grain of mustard seed ye shall say unto this mountain: Remove hence to yonder place; and it shall move'. Gleefully the Caliph latched on to what he saw as a ludicrous boast that a Christian's faith could move mountains, and he called a meeting of the numerous Jacobite and Nestorian Christians of Baghdad (Nestorians are a branch of the Mother Church which does not believe in the divinity of Jesus). There he insisted that they confess on pain of death that they believed this scriptural claim.

They did so, of course.

'So be it,' said the Caliph. 'Prove it. And if you can't find anyone in the land who possesses so small a portion of faith as to be equal to a grain of mustard and can't move this mountain, I shall be justified in regarding you as wicked reprobates and a people without a worthwhile faith.' Then he gave them ten days in which either to move the mountain or to embrace Islam. Otherwise they could expect the cruellest deaths imaginable.

The Christians well knew the Caliph's ruthless disposition (and that he had his eyes on their property) and they quite rightly feared for their lives. But confident of divine intervention, they embarked upon a regime of intensive, endless prayer. Every individual, young and old, prostrated themselves night and day and tearfully begged the Lord to save them.

After eight days relief came in the form of a very mysterious divine revelation. A Christian bishop, known for his exemplary life, had a dream in which he was told to seek out a certain one-eyed shoemaker. This shoemaker would, by divine grace, be able to move the mountain.

When they found the shoemaker he at first didn't want to know, claiming he had not lived a life that could command that much divine grace. But eventually, when he realised how desperate the Christians were, he agreed to try.

As it turned out, this shoemaker was in fact a very pious fellow who regularly attended Christian mass and the other divine offices, observed the fasts, and did much charitable work. He was also well known for an incident involving a beautiful young woman in his shop. The voluptuous creature was being fitted for a pair of shoes when she accidentally exposed a part of her leg causing the shoemaker an instant hard-on!

Appalled at himself, the shoemaker dismissed the beauty from his shop and castigated himself with the Lord's words: 'If thine eye offend thee pluck it out and cast it from thee; for it is better to enter the kingdom of heaven with one eye than, having two eyes, to be cast into hell fire.' And he took his cobbler's knife and gouged out his right eye. Now that's piety for you!

When the Caliph's deadline ran out the Christians held a service first thing in the morning then trudged in sober procession, headed by a cross, to the plain on which the mountain stood. The Caliph was there too, attended by a large number of his guard who knew they would soon be putting the Christians to death if they failed to move the mountain.

The Christians brought out the pious cobbler who knelt before the cross, prayed hard, and cried out in a loud voice: 'In the name of the Father, Son and Holy Ghost, I command thee, Oh Mountain, to remove thyself.'

And it did! Moreover, the countryside all around trembled in a most alarming manner frightening the wits out of the Caliph and his cronies, indeed they were stupefied. It's said that thereafter the Caliph secretly embraced Christianity, wearing a cross beneath his garments. It was found on him after his death and as a result he was not buried in the tomb of his predecessors.

And from that day on, Baghdad's Christians have continued to celebrate the anniversary of the day when the mountain moved.

Let us now move on to the country of Iraq and the large and noble city of Tauris which, of the many cities and forts in the province, is the most densely populated.

The people of Tauris support themselves by commerce and manufacturing and the various kinds of silk produced here, some of them interwoven with gold, fetch high prices. Tauris is well placed for trade with India, Baghdad, Mosul and Cremessor (Hormuz), and merchants from these places as well as Europe come here to trade. You can get all the precious stones and pearls you want here.

The merchants obviously are rich but the ordinary people quite poor. They are made up of a great mixture of nations and sects: Nestorians, Armenians, Jacobites, Georgians, Persians and the followers of Mahomet, known as Taurisians.

Each of these groups has its own distinctive language.

The city is surrounded by delightful gardens producing the finest of fruits.

I found the Mahometans an unprincipled and treacherous lot who believe their faith allows them to keep the goods stolen or plundered from those of other faiths. Theft in these circumstances is no crime, indeed those of their faith who suffer death or injury at the hands of Christians are considered martyrs. Fortunately they are constrained by the powers of the Grand Khan who now governs them otherwise there would be many more outrages.

You should know that these beliefs are common to all the Saracens. For example, when they are at the point of death their priests attend them and ask whether they believe that Mahomet was the true Apostle of God. If they answer in the affirmative their salvation is assured. As a result of these assurances of absolution the Mahometans have succeeded in converting a lot of the Tartars – who are also very taken with the idea of being relieved of the responsibility for crimes!

We'll move on now to Persia, a journey of twelve days, but first let me tell you of a monastery near Tauris which takes its name from the Holy Saint, Barsarmo, and is a very religious place. The abbot and the many monks dress like Carmelites. To keep themselves busy they weave woollen girdles which are placed on St Barsarmo's altar during divine service. Then when they make the rounds soliciting alms they present these girdles to friends and persons of importance. The girdles are much sought after, being reportedly very good against rheumatism.

Persia is a great and noble province but it has largely been destroyed by the Tartars. It is famous for the city of Saba from whence came the three Magi who worshipped the infant Christ in

Jerusalem. They are buried in Saba in a lovely sepulchre where their bodies are said to be unchanged right down to their beards and hair. They were called Baldassar, Gaspar and Melchior and I asked extensively about the three when I was in this city but nobody could tell me anything about them other than that they had been buried in very ancient times.

Three days' journey from here is the castle of Palasata which means 'the castle of the Fire-Eaters' and the inhabitants really do worship fire for reasons, I was told, as follows. The castle people believe in a legend that three kings of that country went to adore a certain king who was newly born, taking with them gifts of gold, frankincense and myrrh. It was believed that the gold would tell them whether he was an earthly king, frankincense would establish his godly status and the myrrh would show if he were mortal or not. When the Magi were presented to Christ, strange things happened. They met him in order of age and when the youngest Magus was presented Christ appeared to be of his own age and stature! The same impression was given to the two older Magi; they saw a man of identical size and age to themselves. They went away and debated this, then came back to devote themselves to Christ who this time appeared as an infant who gave them a sealed box to take away with them.

For several days they carried the box homewards, then they became curious about its contents. It turned out to be just a stone, which they decided was a sign that they should remain as strong as a stone in the Christian faith. When they threw the stone away, however, it burst into flames. They immediately regretted what they had done but, garnering some of the flames, they carried them home and placed them in the church of Palasata. They keep the fire alight and they worship it as a god. Should it be extinguished, they go back to the pit where the original fire (which never goes out) sprang from the stone and they bring new flames home.

The locals actually told this story to me themselves and I also learned that one of the kings was from Saba, the second from the city of Dyava and the third from this very castle of Palasata.

Persia is a large province comprising eight kingdoms, Kasibin and Kurdistan to the south-west, Lor towards the north, Solistan, Spaan, Siras, Soncaria and Timocain. I travelled south to all these places apart from Timocain, which entails a journey to the north near the place called Arbor Secco.

The country is famous for its breed of excellent horses, many of which are taken to be sold in India where they fetch high prices – rarely less than 200 *livres tournois* (1,500 to 2,000 rupees). The largest and most handsome asses in the world also come from these parts, which beasts fetch more locally than the horses because they are easier to feed, can carry heavier burdens and cover more ground in a day than either horses or mules, which tire more quickly. These asses are much preferred by merchants who have to travel through deserts and tracts of sand where there is no fodder and it is a long way between wells and water holes.

Camels are also used here and they too carry great weights and can be maintained at little cost, but they are not as swift as asses.

The horses are traded at Kisi and Ormus and other places on the coast to the merchants who will take them for sale to India, but being creatures of a temperate climate they do not last long there.

The people in some of these Persian districts are savage and bloodthirsty and think nothing of wounding and murdering each other. Thankfully they live in terror of the Eastern Tartars who are in charge here, otherwise no merchant would be safe from them. A rule has been established that if a merchant requests it, guards and guides have to be supplied to provide safe conduct between districts. They get two or three groats for each beast of burden, depending upon the distance to be covered. All are followers of Mahomet.

In the cities they manufacture a variety of cloths of silk and gold. In the countryside cotton grows abundantly, as does wheat, barley, millet and several other sorts of grain together with grapes and every kind of fruit. And don't be fooled by the stories of Saracens not drinking wine because of their religion. They quieten their consciences by boiling it until it is reduced to a very sweet liquid. By changing the taste they change its name and no longer call it wine – although it still is, of course!

Moving on to Yasdi, this is a substantial city on the eastern borders of Persia where much trade goes on. A kind of fine gold and silk cloth known by the name of *yasdi* is sold here and all over the world. Again the people are all Mahometans.

The journey on from Yasdi involves crossing a plain where there are only three places you can find accommodation. The road lies through extensive groves of date palms in which there is an abundance of game animals as well as partridge and quail. If you like hunting there is fine sport to be found here.

You meet a lot of very handsome wild asses on this road and at the end of it lies the Kingdom of Kierman. Formerly ruled by its own monarchs, Kierman today is under the control of governors appointed arbitrarily by the Tartars.

In the mountains turquoise is mined as are rich veins of steel and antimony. The production of fine weapons of war such as saddles, bridles, spurs, swords, bows, quivers and other weapons is a speciality of the region.

Women and young people produce fine embroidery in silk and gold in a variety of patterns especially depicting birds and beasts. They are destined for the curtains, coverlets and cushions of the bedrooms of the rich. The work is so beautifully executed everyone admires it.

In these mountains you find the best falcons that anywhere take wing. Smaller than a peregrine, they are reddish under the breast, belly and tail and so swift no bird can escape them.

It's a pleasant seven-day journey along a plain road that also offers an abundance of partridge and other game. You pass a few villages and frequent towns and castles until you reach a mountain and there is a steep ascent that will take a further two days, but you then find yourself in an area of abundant fruit trees. There were people living here once but now there are only herdsmen grazing cattle. In these high valleys the cold can be so severe you will need lots of garments and a good padded jacket.

Coming out of the mountains you are confronted by a great plain which will take you five days to cross. Here, around the town of Katmandu, where the climate is very warm, they grow wheat, rice and other cereals. It was laid waste by the Tartars and was once a much larger and influential place. On the hillsides, dates, pomegranates, quinces and a variety of other exotic fruit grow, including one called 'Adam's Apple' which is not found in cooler climes. The area is alive with turtle doves who gorge themselves on the fruit and are not hunted by the Mahometans who won't eat them on religious grounds. Also many pheasant and francolin with black and white markings and red legs and beaks, seemingly unique to this area.

They also have a unique species of ox here. Large and white with a short, smooth coat suited to the hot climate, with squat thick horns, it has a distinctive hump about 9 inches wide between the shoulders [first description of Brahmin cattle]. These beautiful animals are strong enough to carry heavy burdens and kneel down like camels for the loading.

And there are sheep the size of asses! Weighing 30lb and upwards they are fat and make excellent eating.

The province is called Reobarle after the river in the valley and has many towns protected by thick, lofty walls of earth. These are defences against raids by people called the Karuanas who rob and pillage all over the area.

The history of these people is intriguing and revolves around the ambitions of a Prince Nagador, a distant relative of the Grand Khan, in fact the nephew of Zagatui, the Grand Khan's brother. Nagador heard that in faraway India there was a province called Lahore, governed at the time by Azzeddin Sultan, which had yet to fall to the Tartars. Nagador recruited about ten thousand men (the most desperate brigands he could find) and taking his leave of his uncle, without a word set off through Badakhshan, through the kingdom of Kashmir where many men and cattle were lost to the terrible roads, and finally to Lahore in the Punjab.

He took Azzeddin completely by surprise, overran the city of

Delhi and a number of others in the area and there began his reign. His Tartar followers (men of light complexion) mixed with the dark Indian women and produced the race known as the Karuanas. The word means 'mixed breed' in the local language and these are the people who terrorise the inhabitants of Reobarle and elsewhere. Moreover, in India they acquired a knowledge of magical and diabolical arts. Chief among these is the ability to produce total darkness in daytime so that they are rendered almost invisible!

They put this skill to work in their raids and are consequently never spotted until it is too late. Reobarle is a favourite target for them because in winter the merchants assemble their trade caravans in Hormuz and await those in passage from India. Horses and mules, out of condition after that long journey, are let out to graze on the rich pastures of Reobarle to fatten them up – only to fall foul of the Karuanas. Those prisoners they take who cannot afford to pay a ransom, are enslaved.

I speak with some authority of this because I was myself caught in one such raid! I escaped to the castle of Konsalmi but many of my people were not so fortunate and were either sold or put to death.

Five days' travel south across this plain you descend for about 20 miles by a road that is extremely dangerous. Travellers are continually assaulted and plundered by a multitude of robbers. Having once descended, however, you come to another plain, the plain of Hormuz which is exceptionally beautiful. It takes two days to cross it, fording a number of streams, through thickets of date palms rich in francolin, partridges, birds of the parrot kind and a variety of other birds not found in colder climes.

At length you arrive at the Persian Gulf where, upon an island no great distance from the shore, stands the city of Hormuz. This is a port used by traders from all parts of the world who bring in spices and medications, precious stones, gold tissue, pearls, elephant ivory and various other items of merchandise. It is a town of middlemen who dispense these goods around the world and the many towns and castles are supported by this commerce. I would say that Hormuz is the most affluent place in Kîrman.

But the ruler, Rukmedin Achomen, who governs with absolute authority while acknowledging the King of Kîrman has a harsh law for unfortunate foreign merchants. If you should die here Achomen will order the confiscation of your property and deposit the return from their sale in his treasury!

It is excessively hot in the city in summer and the citizens of Hormuz retire to their gardens along the shore or the banks of the river where they construct pavilions of reed out over the water. Thus they shelter throughout the morning from a wind off the land so intensely hot as to make it difficult to breathe. People have been suffocated by this wind – known as the Harmatan – and it is certain death if you are caught by it out on the plain. The locals actually immerse themselves up to their chins when they feel the wind blow and stay submerged until it abates!

I was actually in these parts when the following event took place.

The ruler of Hormuz had neglected to pay his tribute to the King of Kîrman, so the King decided to collect his due at the height of the hot season when most of the inhabitants were out of town. A force of one thousand six hundred horsemen and five hundred infantrymen advanced through Reobarle hoping to take the defenders of Hormuz by surprise. Their guides misled them, however, and they failed to reach the town, camping instead in a grove not far from Hormuz.

In the morning that deadly wind found them. They all suffocated. Not one survived to carry the news back to the King! And when the people of Hormuz heard of the disaster they came out intending to bury the carcasses, but found them so baked by the intense heat, limbs separated from trunks, that graves had to be dug right alongside the bodies.

Great traders the citizens of Hormuz may be, but boatbuilders they are not! The vessels built here are the worst I've ever seen and so hard to navigate you use them at your peril. This is because they don't use nails. The local wood is so hard nails would split and crack it as if it were earthenware. Instead, holes are augured at the edges of planks and wooden pins – treenails – driven into them. They are then sewn together with a cord woven from the husks of Indian nuts [coconuts] which are large and covered with fibrous stuff like horsehair.

The fibres are prepared for rope-making by soaking them in water until the softer parts rot away leaving the clean threads used for sewing up the planks. The cords last a suprisingly long time in water. And they don't use pitch for preserving the bottom of boats. Instead, an oil made from fish fat is smeared on and the planks traditionally caulked with oakum.

These vessels have one mast, one deck and a rudder. After loading, the cargo is covered with hides to protect the horses which are carried to India. They have also yet to come up with iron anchors and, as the seas can be very tempestuous around here, vessels are frequently driven ashore and lost.

The inhabitants of Hormuz are again all Mahometans and on the dark side. They sow wheat, rice and other cereals in November and harvest in May. From the fruits gathered (with the exception of dates which come in May) they make a very good wine. People not used to the beverage get very drunk on it, but the more common reaction is just to get fat.

Fresh meat and wheat bread are not popular. They live chiefly on dates and salted fish such as thunnas and cepola which they know to be nourishing. The extreme heat prevents the growth of grass other than in marshy places.

A peculiar custom is attached to the death of men of rank. Their wives bewail them at least once a day for a month and there are professional wailers who can be paid to do the job even though they are in no way related to the deceased.

For the moment I plan to leave the subject of India to a later section of my account, turning now to a journey I made to the north which took me into the kingdom of Kîrman. Outside Hormuz on a different route to the one described previously you come upon the most beautiful valley imaginable producing every kind of food and birds galore, especially partridge, all of which are delicious. Apart from the bread! Made from local wheat it is so bitter no one who isn't used to it can stomach it. The bitter taste is due to the water which is drawn from innumerable salty springs which, admittedly, are otherwise very good for skin conditions and other maladies. Thankfully dates and other fruits exist aplenty.

Three days' north of Kîrman you strike another desert which will take you seven days to cross. For the first three days there is virtually no water and what there is is green as grass, salty and will make you nauseous. Cattle also get sick if they drink this stuff. Travellers must carry their own water as for three days you will not see a sign of habitation. Thankfully on the fourth day you reach a river of fresh water. Most of its channel is underground but the force of the current brings it to the surface in places and there you can get all the water you need. Weary travellers and any cattle that have been brought along stop to refresh themselves after a very tough journey. Then it's back into the desert again until you reach Kobium three days thence.

Kobium is entirely populated by Mahometans and is rich in iron, antimony and zinc from which they make handsome, highly polished metal mirrors. The materials for this work are prepared by taking raw ores and heating them in a furnace. Over the furnace they place an iron grating formed of three small bars set close together. The vapour rising from the burning ore sticks to the bars, hardening as it cools. This is known as 'tutty'. The heavy slag left in the furnace is called 'spodium'.

Leaving Kîrman involves another virtually waterless journey through a desert where not a tree is to be seen for eight days. The little water there is is again very bitter, but if you take cattle they are obliged to drink it. Their owners attempt to make it a little more palatable by mixing it with flour. At the end of a hard week you reach the province of Damaghan on the northern borders of Persia where there are many towns and fortified villages.

On the wide plain here they grow a remarkable species of tree known to Christians as 'Arbor Secco', the dry or fruitless trees. Mahometans call them the Trees of the Sun. Each such tree is lofty with a large trunk. The leaves are green on the upper surfaces and white and sticky on the underside. It produces husks not unlike chestnuts but they contain no fruit. The wood is solid, strong and of a yellow colour and it is the only species of tree for a hundred miles around.

The people of the district report a battle being fought here between King Darius and Alexander the Great, King of Macedonia.

All the towns here, blessed with a temperate climate, are well supplied with the necessities of life. The people – Mahometans to a man – are in general a handsome race; in fact I would describe their women as the most beautiful in the world.

Now let me tell you, as I heard it from a number of people in these parts, the incredible story of the Old Man of the Mountains.

He lived in what became known as the district of Mulehet, which in the language of the Saracen means a 'place of heretics'. Thus his followers were called Mulehetics, or holders of heretical beliefs. His name was Aloeddin and he was Mahometan. In a beautiful valley enclosed by two lofty peaks he created a magical garden offering every delicious fruit and fragrant shrub that money could buy. Pavilions of exotic style, form and size were erected round the garden, furnished with articles of gold, paintings and rich silken drapes.

These pavilions housed beautiful women skilled in music, dance and song – but above all in sex and all the amorous pursuits! Clothed in rich dresses the courtesans sported and displayed themselves in the gardens and pavilions. (Their female guardians were kept indoors.) Aloeddin's purpose in creating so fabulous a place was as follows.

Mahomet, you will recall, promises his faithful followers that if they slavishly obey his will they will enjoy all the fruits of Paradise, including beautiful houris to satisfy every sensual pleasure beyond their wildest dreams. Well, Aloeddin put it about among his followers that he was also a prophet, indeed Mahomet's peer, and he had the power, should he so choose, to admit people to Paradise!

His delicious valley he closed from prying eyes by building an impregnable castle across its entrance, restricting all access to a narrow passage.

Parties of young men from the surrounding valleys aged between twelve and twenty with a martial disposition and a reputation for bravery were selected by Aloeddin and brought before him for daily indoctrination. He also told them of his powers of admission to Paradise.

At different times he had groups of up to twelve of them fed opium and hashish and, when they were deeply drugged, transported them unconscious to the pavilions in the valley. They awoke to the delights Aloeddin had promised. Surrounded by lovely girls who caressed them intimately and sang, danced and fed them delicate food and exquisite wines in an excess of enjoyment played out among rivulets of actual milk and honey, the lads felt they really were in Paradise and were very reluctant to give it up.

In the event, they were allowed four or five days in 'Paradise' before being literally drugged out of their minds again and carried, somnambulant, out of the valley and allowed to come round in Aloeddin's presence.

'Where have you been?' he asked.

'Paradise,' they replied. 'Thanks to you, your Highness.'

'Tell me about it,' said Aloeddin, and before his entire court they did so.

'You know, don't you, that the prophet has promised Paradise to those who defend the Lord,' said Aloeddin. 'Well, if you follow me devotedly and obey my every command, that happy lot is observably yours.'

They all swore they would die for him.

In practical terms, what this meant was that whenever Aloeddin had trouble with local princes they were put to death by a squad of his devoted, fanatical assassins (or 'hashassins' after the drugs they took before attacks). They terrorised and eventually dominated the whole region because, of course, they were all prepared to die for the Old Man of the Mountains. His influence spread as far as Damascus and Kurdistan where he appointed deputies who in turn promoted political murders by drug-crazed assassins. No one, in fact, considered himself safe from the Old Man of the Mountains.

Finally, Mangu, the brother of the Grand Khan and Tartar ruler of these territories, decided things had gone far enough and sent his army to besiege Aloeddin's castle in the mountains. This proved no easy task thanks to the strength of the castle and its suicidal defendants and it was three years before Aloeddin was eventually starved out, imprisoned and put to death. His castle was torn down and the magic garden razed to the ground. That was the end of him.

Leave these mountains and travel eastwards and you enter a spacious plain then a country of hills and dales where there is herbage, pasture and fruits in great abundance. Thereafter you encounter another waterless desert. If you are crossing with cattle, the journey requires very careful planning. Six days of travel bring you to the town of Ashbukan in Khorasan where you will get all the provisions you need and where they grow the best melons in the world. They are preserved by cutting them spirally as we do pumpkins and setting them to dry in the sun. Sweet as honey, they are sent for sale in large quantities to neighbouring countries where they are snapped up. Game is also plentiful here, both birds and beasts.

In the far north of Khorasan is the royal city of Balach which while yet large and magnificent was, until the Tartars sacked it, even grander. Many buildings are partially demolished after their repeated attacks. It still has many palaces constructed of marble and spacious squares the dimensions of which can even now be made out, although they are mostly in a ruinous state. Local legend has it that it was in this city that Alexander the Great married the daughter of King Darius.

Balach is an important Islamic centre but still within the domain of the Eastern Tartars and it marks the north-eastern limits of Persia.

Continuing north-east, a journey of two days brings you to a depopulated section of country. The people who once lived here have fled to strongholds in the mountains to protect themselves from the bandits who have overrun the area. Numerous large lions are still to be seen in this country of lakes and streams, probably because there is such a lot of game. It's difficult getting provisions in these hilly parts however and the traveller is well advised to pack ample supplies for himself and his cattle before he sets out.

Two days from Balach you come into fine fruitful country where, near the castle of Thaikan, a great market for corn is held.

Steep, large hills are to be found to the south. These turn out to be composed entirely of compacted salt. It is regarded as the purest in the world and people come from miles around (sometimes travelling for as long as thirty days) to avail themselves of it. It is so hard you need iron implements to break it up, but there is nearly enough salt here to supply the whole world.

There is a considerable trade also in almonds and pistachio nuts which are grown in the hills. North-east of Thaikan, a journey of three days will bring you to beautiful, densely inhabited country abounding in fruit, corn and vines. The trouble is the people here, all Mahometans, are bloodthirsty and treacherous.

The excellent wine, which is very sweet, results in drunkenness and debauchery.

They wear peculiar headdresses, basically a cord, about 10 spans in length, which they bind around their hair.

Keen sportsmen, they are taught how to cure the skins of the game they hunt and frequently wear nothing but these skins. They also make shoes out of them.

The city of Scassem is to be found three days from here after a journey through an area of numerous cities and castles. Scassem is governed by a chief, who is the equivalent of our barons and counts, and his fiefdom extends to other towns and strongholds in the mountains. There is a river of tolerable size.

I saw porcupines here who roll up in a ball when the hunters set their dogs on them and shoot out their spines with such fury both man and dog can be wounded.

The people have their own peculiar dialect. The herdsmen live in caverns that they dig in the mountain sides which are fortunately of clay rather than stone.

The road to Balasham is a further three days through country where there is water and sufficient pasture for horses but none of the necessities required by the traveller so you have to take everything with you.

This is an extensive kingdom that takes all of twelve days to cross and is governed by hereditary princes descended from Alexander and the daughter of Darius, King of the Persians. These princes have the name of 'Zulkarnen', being the equivalent of Alexander in the Saracenic language.

The precious stones called balas rubies are found in the high mountains here, but mined on only one, Sikinan, under licence from the King (just as he prescribes for gold and silver), which means he controls the market. Woe betide any miner who attempts to dig without such a licence: he would be put to death. Nor can you buy these rubies on the open market or even export them without the King's permission. Occasionally he gives them as presents to visiting dignitaries, otherwise they are used as gifts to kings and princes, some as tribute to his superior lord, and some he allows to be exported in exchange for gold and silver. The King has cornered the market in this way in order to keep the price up. In fact there is an abundance of rubies, which would of course drop in value if mined indiscriminately.

These mountains also offer rich veins of lapis lazuli of the finest colour of ultramarine in the world. The mines of silver, copper and lead are also very productive.

The country is extremely cold. Horses of superior quality and great speed are bred here with hoofs so tough they do not need shoeing. The locals race them down slopes where other animals could not or would not gallop, and they claim they are the descendants of Alexander's famous horse, Bucephalus, and that the foals bear a distinctive mark on their foreheads. It is said that the whole breed was once owned by one of the King's uncles, who refused to give any to his nephew and was murdered as a consequence. The widow, incensed by the murder, had them all put down and thus the breed was lost to the world!

The powerful saker falcon is to be found in these mountains as well as lanner falcons, perfect goshawks and sparrow hawks. The local people are fine falconers, hunting both birds and beasts from the wing.

This is good wheat-growing country and also produces a huskless variety of barley. A want of olive trees means oil has to be produced from certain nuts and from the grain called sesame. Sesame resembles the seed of flax but is lighter in colour. In my view it is better than olive oil and has more flavour than any oil I have ever tasted; it is a view shared by the Tartars who use it extensively as do the other inhabitants of these parts.

The country abounds in narrow and easily defended passes which deter foreign invasions. The men are also good archers and from the skins of the wild animals they hunt make most of what they wear, other fabrics being scarce here.

Innumerable wild sheep find pasture enough in these mountains, rambling about in flocks of four, five and six hundred, all wild. Hunting makes no apparent impact on their numbers.

These peaks are very lofty. A man can easily take a day getting to the top of one of them. Separating them are wide plains of grass, trees and large streams of the purest water where there are trout and many other delicious fish. The air is so pure and healthy, sick people from the towns and valleys below come up here to recover their health, indeed I had to do just that myself after being here for a year.

The local women have a very odd fashion. In place of drawers they wear below their waists a garment fashioned, according to their means, from 60, 80 or 100 ells of fine cotton cloth. It is gathered and plaited to increase the apparent size of their hips. Hereabouts the women with the largest hips are judged the most attractive!

Ten days' journey away to the south you reach Bascia where the people have a distinctive language and are very different in appearance. They have dark complexions, worship idols and are, frankly, evil-natured. They practise magic, call up demons and are then possessed by them. In their ears they wear pendants of gold and silver adorned with pearls and precious stones. In some parts the climate is extremely hot. Their diet is meat and rice.

Now let me tell you about Kesmur to the south-east, which took me a week to get to and where there is a race of magicians whose skills excel all others. They can make their idols speak, hide the light of day and procure many other miracles. Most of the idols in this part of the country are made in Kesmur. The river, from here to the Indian sea, is navigable.

The people are a little on the dark side but the women, while dusky, are gorgeous. They eat, in moderation, meat, cereals and rice. The climate inclines to be warm but there are areas of woodland as well as tracts of deserts. Some of the mountain passes are difficult to negotiate. There are many towns and fortresses and the king here does not have to answer to anyone.

There is a class of priest, devotees who live in closed communities and observe great restraint in their drinking and eating. Sex and sensual delights they do without altogether to avoid giving offence to the idols they worship. They live to a considerable age. There are here also several monasteries where certain superiors exercise the role of abbot and generally they are highly revered by the mass of the people.

The natives here adhere to strict dietary rules and no blood is shed from slaughtered animals. They get the Mahometans to do their butchering for them.

The coral from here fetches the highest price in the world.

If I had kept going in the same south-easterly direction I would have ended up in India, but I have decided to save that account for later. We will go back now to Balashan and I will describe the road I took to China.

Striking out to the north-east, three days' travel through country where castles and villages are set alongside a river, brings you to the province of Vokhan. These people, Mahometans, have a distinct language and are generally civilised in their manners, are said to be valiant in war and quite famous for capturing wild animals. Their chief is in the fiefdom of the prince of Balashan.

Mountain after mountain greets the traveller who proceeds from here in a north-easterly direction. Eventually you come to the point on the road where the surrounding peaks are so lofty you feel you are on the roof of the world. Here, between two ranges, there is a vast lake from which flows a fine river which pursues a course across an extensive plain covered with greenery. Indeed, such is the quality of this pasture it would only take about ten days to fatten up the thinnest of cattle.

Wild animals abound, particularly mountain sheep with huge horns. The shepherds make ladles and vessels for food from their horns. The same material is fashioned into a wolf-proof fence for containing the herds that would otherwise be plagued by huge numbers of wolves. You also find piles of these horns and bones stacked by the sides of the road to help travellers when there have been heavy snowfalls.

For twelve days you slog across this elevated plateau known as the Pamir and because there is a complete absence of human habitation, it is vital you are properly provisioned. So high are these mountains there are no birds to be seen.

I must tell you of an observation I made: due to the thinness of the air, fires do not give out the same heat as they would at lower altitudes, nor do they cook food so well.

And this is only the introduction to the mountain vastness! You still have another forty days ahead of you climbing mountains and traversing valleys in unending succession, passing many rivers as well as stretches of desert without meeting a single human being or anything green, until you get to Beloro. Here, high in the mountains, dwells a tribe of savage, ill-mannered people who worship idols, subsist on wild game and dress in the skins of their prey.

At the end of this difficult journey you finally come to Kashgar where the inhabitants are Mahometans, their language is peculiar to themselves and they exist on trade and commerce particularly in cotton stuffs, flax and hemp which is produced locally. Kashgar is an emporium for the trade carried on between Tartary, India and China and is now subject to the domination of the Grand Khan. What a relief to be among the gardens, orchards and vineyards you find here.

Merchants from Kashgar travel all over the world but I found them to be a grasping, sordid lot who eat rudely and drink worse. Admittedly, a few Nestorian Christians are permitted to live by their own laws and worship in their own churches. I crossed Kashgar in five days keen to get to the famous ancient city of Samarkand.

What a place this is! Beautiful gardens produce all the fruits a man could desire and the city itself can only be described as noble. There is a mix of Mahometans and Christians, all of whom offer allegiance to a nephew of the Grand Khan. The two groups do not live happily together, in fact there is perpetual strife and frequent wars between them.

Let me tell you of a miracle that is supposed to have happened here. Not so long ago a local chief, Zagata, who was the brother of the then reigning Grand Khan, became a convert to Christianity. This delighted the city's Christians, of course, and they decided to commemorate the event by building a church dedicated to St John the Baptist. Obviously the sanctuary enjoyed the support and protection of the newly converted Zagata.

It was elegantly constructed so that the whole weight of the dome rested on a single central column which in turn was supported by a single square stone which, with Zagata's permission, they had taken – in an act of great provocation – from a Mahometan temple. And then Zagata died! His successor showed no inclination to become Christian and the Mahometan Musselmen demanded their sacred stone back, knowing full well that this would bring down the Christian church. The Christians tried hard to buy them off, but to no avail. Eventually, all they could do was to rely on the protection of the glorious John the Baptist.

Came the day when they were due to return the stone, the saint answered their prayers. The pillar raised itself a foot, the stone was hauled out and there, without any kind of support, the pillar remains to this day!

Anyway, be that as it may, let us proceed to the province of Karkan. It is a five-day journey and the inhabitants are mostly Mahometans with some Nestorian Christians, all subject to the Grand Khan. Plenty of provisions are to be had here, particularly cotton goods, and the people are expert artisans. But they suffer a great deal from swellings of the legs and tumours of the throat brought about by the quality of the water they drink.

There is nothing else worthy of comment so I will move on, taking a course north-east of east to the province of Kotan, a place of many cities and forts, eight days' journey away. Again it is a dominion of the Grand Khan and the people are all Mahometans but the essentials of life are to be found here in great abundance: flax, hemp, grain, vines and other produce. There are in addition to the farms, numerous gardens. Excellent traders certainly, but not much good as soldiers, I'm told.

Now to the province of Peyn which is east-north-east of here in the direction of China. The city of Peyn is one of many cities and castles with a river running through it, in whose bed may be found jasper and chalcedonies. Again, you can get all the provisions you will need here, in fact the inhabitants live by manufacturing and commerce, particularly in cotton goods.

And they have this custom! If a husband is away from home for twenty days his wife, if she so wishes, may take another. Similarly the husband, which means that a man may marry wheresoever he resides.

All the provinces I have described thus far, Kashgar, Kotan, Peyn and the country as far as the famous Desert of Lop are in Turkistan.

East-north-east again, still within Turkistan, is the province of Charchan. It was a flourishing place in the past but the Tartars have laid it waste. Its chief city is Churchman and its people are exclusively Mahometans. More chalcedonies and jasper are to be found in the several large streams running through the province. They find a ready market in China and make a major contribution to the local economy. The place is otherwise desert and the water is mostly bitter and unpalatable. Tartar armies pass through here plundering the goods of the inhabitants and killing and devouring their cattle. When the people get warning of the approach of a body of troops, they flee deep into the desert to places where they know there is fresh water to sustain them. Fearful of these same Tartar raids when the harvest is being gathered, the inhabitants deposit the grain in caverns in the sands from where it is taken out monthly as need dictates. The wind blows away their tracks so only the locals know the hiding places.

At the end of a five-day journey you arrive at the city of Lop, on the edge of the great desert. You will need to spend a considerable time here if you are planning to cross the desert, both to gather your strength and to make your preparations for what lies ahead. Camels and strong asses are needed for this journey especially if you are carrying commercial goods and, if your provisions run out, you will need to kill both types of beast to survive. Camels are the preferred means of transport because they can carry heavier loads and eat and drink less. You need enough provisions for a month; in fact were you to attempt to traverse the desert's full length it would take almost a year, which is obviously not practical.

The thirty-day transit is across sandy plains and barren mountains, stopping every twenty-four hours at known water holes. This water is limited, enough to provide for about one hundred people and their beasts. Three or four of the water holes offer only salty, bitter water, but at the other twenty it is sweet and good.

You will not see a single bird or beast; there is simply not the food for them.

People hereabouts will tell you that the desert is home to many evil spirits who employ extraordinary deceptions to tempt travellers to their deaths. If, for example, you fall behind to take a pee or fall asleep and the caravan passes behind a hill, you will hear yourself called – by name! What's more, it will be in a familiar voice which leads the victim to believe it is one of his own companions. If you follow the voice off the direct road – as many do – you can quickly lose yourself and die. At night the desert traveller is convinced he hears the march of a large cavalcade on one or other side of the road. But if you go in search of it when day breaks, again you find you have been lured into danger. During the day these spirits can actually assume the appearance of a companion and again using a familiar voice, will address you by name and try to lure you off the beaten track. Others claim that there are those who in broad daylight have seen a body of armed men advancing towards them and, apprehensive of being attacked, have fled into the wilderness, only to become lost and die miserably of hunger.

I have my doubts about these stories but there is a seemingly endless number of them. I heard too of spirits who fill the air with the sound of all kinds of musical instruments, drums and the clashing of arms with the result that travellers close ranks against an attack. Finally, at night you are obliged to set up a marker indicating the right course to be taken on the morrow and to attach a bell to each beast of burden to prevent them wandering off.

Crossing this desert is no picnic. In fact the troubles and dangers I have described are unavoidable.

The thirty-day journey across the desert at its narrowest point is rewarded by your arrival at the city of Sachion not far from the Chinese province of Shen-si and subject to the Grand Khan. It is in the province of Talguth and the inhabitants are Turkomans, Mahometans and a scattering of Nestorian Christians. The ones who worship idols have a distinctive language. In the main this is an agricultural community growing a lot of wheat.

You see monasteries and abbeys featuring a great many idols of various descriptions including some especially revered to which sacrifices are made. When a son is born here he is placed under the protection of one of these idols. A sheep is raised in the father's house and a year later on the day of the idol's own festival the boy will be taken into its presence and the sheep sacrificed. They cook the flesh, lay it before the idol and pray at length for the health of the child.

During the prayer the idol is thought to suck the savoury juices from the meat. The remains are carried home where they are consumed, reverently, at a feast. The bones are preserved in handsome urns. The priests take the head, feet, intestines, the skin and some flesh to eat.

There are also rituals for the dead. On the death of a man of high rank whose body is to be buried, his relations call in astrologers and, based on the year, day and hour in which the deceased was born, they examine his horoscope. Taking into account the constellations and the positions of planets they set a propitious date for the funeral. If the right planet is not then in the ascendant they will keep the body for a week or more and sometimes as long as six months. Fearful of the effect of adverse influences, the relatives absolutely refuse to burn the corpse until the astrologers say the time is right.

You can imagine the state of some of these corpses! They attempt to stave off putrefaction by building a coffin of planks 6 inches thick, well fitted together and painted. In with the corpse they place quantities of sweet-scented gums, camphor and other potions. The joints are also sealed with a mixture of pitch and lime and the whole thing covered with silk. Every day the table on which the coffin rests is spread with bread, wine and other provisions. The family take meals here but the food is also there to sustain the spirit of the deceased, which is believed to rely on the fumes from the victuals.

If the astrologers direct that it would be bad luck to take the corpse out through a particular door, the relatives will break down a wall to ensure it departs opposite the propitious planet. Not to so do would enrage the spirits of the departed against the family and it would do them injury. Should any member of the family subsequently suffer a loss or an untimely death the astrologers are quick, of course, to blame it on the dearly departed not having exited through the right opening!

The ceremony of cremation must take place outside the city and this too is accompanied by much ritual. Alongside the road on which the body will pass they build little pavilions with porticos covered in silk. At each of these the body is set down and presented with meat and drink so that the departed will arrive at the cremation site with the energy to attend the pyre.

Pieces of paper are circulated (made of the bark of a certain tree) upon which the figures of men and women, houses, camels, pieces of money and dresses have been painted and these they burn along with the corpse so that the deceased may enjoy all these things in the afterlife. Throughout these ceremonies every musical instrument in the place is sounded in an incessant din!

We proceed to the north-west again, this time to the district of Kamul which occupies a tract of cultivable land between the Lop and Gobi Deserts. Food is abundant and there are ample supplies for travellers. The people have their own unique language and they worship idols. The men are a jolly lot and enjoy little else but singing, dancing, reading and writing; in short every kind of amusement open to them. This extends to their wives!

Wives, daughters, sisters and other female relations are ordered to attend to the visitor's every whim. When I was there the husband of the house actually went off into the city and the men do not come back the entire time there is a stranger in residence. They will also supply necessities for which they expect payment. I am talking here of all the conjugal rights and privileges a man would expect of his own wife! Nor is this regarded as scandalous behaviour; on the contrary they believe that it brings honour to the family in the eyes of their gods to provide weary travellers with this hospitality.

And the women are, in truth, very beautiful, very sensual and seem well disposed to carry out their husband's orders. However, when this custom came to the notice of Mangu Khan, while he was holding court in the province, he was scandalised and issued an order to the people of Kamul banning such goings-on. They were actually prevented from furnishing lodgings to strangers who were obliged instead to seek inferior lodgings at inns or caravanserai.

Matters went on like this for three long years until the ban was shown to be reducing agricultural production! In fact it caused so many family problems a deputation was sent to the Grand Khan to beseech him to let them resume a custom which they insisted had been solemnly handed down by their fathers from remote ancestors. They stated unequivocally that the ban was progressively ruining family life!

The Grand Khan washed his hands of the whole affair. 'If you are so anxious to persist in bringing shame and ignominy upon yourselves, I will not stop you,' he said. 'But I think these are base customs and your wives are earning money as prostitutes.' But I can tell you that the people of Kamul were delighted and have been practising their ancient 'rights' right up to the present day.

Adjoining Kamul is the district of Chinchitalias which takes sixteen days to cross and in its northern parts borders on deserts. Still under the domination of the Grand Khan, there are three distinct religions practised in the forts and cities here: Nestorian Christianity, Islam and idolatry.

In the mountains they mine iron, zinc and antimony and you also find a strange substance which has the attributes of the legendary salamander. When woven into a cloth it is incombustible! When extracted from the mountain the fossil material has fibres not unlike wool. (I was told this by a Turkoman travelling companion, one Curfilar, a very intelligent fellow, who for three years had been in charge of mining in these parts.) The material is first dried in the sun, then pounded in a brass mortar and washed leaving fibres that can be spun into cloth. The cloth is placed in a fire for about an hour until it is as white as snow. When it gets dirty you can clean off the spots by exposing it again to the fire. Nothing else works.

Incidentally, I never found in the East any traces of true salamanders that are supposed to be able to exist in fire. But there is a report that they preserve in Rome a napkin woven from the salamander material I have just described, in which was wrapped the sudarium of our Lord, sent as a gift from one of the Tartar princes to the Pope.

Off again, still heading north-east towards China sometimes called Cathay (indeed I may be in it by now), where a journey of ten days through unremarkable country brings one to Succuir province, a place of many towns and castles of which the capital is likewise named Succuir. The inhabitants are mostly idolaters with a few Christians and are subject to the Grand Khan. Throughout this province, and two others I will get to in a moment, all rather mountainous, they grow large quantities of the most excellent rhubarb. Merchants ship it from here all over the world.

But there is a real problem here with a poisonous plant which grows throughout the area and exposure to which causes the hoofs of pack animals to drop off. Traders do not dare go into the mountains with pack animals for fear of this plant, but the locals know how to avoid it.

The inhabitants of Succuir – who are quite dark – depend on

meat and what they grow, not bothering much with trade. The district is very healthy.

As promised, I want to move on to the adjoining province of Tangut and the city of Kampion, which is large and magnificent. Again there live here a mixture of Christians, Muslims and idolaters and we are far enough east to find religious houses of the latter (monasteries and abbeys). A multitude of idols made of clay, stone and wood, all gilded, some huge, others tiny, are housed in these places. The big figures are almost 30 feet high and are mostly lying down. The small figurines stand behind these giants, like disciples in reverential postures. Size is not important, small and large are highly venerated.

Very religious idolaters lead more correct lives than the other classes (according to their ideas of morality) and abstain from anything sensual or carnal. Unlicensed intercourse is not generally considered a serious offence, however, and the general rule is that if a woman makes advances that's fine. Not so for men, however!

They consult an almanac much like we do according to the rules of which there are days when they do not shed blood, eat flesh or fowl (as we do not on Fridays) and mark the Sabbath and saints' days. A husband may take as many as thirty wives according to how able he is to afford them. They do not receive dowries with their brides; on the contrary, the wife expects a marriage settlement of cattle, slaves and money. The first wife is the highest ranked but the husband can send away any of his wives who does not get on with the rest and is generally disagreeable. They mostly take to their beds close relatives, even mothers-in-law!

With my uncles I was obliged to live in this city for almost a year and from a Christian point of view these people really live like animals and commit mortal sins with indifference.

We now strike out due north on a journey of twelve days to the city of Ezina on the borders of China at the commencement of the vast Gobi Desert. Here the inhabitants are all idolaters. They raise camels and various kinds of cattle and in the mountains are excellent lanner and saker falcons. They get enough from the land to meet their needs and they are not really concerned with trade.

Here you must invest in provisions for forty days because the road to the north heads straight into the desert. Say goodbye to human company also because, apart from a few grazers in summer in the mountains and valleys, the place is otherwise deserted. These same retreats are home to wild animals and wild asses that find water somehow in the pine woods. But the journey is well worth it because having survived the desert you reach the city of Karakoran on the northern side where the first Tartars settled in ancient times and established their rule.

Karakoran is about 3 miles in circumference and is defended by a massive rampart of earth (there being no good stone hereabouts) and boasts a huge castle in which there is a handsome palace occupied by the Governor.

The history of the Tartars is an extraordinary tale well worth the telling. They originated around the towns of Jorza and Bargu between Lake Baikal and the Gobi Desert where there are immense steppes, good pasture, large rivers and plenty of water. They had no king of their own but gave allegiance to a powerful prince whose name, I am told, was Unc-Khan but who remains a rather mystical figure and may have been the person we know of as Prester John. Over the course of time these Tartars (or Moghuls) multiplied to such a massive extent that Unc-Khan grew apprehensive of their strength and came up with a plan to split them up and confine the groups to different corners of the country.

Rebellions and such like were put down by a conscripted force and slowly the power of the provincial groups was diminished. The irregulars were made more effective and followed Unc-Khan's orders better when he appointed his own officers to lead them. Eventually the Tartars came to recognise, however, that what Unc-Khan really had in mind was their enslavement and that their only salvation was to form themselves into a strict union and move out. They went north across the great desert until they had put enough distance between the Tartar Union and Unc-Khan for them not to have to pay him the traditional tribute.

Some time before the migration to Karakoran, in about the year 1162, they elected as king one Genghis (or Jengiz) Khan, a leader known for his integrity, great wisdom, commanding eminence and reputation for valour.

Initially Genghis dispensed such justice and practised such moderation that the Tartar tribes revered him as a deity. As his fame spread more and more of them, no matter how distant, gathered to his banner until eventually he was leading so many brave men he decided it was time for the Tartars to emerge from the wilderness.

He instructed the Tartars to arm themselves with bows and at the head of a vast, very mobile army set about the conquest of cities and provinces. Genghis continued just and virtuous so that wherever he went the people submitted to him and professed themselves happy with his protection and favour. This is not surprising because previously towns and districts had either been ruled by district councils or by petty officials. Anyway, there was really no way to resist so formidable a power as Genghis Khan and he was soon in possession of some nine provinces. Governors were appointed, of whom Genghis demanded exemplary conduct in terms of those whom they governed and their property. He also relocated key individuals to other provinces (always paying them well).

Finally, he decided he was strong enough to take on Prester John. Ambassadors were sent from Genghis to the court of Prester John demanding his daughter's hand in marriage, even though he knew that the demand would be indignantly refused. In fact the King replied: 'Whence arises this presumptuous Genghis Khan, who, knowing himself to be my servant, dares to ask for the hand of my child? Let him know from me that if he repeats such a demand, I shall put him to an ignominious death.'

This did not go down very well. Genghis led a vast army into Prester John's kingdom and encamped in strength on the plain of

Tenouk and had the message conveyed: 'Prepare to defend yourself'. In response, John advanced at the head of a huge force and took up a position about 10 miles from the Tartars.

Genghis called in astrologers and magicians to predict the outcome of the forthcoming battle. They took a Greek reed and split it in two, writing on one half the name Unc-Khan and on the other, Genghis. They placed them on the ground some distance apart and gave notice to the King that he would hear incantations during which time the reeds would move together, with victory going to the reed that successfully mounted the other.

And so it came to pass, watched by both armies! The shamans chanted from their books of necromancy and in the course of time Genghis Khan's reed came out on top. Upon witnessing this, Genghis, at the head of his Tartar army, marched through his opponent's ranks and entirely routed them. Unc-Khan himself was killed, his entire kingdom was taken over and Genghis got his daughter after all. He ruled for another six years, expanding his empire all the time until at the battle of Thaigun he suffered an arrow-shot in the knee and died of the wound. He is buried in the mountains of Altai.

Here is the accession after that: Cyhn-Khan, Bathyn-Khan, Esu-Khan, Mangu Khan and finally the most powerful of all, Kublai Khan (for whom I worked). He inherited all his predecessors' possessions and during his long reign of almost sixty years acquired quite literally almost all of the rest of the world.

It has invariably been the custom that all the Grand Khans and chiefs of the race of Genghis Khan are interred near him in the lofty mountains of Altai. Here the chosen few are brought even if it involves a journey of a hundred days or more. During these extended funerary processions to the deceased's grave site his escort kill (or rather sacrifice) such persons as they may chance to meet along the way. 'Depart for the next world and there attend your deceased master,' the unfortunates are told. (The escorts actually believe they are doing these poor souls a favour and that they will be so employed!) They do the same with horses, killing the prime stud animals for the Khan's use in the afterlife.

When the corpse of Mangu was transported to the mountain the horsemen who accompanied it killed, in this horrible fashion, upwards of twenty thousand innocent people whom they just happened to come upon.

You might like to know some of the social patterns of the Tartars. They are of no fixed abode and, as soon as winter approaches, migrate with their cattle to warmer regions in search of better pasture. In summer they retrace their steps, often to cold parts of the mountains where it is green and there is plentiful water and their cattle can be free of horseflies and other biting insects. They tend huge herds and flocks and need to keep moving them ever higher in search of adequate pasture.

Their huts or tents are made up of poles covered with a felt of coarse wool and hair. They are round and nicely constructed and they can be quickly disassembled into one bundle which, when packaged up, can be easily transported in a four-wheeled cart. There is also a rather better two-wheeled cart covered with black felt which I know from experience can keep out the rain for a whole day.

Drawn by camels or oxen these carts carry the Tartars' wives and children, utensils and essential provisions. It is the women who also attend to all the trade. Busily buying and selling, they provide everything necessary for the family, leaving the husbands free to devote themselves to their military obligations (and a good bit of hunting and hawking).

They have the best falcons and hunting dogs in the world and the spoils of hunting make a useful contribution to a diet otherwise exclusively meat and milk. Marmots (we call them Pharaohs' mice) provide ready meat as they are found in great abundance on the steppes. The favourite drink is fermented mares' milk called 'Kemurs' which when properly prepared has the quality and flavour of white wine.

The women? Well what can I say? They are exemplary when it

comes to chastity and decency and in the love they extend to their husbands. It is true to say that they regard infidelity as a vice. I mean it; they regard it as infamously dishonourable. And you cannot help but admire the loyalty of the husbands to their wives. Even though there may be ten or twenty of them, they maintain a quiet union among themselves that is admirable. No offensive language is ever heard and they are kept busy caring for their families. The modesty and chastity which can exist in these marriages result I am sure from the husband being able to choose as many wives as he likes.

The wives do not cost him much either, in fact they make a valuable contribution via crafts and trading to the family finances. In recognition of this, when a man takes a wife he pays a marriage settlement to her parents.

The first wife, as I have said, is considered superior, and is held to be the most legitimate and commands the most attention. This extends to her children. It is inevitable that this unlimited number of wives results in more children being born than elsewhere in the world. And, if the father dies, the son may take his wives, although not his own mother. They can also take their sisters-in-law, but not their sisters. All these marriages are solemnised with great ceremony.

The doctrines and faiths of the Tartars are as follows.

They believe in a sublime, heavenly deity. They burn incense in censors and pray for spiritual and physical wellbeing. They worship a second deity, Notigay, whose image, usually covered with felt or cloth, everyone keeps in their houses. They accord this deity a wife and a child, placing the wife on his left side and the child before him. He is the deity responsible for their day-to-day concerns such as their children, their cattle and their grain. At meal times they take a fatty morsel of meat and grease the lips of the idol and those of the wife and the child. They then throw out of the door some of the gravy as an offering to the other spirits. Once Notigay and his family are considered to have had their proper due, everyone else may eat and drink.

The wealthy dress in cloth of gold, silks, sable, ermine and other rich animal skins. They have expensive accoutrements: bows, iron maces and, occasionally, spears. The bow is far and away their most effective weapon since they have practised with it since childhood. They wear armour of buffalo hide and other skins dried in fires to render them extremely hard and strong.

These people are valiant in battle – almost fanatical – setting little value on their own lives and exposing themselves without hesitation to all manner of danger.

It has to be said that the Tartars have cruel dispositions. They are used to extreme privation and if called upon to do so, can live for a month on the milk of their mares and any wild game that might come their way. Their horses graze where they can and do not require supplementary food such as barley or other grains.

The men can stay in the saddle for forty-eight hours, sleeping while their horses graze! The truth is that no people on earth can surpass them in terms of stoicism or fortitude under duress and as an army they are obedient to command and maintained at little expense. Small wonder that they have subdued so considerable a portion of the world.

Let me describe now how a Tartar army works. We are talking now of a force of perhaps a hundred thousand men with its leader at the head. Officers command every ten, every hundred, every thousand and every ten thousand men. The command structure goes up the line and by this means each officer is responsible for his unit and each can be progressively called upon to commit their troops to the line. The system makes for excellent control of all the elements, large or small, of the available army.

The drafting of troops is done expeditiously, based on the explicit obedience of each man to this squad. Squads of ten are called 'tuc' and ten of these constitute a 'toman'. When the campaign begins a body of men is sent out two days in advance to guard the main army's flanks and rear against surprise attack. This advance guard travels very lightly carrying light rainproof felt tents and their cooking utensils. They subsist, as I have said, upon mares' milk. Each man has a big group of horses, at least eighteen horses and mares which they ride in relays. Should circumstances demand, I have seen these troops go for ten days without a cooked meal surviving on blood drunk directly from a vein opened in a horse!

These field rations are supplemented with a dried milk curd which is prepared as follows. The rich creamy part is skimmed off the boiling milk and set aside as butter. The curds are sun-dried and each serviceman carries about 10lb of it. Half a pound of this is placed every morning in a leather flask of water and violently shaken (by dint of hard riding), a procedure that turns it into a thick porridge which constitutes their dinner.

The Tartar method of doing battle is entirely different to ours. When they engage the enemy they never enter the throng but weave about, aiming arrows first from one flank then the other. Now and then they pretend to flee, shooting arrows backwards, so killing as many men and horses as if they were fighting face to face! Their adversary thinks he is winning but, having already inflicted considerable mischief, the Tartars wheel about, overpowering the pursuing troops and, even though they have fought steadily, taking them prisoner.

Tartar horses are marvellously well trained. They are used to quick changes of course and turn on command instantly and in every direction. Many victories have been achieved through the agility of the horses.

I have to say, though, that all the above is a description of old classic Tartar traditions. Nowadays the tribes are much corrupted. Those dwelling at Ukalka, for example, have become idolaters and over the eastern provinces they have adopted all the mannerisms of the Saracens.

Tartar justice is also quite specific to their society. When a person is convicted of robbery not meriting the death sentence, the criminal is caned. The number of strokes depends upon the seriousness of the crime and can run to over a hundred. A great many die! Stealing a horse earns capital punishment, the guilty party being cut into two parts with a sword. You can buy your way out of these punishments by paying nine times the value of the stolen goods.

Horses, mares, camels, oxen or cows, all bearing their owners' mark, graze at large anywhere in the plains and mountains without herdsmen to look after them. If they get mixed up they are restored to the owner by identifying his mark. Sheep and goats are tended. Tartar cattle are of a good size, fat and very handsome.

They have this strange custom of arranged marriages between the dead. Boys and girls who have passed away are contracted in marriage and there is a ceremony at which human figures representing attendants with horses and other animals, dresses of all kinds, money, and every item of furniture are drawn on pieces of paper, then burnt. The marriage contract also goes up in smoke. It is the belief that all these items pass to the couple in the Other World through the smoke. After such a ceremony, which fully formalises the marriage between the dead couple, their fathers and mothers consider themselves duly related.

In this description of the Tartars I have not mentioned their lord, the Grand Khan, his brilliant acts and enterprises, as I intend to save these for later. Meantime, let us return to our journey, heading north for forty days through the plain of Bargu in the direction of Siberia.

The people here, called the Mekriti, are a cruel lot, living on the flesh of large deer, some the size of stags, which also provide them with transport. Another rich source of food is the fish and fowl of the numerous lakes and marches. The birds come here in the summer when they have moulted and their lack of feathers makes them easy prey for hunters.

This huge plain has a frozen ocean at its northern extremity and in winter the cold is so severe neither bird nor beast can survive here. The people resemble the Tartars I have just described and are subjects of the Grand Khan.

At the end of forty days I am told you reach mountains from

which this ocean can be seen. Here vultures and peregrine falcons have their nests but of people and cattle there are none. The falcons are about the size of a partridge with a swallow-like tail, claws resembling those of parrots and are swift in flight. They feed largely on the only species of bird in the area, called 'bargelak'.

This is where the Grand Khan gets his hunting falcons from; broods of peregrines from the mountains and plenty of gerfalcons from an island lying off the coast. The suggestion that the Grand Khan gets his gerfalcons from Europe is untrue, although some Western Tartars and other chiefs of the Levant acquire their birds in this way. The gerfalcon island is so far north the Polar star appears to the south, or behind you.

We are at last approaching the provinces near to residences of the Grand Khan. Leaving Kanrion (of which I shall have more to say later), a journey of five days eastwards brings you to the Kingdom of Erginul subject to the Grand Khan in the province of Tangut. This can be a somewhat terrifying journey because at night one is troubled by the voices of spirits.

There are several principalities in the kingdom and it is a land of idolaters, Mahometans and a few Nestorian Christians. The principal city is also called Erginul and the road that leads east from here via the city of Singui is the road to China. This is the territory of the musk ox and large numbers of them are eaten. The flesh is said to be very good. (I was able to take back to Venice the dried head and feet of one of them.) It is a journey of twenty-five days across this province.

The people are mostly traders and manufacturers. They have grain in abundance and you find pheasant here that are twice the size of ours, and a great variety of other birds some of which have beautiful plumage.

The people are generally rather fat, have small noses, black hair and in place of beards sprout a few scattered hairs on their chins. Upper-class women are likewise free of superfluous body hair, are fair skinned and shapely, but they have rather dissolute natures.

The men are very fond of women and have as many wives as

they please (in practice as many as they can afford). They will marry a poor woman if she is attractive and hand over rich presents to her parents and relatives. Beauty is everything!

Let us head east. Eight days from Erginul brings the traveller to Egrigaia, still part of the huge province of Tangut and still subject to the Grand Khan. This is a place of many cities and castles, the principal one being Kalacha. It is the same religious mix as before; while primarily the home of idolaters, the Nestorian Christians have three churches in Kalacha.

They make the finest shawls in the world here, called 'camelots' from the hair of camels and also a beautiful white wool. Merchants snap them up and ship them abroad, especially to China.

A small deviation to the north will take you to Tenduk, the territory of Prester John. All the princes of Tenduk have been subject to the rule of the Grand Khan since Genghis subdued the country. The king, who rules from a city also named Tenduk, is a direct descendant of Prester John, indeed is known as King George. He is both a Christian and a priest. George rules territories somewhat smaller than those of Prester John and he has a privileged arrangement with the Grand Khan whereby he and the other princes of Tenduk may marry his daughters and other women of the Grand Khan's family.

The colour azure, made from a stone, is found here in great abundance and is of fine quality. Camelhair cloth is also manufactured and there is extensive agriculture, trade and mechanical work.

Both the King and the government, as I have said, are Christians. There is also, apart from idolaters and Mahometans, a race known as 'Argons' who are a mixture of idolaters and Mahometans. I must say that King George's people are fairer complexioned and better looking than those of the other countries through which we have passed; better educated, too, and more skilful traders.

Originally the sovereigns who bore the title 'Prester John' ruled over all the neighbouring countries including those of the Tartars.

The current 'George' is the fourth in descent from Prester John and is head of the family of the patriarch. The family controls two large regions, Gog and Magog (known locally as Ung and Mongul) and each had its own distinctive people; in Ung they were known as Gogs and in Mongul they were Tartars. Subsequently the Monguls and the Tartars became indistinguishable.

The people of Tenduk are fine manufacturers and traders of woven goods, especially wools, fine gold tissue ornamented with mother-of-pearl known as *nasici* and silks of different textures and colours as good as those of Europe.

One of the towns, Sindichin, is famous for the manufacture of all manner of arms and military accoutrements and ordnance. Up in the mountains the village of Idifa produces large quantities of silver from a rich mine. The whole area teems with birds and beasts.

China at last! First you come to the important city of Changa-nor or 'White Lake'. Here the Grand Khan has a grand palace that he is very fond of visiting. It is quite beautiful, surrounded by lakes and streams that are home to many swans. In the surrounding plain, cranes, pheasant, partridge and other birds abound. The Grand Khan much enjoys hunting from here (thanks to the abundance of the game) with gerfalcons and other hawks.

There are five species of cranes, some black as night with long wings. Then there is a magnificent bird that is white with even longer wings marked with golden eye shapes like those of peacocks; the head is red and black and it has a formed neck of black and white. You also see many birds that look like the cranes we have in Italy. Then there is a small crane with pretty red- and azure-streaked feathers and, finally, a very large bird of grey colour with a head of red and black.

One of the nearby valleys is famous for its large number of partridge and quail. The Grand Khan has the sides of the valley sown with millet and panicium which are both grains the birds like. Strict orders are in place that no one should harvest these seeds lest the birds go hungry, and numerous keepers are posted here to make sure the birds get the seed in winter and to protect the game in general. Hence they have become completely used to being fed. The gamekeepers have only to whistle to find themselves surrounded by birds flocking from every direction!

A number of small buildings have been erected in which birds shelter for the night. All in all the Grand Khan is always assured of finding abundant sport here even in winter, although he does not actually live here in winter because of the extreme cold. Camel loads of frozen birds are, however, sent to him wherever his court may be at the time.

From Changa-nor to Shandu in the north-east is a journey of three days. Shandu was built by Kublai Khan and it boasts a grand palace of marble and other fine stones, beautifully wrought and very elegant. Gilded halls and chambers make it very handsome. The palace grounds are contained within 16 miles of wall!

Within the bounds of this royal park, beautiful meadows are watered by many little streams providing rich pasture for small deer who, in turn, are good for hawks and other hunting birds nesting here. More than two hundred birds are kept for sport and the Grand Khan goes there at least twice a week to inspect them.

On his rides around this private forest, Kublai has one or more small leopards carried on horseback in cages behind their keepers. Kublai personally gives orders for them to be released and he loves to see them swiftly take a stag, fallow deer, or a goat. The kills are fed to his hawks.

Amid a beautiful grove of trees in the middle of the park the Grand Khan has built a royal pavilion. Gilded and burnished columns support a roof of bamboo cane, also varnished and gilded. Around each of the columns a dragon winds its gilded tail and its talons grasp the wood. No rain can penetrate the roof because of the complexity of its construction. Thick bamboos, 40 feet in length, are cut at their joints and split in half. The pavilion is covered with these split bamboos, convex and concave, and tied to the roof frame at their ends to make the roof windproof.

The building is held together like a tent by more than two hundred exceptionally strong silken cords and although the structure is very light, it can withstand the strongest winds. It is also so cleverly constructed it can quickly be dismantled and re-erected according to his majesty's pleasure.

He has selected this spot for his sporting summer retreat because of the beneficial mountain air and the mild climate and is in residence here for three months, June, July and August. On 28 August it is the custom to proceed to an appointed place to perform traditional rituals.

You have to understand that Kublai keeps a stud of ten thousand mares and horses, all as white as snow! Nobody who is not a descendant of Genghis Khan may drink the milk from these mares other than the family of an honoured military veteran, Boriat, who fought very bravely at Kublai's side. You show respect for these horses! Even when they are just grazing in the royal meadows or pasture no one dares get in their way.

Kublai also employs astrologers exceptionally skilled in diabolical magic. On the 28th day mentioned, Kublai regards it as his traditional duty to scatter mares' milk to the winds as a libation to all his spirits and idols. This gesture is supposed to calm the spirits and ensure their protection for all the population: men and women, their cattle, chicken, grain, in fact all the fruits of the earth.

Sometimes the shamans or, if you like, magicians, give wonderful demonstrations of their powers. If, for example, it should cloud over and look like rain, they go up on the roof of the palace where the Grand Khan is living and by the power of incantation, stay the tempest and prevent the rain from falling. It can be blowing a gale over the surrounding countryside but not a drop falls on the royal palace.

These yogis are of the cults of Tebeth and Kesmir and are more skilled in the black arts than any of the other groups of idolaters. They convince the ordinary people that they draw their powers from performing penances and maintaining the sanctity of their own lives. They actually go around filthy and in an indecent state, indifferent to the respect they should be showing to the people before whom they appear. They do not wash or comb their hair and they live in very squalid circumstances. Moreover, they are addicted to the foul practice of cannibalism. When a criminal is sentenced to death they carry off the body, cook it and eat it! (I should say that this does not happen to the bodies of people who die of natural causes.) These yogis have the name *baksi* (in Tibet they are called lamas) and I will tell you a story of their powers that you may believe or not.

The Grand Khan dines at an elevated table some distance away from a large sideboard where the drinking vessels stand. By means of the supernatural, the *baksi* priests cause a cup of wine, milk or other beverage to fill spontaneously without being touched by the attendant and then transport itself majestically to the Grand Khan, a distance of ten paces! When he has finished it floats back. Kublai usually invites witnesses to watch this performance.

On their feast days the *baksi* descend on the palace of the Grand Khan and demand of him: 'Sire, if a sacrifice is not made to the gods they will be angered and inflict on us bad seasons, blight to our grain, pestilence among our cattle and plagues. Please give us a number of black-headed sheep, several pounds of incense and lignum aloes in order that we may appease him with the customary rites and due ceremony.' (These words are not put to the Grand Khan directly but via senior officers.)

The Grand Khan never fails to meet all their requests and on the appointed day they sacrifice the sheep in the presence of their idols (first having poured off the liquid in which they have been steeped) and conduct the rituals of worship.

There are many great monasteries and abbeys in this country, some of them so extensive as to pass for small cities, housing populations of some two thousand monks. They dress better than the ordinary folk; they shave their heads and beards and carry on their religious services and festivities with choirs, the burning of incense and great solemnity. Some of these monks take wives.

There is also a much stricter religious sect, the Sensim, who lead austere lives and practise virtual abstinence. They have no other food than a kind of porridge, the grain of which is soaked in warm water until the farinaceous part is separated from the bran and in that state they eat it. This sect worships fire and is considered by others to be a breakaway religion worshipping different idols.

The Sensim never marry although they still shave their heads and beards. They wear garments of hempen material – sometimes silk – but it is always of a dull colour, mostly black. They sleep on coarse mats and, in my opinion, have a harder life than anyone else on earth.

But it is time I got on to the subject of the great, indeed, wonderful acts of the supreme lord and emperor of the Tartars, Kublai Khan.

BOOK TWO

Introduction

Marco was awe-struck by the Great Khan, Kublai, his splendid court and the palaces and cities gracing his vast empire. And as a result he had been judged a subjective and biased witness to the wonders of the East and its mighty ruler.

In fact, this awe was partly a reflection of the degree to which the Western world was ignorant of this Lord of Lords ruling a world of which their knowledge was all but non-existent. In Pre-Crusades Europe, Kublai was still the dreaded son of Genghis, who had terrorised eastern Europe and terrified the west. And this reputation had been well founded. Tartar conquest was based on a single ultimatum: lay down your arms and accept the rule of a Tartar lord or be exterminated by his army. Men, women and children were ruthlessly killed and their skulls piled in vast mounds to remind the next intransigent city of its inevitable fate.

When they came the Tartar hordes were widely regarded as unstoppable.

Marco discovered that this was observably not the case with Kublai. Tartar (Moghul) rule had matured by the time he reached the court of the Lord of Lords. Arguably, in fact, Kublai's tenuous control of an essentially vast and ungovernable area of land had begun to slip. Most of Book Two is devoted to setting this record straight and it is much the largest part of the manuscript.

Marco and his family would (they claimed) actively participate in the expansion of Kublai's empire, Nicolo and Maffeo building huge siege engines of European design which brought about the sub-mission of one of China's larger, most strongly fortified cities.

Marco appears to have been content with winning a place in the Great Khan's diplomatic corps and in the old man's heart. Great Emperor Kublai might have been, but for much of his life he was at war with his many influential sons to whom he had given vast lands to govern. He was also surrounded by a stifling plutocracy, so the stories Marco bought him from remote lands must have been a refreshing relief.

I believe that we are fortunate that Marco Polo was young and impressionable. The collapse of Kublai's Empire was still some time in the future and the young Marco toured the mighty kingdom when it was in its fading but still glorious prime. He gave his sense of wonder free rein, uninhibited by much experience or worldly comparisons.

Most of the time he quite literally could not believe his eyes. He probably kept careful notes, knowing Kublai's voracious appetite for news and gossip. How extraordinary it all was can be judged by the fact that when he returned home and, with Rustichello's help, published it in a book, few readers believed him.

But as I have said previously, the details have in so many cases, including the most extraordinary, proved remarkably accurate. For example his story of twenty thousand innocents being killed en route to serve as companions to the dead when the body of Mangu Khan is conveyed to Mount Attai, was treated with outright derision.

Chinese annals which have come to light since support this grisly tale, in fact Marco may have understated the numbers by as many as ten thousand souls. As recently as 1661 the Tartar emperor, Shun-chi, ordered a huge human sacrifice upon the death of a favourite mistress. Similarly, seemingly minor details such as his description of 'a certain small animal not unlike a rabbit called by our people Pharoah's mice' was confirmed by several subsequent travel accounts as areas of large marmot populations.

Even the apparently ridiculous story of drinks floating back and forth to Kublai's table has been checked out and is now thought to have been a mechanical conjuring trick. The French traveller, Rubruquis, reports that the Tartar princes were fond of such tricks and that one of them had hired a fellow countryman of his to design a curious bit of machinery which conveyed into the dining hall a variety of beverages which issued from the mouths of silver lions.

Book Two is, in reality, a eulogy to a benign, just and civilised elder statesman, as far a cry as you could get from a man others believed could have been the scourge of Europe, with a taste for blood-letting and savagery. No doubt Marco's early impressions were naïve (he was after all in his early twenties), but when he was influential at court he found Kublai Khan remarkably even handed on vexing subjects such as religion.

Quite who this Lord of Lords actually believed in has never been satisfactorily established. He certain wasn't a Muslim, although much of his empire was, and he seems to have carefully observed most of the important religious festivals of the major religions in the lands he ruled.

Marco Polo likes to give the impression that Kublai considered becoming a Christian, on one occasion sending Nicolo and Maffeo for oil from the lamp of the Holy Sepulchre and with a request to the Pope to send him one hundred 'learned men' who could prove that the Christians worshipped the one true God.

The history of the world would indubitably have been changed had that request ever been followed up, but Christianity failed to make its greatest leap forward when the Pope's representatives – admittedly just two of them, but with the power to create priests – lost their nerve when they heard reports of the ever-warring Tartars in their path.

The truth seems to be that Kublai was an eclectic on the subject of religion and openly fascinated by the magic claimed for the religious artefacts of the various religions. Apart from the holy oil from Jerusalem, he also tried to buy Buddha's begging bowl. He kept teams of necromancers, sooth-sayers, wizards and astrologers at the court and seems to have had as much faith in their miracles as in the Christian faith. When it comes to religious content and emphasis in the Marco Polo manuscript one also has to take into account the fact that in the first years of its long life it was translated, copied and illuminated exclusively by clerics of the Christian church.

Marco further suggests that Kublai had huge and very wide interests particularly in nature and natural history, a field of interest to which I have been professionally attached for some years. It is my view, however, that it is Marco who has the real interest in the flora and fauna of the vast empire, rather than Kublai, whose interests were mostly sporting. Admittedly Marco reports that the Emperor once sent a team of ambassadors to the island of Madagascar to get him a giant feather of the mythical great auk, but this again seems more an interest in curios than ornithology.

Book Two is extraordinarily rich for a manuscript of this vintage in 'pure' natural history. It gives the first documented instance of elephants used as fighting machines, detailed descriptions of the training of the Tartar fighting horses and how armies of hundreds of thousands rode, milked and bled their animals for food. The extraordinary mobility of the Tartar armies was dependent entirely on their remarkable horsemanship and the fact that they could live on a rich whey porridge of mares' milk mixed with blood.

Rather than a merciless killer, Kublai is revealed as being a collector of exotic trees, the pioneer of large arboretums and of public roads planted with trees two feet apart to provide shelter for travellers.

Kublai, a Tartar, has a passion for horses and he can afford the very best. At the New Year festivals, the Great Khan is given upwards of one hundred thousand horses – all of them pure white.

There are descriptions of royal hunts conducted with trained leopards, lynxes and even tigers. These big cats are carried around in special wagons – along with a little dog to keep them company. Buck, bear, boar, wild asses and oxen are the fair game of these royal sporting outings.

Marco describes with wonder two influential Masters of the Hunt each with a staff of ten thousand huntsmen. They take Kublai hunting in the frozen north of his vast empire (towards Siberia) with a host of gerfalcons, peregrines, sakers and hunting vultures so numerous ten thousand 'taskoal' or bird-handlers are required to look after the raptors. Five thousand dogs are also involved in the chase and some of the eagles are so large they can pull down a wolf. The two Masters of the Hunt have a contract to supply Kublai's court with one thousand pieces of game a day. Quails, Marco adds (with his usual care for the detail which adds such credibility to his accounts), don't count.

Kublai's hunting pavilion is a handsomely carved affair covered with wild cats' skins mounted on the backs of four elephants. The royal quarters are covered outside with tigers' skins with an inner lining of ermine and sable. The concept of conservation was, of course, still hundreds of years in the future.

Marco visits lands where the air is redolent with the smell of musk and he explains in detail how the musk-ox produces it once a month 'like a boil full of blood'. In many of these lands wild game is the only source of food and clothing. We also learn in Book Two of silk-worms and how they are fed exclusively on mulberry leaves, a trade secret that could have led to silk being produced elsewhere than in India and China.

There are graphic descriptions of huge serpents with claws like those of the tiger, and glaring eyes 'larger than a 4-penny loaf'. This is the first recorded description in Western literature of the Asian crocodile. Tigers (which Marco calls lions) are a constant danger to the traveller, some so huge and predatory it is safer to spend your night moored in mid-stream rather than venture to the river bank. Marco also tells of a species of huge dogs, a couple of which can overcome a tiger.

Plants also attract Marco's constant attention and he describes cane 90 foot long that can be split and twisted into ropes 900 feet in length. In the wondrous city of Kinsai, the 'celestial' city which was then the capital of southern China, surrendered to Kublai's army by the Song dynasty, he finds bamboos a foot thick. Ever the Venetian merchant at heart he notes the prices of all the medicinal plants like ginger, tea, ganganal and rhubarb. We learn how fine sugar is made from cane using a process of refining which uses wood ash introduced by experts from ancient Babylon.

The mundane is dutifully recorded along with the exotic: Marco points out that Kublai gets a huge amount of his revenue from the production of salt. The tightly controlled production of salt, which is cast in moulds, is used as currency in certain parts.

Marco relates in this book how fine porcelain is made from certain earths laid down for years, but it would be several hundred years before any western manufacturer was able to produce porcelain. It was Marco's degree of pure revelation which so stunned a sceptical Western world when the first handwritten copies of his book appeared. Almost every page of Book Two has something on it which was new to Europeans.

The most startling of these is that this mighty empire which then covered three-quarters of a world known to very few people, was run not on gold, stones, or cowrie shells but on scraps of paper. This printed money, Marco revealed, was accepted throughout Kublai's kingdom 'on pain of death'.

We hear also of a similarly unique communication system (an early, infinitely more extensive version of the American Pony Express) serviced by messengers on foot and mounted. This countrywide courier service had its own roads, boats and lavish guest houses. Messengers covered up to 250 miles in one day, running or riding in relays.

Book Two slips in the first reference in Western literature to coal: 'a sort of black stone which burns like charcoal and gives out much more heat than wood.' Coal was completely unknown in Europe at this time. For good measure he confounds his Western readers with the news that, with such an easy source of heat, those who can afford it take a hot bath at least three times a week.

It is a tragedy but small wonder that poor Marco, in his own lifetime, was regarded as the biggest liar that had ever been and was lampooned at medieval fairs by clowns as a teller of a million tall tales. But were these attacks not simply egocentric Europeans refusing to accept that behind the veils of the mysterious, apostate East, two wild horsemen from the steppes had built a civilisation to equal anything the West had to offer? Book Two is Marco Polo's irrefutable affidavit to all this and it must have been very hard, not least for the all-powerful Christian church, to stomach.

BOOK TWO

Lord of Lords

The epithet Kublai Khan means 'Lord of Lords', one to which he is quite entitled, I would say, in that he surpasses any sovereign who has ever lived in terms of the number of his subjects, the extent of his territories and the size of his income. I hope I can also persuade you that he indeed commands more obedience from his subjects than any monarch who has ever lived.

Kublai Khan is directly descended from Genghis Khan, founder of the Tartar empire. He is the sixth of his line and began his reign in 1256. Even though he is the legitimate heir he had to fight for the throne against his brother and his officers of the court. But his courage, virtue and prudence carried the day.

Today in the year 1288, he has been on the throne for thirty-two years and is eighty-five years of age. Prior to ascending the throne he served industriously in the army where he had a reputation for bravery and daring. His judgement and military skills earned him a reputation as the most able and successful commander that ever commanded the Tartar army.

Once on the throne he quit the field and entrusted the conduct of military expeditions to his captains and his sons, with one vital exception. One of Kublai's nephews, a young chief called Nayan, took over a number of cities and provinces gaining resources that enabled him to raise an army of some four hundred thousand horse. Pride got the better of him when he found himself at the head of so many men and he resolved to throw off the allegiance he and his predecessors had paid to the Grand Khan and usurp the sovereignty.

Nayan secretly despatched messengers to Kaidu, the powerful chief of Turkistan and the nephew of Kublai, who was rebelling against the Grand Khan. (He hated Kublai, who had punished him for several serious offences, with a passion.)

To Kaidu, therefore, Nayan's proposals were very attractive and he promised to bring one hundred thousand horses into the alliance. But the assembling of so large a force could not be kept hidden from the Grand Khan and he immediately reacted by closing all the passes leading to the countries of Nayan and Kaidu to cover his own preparations. He assembled a force of three hundred and sixty thousand horse from troops stationed within ten days' march of the city of Kanbula and another million infantrymen were enlisted from among his private guard, his falconers and domestic servants. Within twenty days they were ready. This was clever planning. Had Kublai relied on the standing army charged with the protection of the provinces of China, they would have required thirty or forty days to assemble and this would have allowed time for the enemy to establish commanding positions. As it was, Kublai fell on Nayan before he had joined forces with Kaidu and destroyed him absolutely.

It is worth noting here that in North and South China, as well as other parts of the empire, there are many disloyal and seditious people ranged against the Grand Khan. There is an ever-present threat of rebellion that obliges Kublai to maintain Tartar armies a few miles outside the large cities and centres of population ready to move in at a moment's notice. He changes these armies and these officers every two years.

Such precautions result in the population being kept in quiet subjugation and few uprisings are attempted. The troops are paid out of imperial revenues and they have their own cattle and milk which they sell in city markets to provide them with all they need. You thus have a string of Tartar troops across the country at distances of thirty, forty and sixty days' journey. Even if half of them were collected in one place you would not believe the multitude.

Kublai's advance on Nayan was carried out in complete secrecy even though it involved a forced march that continued night and day for over a fortnight. Road blocks were set up and all who sought to pass were made prisoner. Kublai halted his troops on a plain overlooking Nayan's encampment and rested them for two days. Astrologers were called in and declared before the whole army that Kublai would win. (The Grand Khan routinely brought in astrologers to inspire the troops with a promise of victory.)

The following morning the army tore down the hill springing on an unprepared enemy, with no scouts, or advanced guards. Nayan himself was asleep in his tent with a wife. By the time Nayan awoke, it was too late to get his army into proper fighting order and all he could do was curse the fact that he had not yet joined up with Kaidu.

Kublai advanced in a huge wooden castle mounted high on the backs of four elephants armoured with thick, hardened leather and livery of cloth of gold. The castle housed many crossbowmen and archers and bore the royal standard adorned with the sun and the moon. Thirty battalions of horse, each ten thousand strong, and troopers armed with bows, followed behind. Two wings swept out to outflank Nayan's army.

Five hundred infantrymen, armed with short lances and swords, marched in front of each battalion of horse. If the enemy took flight these men were trained to mount behind the horse soldiers until they caught up with the enemy, whereupon they set to work killing the enemy horses with their lances.

Once the Grand Khan's army was in position all manner of wind instruments, a seemingly infinite number, were sounded, followed by the singing of songs as was the Tartar custom before battle commenced. The start of the battle was signalled with the clash of cymbals, the beating of drums and more singing. I tell you, it was wonderful to hear.

Kublai first ordered the flanking troops to attack and they were soon involved in bloody conflict. The air was filled with arrows which rained down causing huge casualties of men and horses. The shouts of the combatants, the hiss of weapons and the screams of the horses were enough to strike terror in the strongest hearts.

With their arrows discharged, the armies locked in hand-to-hand combat wielding swords, lances and maces shod with iron. Such was the slaughter that men and horses were piled in vast heaps and neither side could advance. For a long time the outcome was undecided and victory wavered between the contestants from morning until noon. Nayan, who had the reputation of a liberal and indulgent leader, commanded such zealous devotion from his troops that they were all prepared to die rather than turn their backs on the enemy.

Finally, Nayan realised he was completely surrounded and attempted to save himself by flight. He was soon captured, however, and brought before the Grand Khan who ordered that he be put to death. The actual execution was bizarre. Kublai believed that the sun and the air should not witness the death of a prince of royal blood so Nayan was enclosed in two carpets which were beaten and shaken until life had departed from his body.

Those of Nayan's troops who had survived the battle (all inhabitants of the provinces of Chorza Kauli, Banskol and Sitinque) submitted and swore allegiance to Kublai.

Nayan, it turned out, had privately undergone the ceremony of baptism although he never openly admitted to being a Christian. He bore the sign of the cross on his banners and lost a vast number of Christians in the battle. Saracens and Jews who saw these banners taunted the surviving Christians: 'Just look at the state to which you and your Christian banners are reduced.'

They complained to the Grand Khan and he ordered the taunters to appear before him and handed out this sharp rebuke, 'If the cross of Christ has not performed to Nayan's advantage that is because he defied justice and reason by rebelling against his Lord. He was a traitor and to such wretches it could not afford protection. Let none presume to charge with injustice the God of the Christians who is Himself the perfection of goodness and justice.' The Grand Khan was always very even-handed in his treatment of the several religious faiths in the empire.

After his victory over Nayan he returned in triumph and with great pomp to his capital city of Kanbula and remained there until March. This was our Easter and being aware that it was one of our principal religious occasions, he commanded all the Christians to attend him and bring with them their book containing the four gospels of the evangelists. He had it repeatedly perfumed with incense, he kissed it and directed all the nobles who were present to do the same. This was his usual practice with the principal festivals of the Christians and he also observed the festivals of Saracens, Jews and idolaters. Asked about his motives he replied, 'There are four great Prophets revered and worshipped by the four different classes of mankind: Jesus Christ who is held to be divine by Christians, Mahomet for the Saracens, Moses to Jews and the idolaters have Sogomombarkan. I honour and respect all four and look for help to whomsoever among them is supreme in heaven.'

But you only have to see the way he behaves in the presence of Christians to know that he regards Christianity as the truest and the best; nothing, he's been heard to say, was professed by its followers that was not replete with virtue and holiness. He will not, however, allow Christians to carry the cross before them in their processions, arguing that it was the device on which Christ was scourged and ignominiously put to death.

One might ask why, having shown such a preference for Christianity, he did not get himself baptised. He once gave this answer to my father and uncle when he sent them as his ambassadors to the Pope:

Why should I become a Christian? You yourselves have seen that the Christians of these countries of mine are ignorant, inefficient people who do not seem able to perform miracles, whereas the idolaters can perform them at will. When I sit at table the cups in the middle of the hall come to me (of their own accord) filled with wine for me to drink, without being touched by human hand.

The yogis of the idolaters can control bad weather and direct it anywhere they want in the heavens. They are wonderfully gifted with things of that nature. You yourselves have seen that their idols can speak and have the power of prophecy. But what extraordinary powers, what miracles have been displayed by the priests of Christianity, the nobles of my court who do not believe in Christianity will ask. The idolaters can make the claim that miracles are the product of their sanctity and the influence of their idols. The nobles will think I am making a grievous error not acknowledging the power of the yogis to forecast my death.

But then he said to my father and Uncle Maffeo,

So I want you to return to your Pontiff and ask him to send me a hundred persons so skilled in your laws as to be able to convince the idolaters that they too can perform miracles if they want but refrain from doing so because they involve conjuring up evil spirits. If these holy men can get the idolaters not to engage in such practices in their presence, I will ban idolatry and get myself baptised. I expect my nobles will want to follow my example, indeed my subjects in general. We will have more Christians than you do in your country.

If only the Pope had been prepared to send us people really qualified to teach the gospel I think the Grand Khan would have embraced Christianity. He certainly seems to have had a strong liking for it.

But I have rather wandered off the subject. I wanted to tell you about the rewards and honours Kublai bestows on those who distinguish themselves by their valour in battle. A council of twelve of the most intelligent of his nobles is appointed to assess the conduct of the officers of the army. Their reports are presented to Kublai and he makes his promotions accordingly, from among those who have commanded a hundred to those commanding a thousand, and so on. They also get presented with silver trophies as well as the customary warrant to command or govern. These warrants are in the form of valuable metal tablets, silver for the commander of one hundred, gold on silver gilt for one thousand and gold embossed with the head of a lion for those chosen to take on a command of ten thousand. The silver tablets weighed 20 ounces and those with the lion's head almost 40 ounces. They specify the privileges, duties and powers of the holder.

Those given the command of one hundred thousand men are honoured with a gold tablet weighing about 60 ounces, embossed with the image of a lion and the moon. Whenever such a person rides in public an umbrella is carried over his head in recognition of his high rank and when he sits it is always upon a silver chair. On certain of his nobles the Grand Khan confers tablets bearing an impression of a gerfalcon. These honoured few are authorised to command, as a guard of honour, the entire army of any great prince. They can also make use of the horses of the imperial stud at their pleasure and appropriate the horses of any officer inferior in rank.

Kublai, who, as I have said, is styled Grand Khan or Lord of Lords, is neither tall nor short but of middling stature. He is well formed and well proportioned. He has a fair complexion that is occasionally suffused with red, like the flush of a rose, which adds much grace to his countenance. His eyes are black and handsome and his nose well shaped and prominent. He has four principal wives and the eldest born son of any of them may accede to the throne. They all bear the title of empress and have their separate courts. They are each attended by no fewer than three hundred young female attendants of great beauty. Then there are a multitude of young pages, eunuchs and ladies of the bedchamber. Each of the courts has a total staff of some ten thousand!

When the Grand Khan desires the company of one of his empresses he either sends for her or goes to her palace. Many concubines are also provided for his pleasure. They mostly come from a province of Tartary called Ungut where there is a city of the same name and the women are famous for the fairness of their complexions and their beauty.

The Grand Khan's officers go to Ungut every other year, sometimes more often, to collect for him four or five hundred (or more!) of the most beautiful young women. They are chosen in the following way. Qualified persons are appointed to inspect the girls for facial beauty, quality of the hair, eyebrows, the mouth and lips and other features. The overall look of the first is also judged and then they are valued – 16, 17, 18 or 20 or more carats. The Grand Khan usually takes girls of 20 or 21 carats. When they arrive at court a new set of inspectors makes a further selection. About thirty or forty are usually selected for the Grand Khan to have his way with. Ahead of that, however, these chosen few are placed in the care of the wives of certain noblemen who watch them at night to make sure they have no concealed imperfections, do not snore, have sweet breath and are free of unpleasant body odours.

Finally the first who pass all the rigorous tests are split into groups of five. For three days and nights they attend the Grand Khan in his private apartments where they are expected to perform every service that is required of them. Quite literally, he does with them as he likes.

Each party takes its turn and then the first five go in again. A group is also on duty in an outer chamber to provide the Grand Khan with anything he wants in the way of food and drink. Essentially he is waited on hand and foot by these obliging young females.

Those he does not fancy are given to the different lords of the household and they are taught cookery, dressmaking and other suitable tasks. Courtiers looking for a wife can have one of these young ladies together with a handsome settlement if the Grand Khan says so. One way or another they are all disposed of to noble households.

You might think that the people of Ungut would feel aggrieved at their daughters being commandeered by the sovereign in this way. Not a bit of it. They regard it as an honour and a favour, particularly the fathers of beautiful daughters who are especially pleased. 'If', they say, 'my daughter is born under an auspicious planet to good fortune his majesty can fulfil her destiny with a noble match; which I could not do.' On the other hand if the daughter is guilty of misconduct or falls out of favour in any way, the father blames it on the malign influence of the stars.

The Grand Khan has had twenty-two sons by his four legitimate wives. The eldest was Genghis (named after his great ancestor) who, had he lived, would have inherited all Kublai's titles and the government of the Empire. Genghis fortunately has a son, Themur, who will succeed in his place. Themur is in good health and he has wisdom and valour, having proved himself in several successful battles. Besides this Kublai has twenty-five sons by his concubines and they are all continuously employed in the army where they have also proved to be brave soldiers. They have the rank of noblemen. Seven of his legitimate sons run extensive provinces and kingdoms. In my view, they all govern with wisdom and prudence as is only to be expected of the children of the greatest of the Tartars.

I want to return now to where Kublai usually resides from December to February, the great city of Kanbula, in the north-east corner of China, also known as Cathay. On the southern side of the city stands Kublai's vast palace that is enclosed by a wall and a deep ditch. The walls form a square each side of which is 8 miles long. There are four equidistant gates set in these walls. At the heart of the complex a second wall encloses a space a mile across where the troops are billeted. Outside this another mighty wall encompasses a 6-mile square which has three gates on the north side and three to the south. The middle gates are larger than the outer two and are always kept shut other than when the Emperor uses them to come and go. The smaller gates provide public access.

Eight handsome and spacious buildings house the royal military stores. Each contains a separate category of stores: cavalry ordnance such as bridles, saddles and stirrups in one; archery requisites such as bows, strings, quivers and arrows in another; leather armour corselets and other protective gear in a third.

Finally there is a fourth enclosure with walls of great thickness 25 feet high and topped with pure white battlements. Its walls are each a mile long containing six gates and it also has eight buildings devoted to the royal wardrobe!

Handsome trees and meadows fill the open spaces between the walls, and stags, musk ox, roebuck, fallow deer and other species roam here. The roads traversing these pastures are raised some 3 feet and paved so that no mud or rainwater collects on them, indeed they act as conduits to help water the abundant grass.

Within the 4-mile enclosure stands the palace of the Grand Khan, the largest I or anyone else has ever seen. It bridges its north and south walls leaving a single opening which is used by military guards and persons of rank. The building is of a single storey with a very high roof. It is raised on a platform some 30 spans high bordered by a 6-foot wide marble wall. The wall serves as a terrace for people to walk about on. There is a handsome balustrade and pillars that the public may approach along the outside of the marble wall.

The towering sides of the great halls and apartments are decorated with carved dragons and gilded figures of warriors, birds, beasts and battle scenes. The four sides of the palace are served by grand flights of marble steps from ground level to the marble terrace.

The palace's grand hall is big enough to hold dinner parties for huge multitudes of people. There are a number of other chambers, all exquisite; indeed it would be hard to suggest how they might be improved. Even the roof is decorated with a variety of glazed tiles coloured red, green, azure and violet. The windows are glazed with I know not what, but whatever it is is so fine and delicate as to be as clear as crystal.

To the rear are large buildings with several apartments where Kublai keeps his private treasure; a fortune in gold and silver bullion, precious stones, pearls and gold and silver plate.

The wives and concubines occupy the apartments and here, in complete privacy, Kublai is able conveniently and without interruption to conduct the business of the state. Opposite the Emperor's palace and very similar is another palace which is the residence of his eldest son, Genghis. The court observes all the ceremonials befitting a prince who is to succeed to the government of the Empire.

About a bow-shot's distance from the palace a huge artificial mound of earth rises to a height of at least 300 feet with a circumference of about a mile. It has been planted with the most beautiful evergreen trees. Whenever Kublai hears of a handsome tree growing anywhere (no matter how large and heavy) he has it dug up, roots, earth and all, and has it transported to the verdant mound by means of elephants!

On the summit of what is known as the Green Mount is an ornamental pavilion also bright green. The view from here – the lovely trees and elegant, decorated buildings – is truly wonderful.

In the northern corner of the city precinct, where the earth was removed for the mound, is a large fishpond, also used for watering cattle. The small stream that feeds it passes then along an aqueduct, past the Green Mount into a much larger excavation between the palaces of Kublai and Genghis. (The earth from here was also used to heighten the mound.) This lake is full of fish, providing Kublai's table with an unlimited abundance. The stream flows through the lake and there are iron or copper grills to prevent the fish escaping. A bridge spans the lake from one residence to the other. This is most certainly a great palace.

Kanbula is situated near a large river and was in ancient times the most magnificent and royal of cities. The name means 'the city of the sovereign', but Kublai was told by his astrologers that it contained rebellious elements and he elected to build another city, the one I have just described, on the other side of the river. The new city was called Tai-du and Cathayans were forced to move from the old city to the new. That proved difficult because old Kanbula was vast, so inhabitants who were judged to be above suspicion were permitted to stay where they were.

The new city forms a perfect square 24 miles in extent with each of its sides exactly 6 miles long. It is enclosed by walls of terracotta, 30 feet thick at the base and about 9 feet at the top surmounted by brilliant white parapets. Inside, the streets are so perfectly aligned if you stand on the wall above one of the gates you can see the gate opposite you on the other side of the city. The public streets have shops and stalls of every kind. Houses are lined up on perfectly square plots spacious enough for handsome buildings, generous gardens and courtyards. The heads of each local tribe have one of these mansions assigned to them and these rights are passed on.

The entire interior of the city looks exactly like a chessboard. I find it difficult to describe how beautiful is the effect of this precision.

The vast outer wall of the city has twelve gates, three on each side of the square. Over each gate is a handsome building where they keep the city's arms. Every gate is guarded by one thousand men. This is really an honour guard for the Grand Khan and does not reflect any perceived danger to the city. (That is not to say that the astrologers have not caused him a degree of suspicion about the Chinese.)

A great bell hangs in a lofty building in the centre of the city. It sounds a curfew of three strokes every night after which woe betide anyone out on the streets unless their business is urgent, like a man falling sick or a woman requiring help in labour. Even these people are required to carry a light.

There are suburbs spreading out 3 or 4 miles from the city walls. The number of people in these suburbs exceeds that of the city itself. A mile or so out, inns and caravanserai provide accommodation for merchants. These are segregated just as, for example, we would provide different billets for Lombards, Germans or French.

In the New City and suburbs there are some twenty-five thousand prostitutes and they are supervised. Each hundred and each thousand have their own officers who are responsible to a captain-general. This kind of control is necessary because here the ladies of the night are allocated out. When an ambassador who has business with Kublai comes here it is customary for him to be entertained at the Grand Khan's expense. The captain-general allocates to each member of the embassy one girl every night. The girls do not get paid – it is their tribute to the sovereign.

Guards in parties of thirty and forty patrol the streets throughout the night keeping an eye open for people not observing the curfew. Any trouble and the offender is immediately detained for the night, appearing before magistrates in the morning. Depending upon the seriousness of the delinquency they are flogged and this can sometimes result in death. Flogging is a traditional way of punish-ment for these people, because they are encouraged by their astrologers not to shed blood.

But, as I have said, these people have a rebellious disposition. Here is one famous story. The disposition of land, government and everything belonging to the state was in the hands of a committee of twelve, one of whom was a Saracen named Achmac. He was a crafty, bold man with more influence over the Grand Khan than any of the others, to such a degree that Kublai was much taken with him and indulged him royally. Indeed, it was discovered after his death that he had beguiled his majesty with spells obliging him to hear and grant anything he asked. By the same means he did whatever took his fancy.

Government and public offices were given away, judgment pronounced on offenders and, if he encountered ill-will in anyone, he had only to say to the Grand Khan, 'This person has committed an offence against you and deserves to die,' and Kublai would reply, 'Do as you judge best.' Immediate execution followed!

Kublai believed in him so absolutely that no one dared say anything against him. Everyone stood in awe of him. Even those accused of capital crimes had little hope because they could not find an attorney who would represent them. No one dared oppose the will of Achmac and numerous people died unjustly because of him.

Similarly, any handsome woman he desired, and who became the object of his lust, he had; if she was single, he took her as a wife, otherwise he simply compelled her to yield to his desires. Fathers of beautiful daughters were particularly vulnerable. He would send emissaries to ask, 'How do you see you daughter's future? You cannot do better than give her in marriage to the Lord Deputy or the Vice Regent (meaning Achmac who used these titles). Moreover we will guarantee you a three-year government appointment.' Achmac then arranged with the Grand Khan for the job to be made available. The fathers are thus tempted to part with their child. Many a young, beautiful girl was sacrificed to be the slave of his pleasure by these means.

He had twenty-five sons holding the highest offices of state, some of them using his influence to indulge too in his lecherous habits and committing many other unlawful and atrocious acts. Those who obtained appointments gave him a generous kickback and he accumulated great wealth. For twenty-two years he exercised uncontrolled sway until finally his people rebelled against the wickedness committed against their families and held a meeting to decide how they might bring about his and the government's demise.

A Chinese chief named Chen-ku had an army of six thousand men and he burned with resentment at the multiple violation of his mother, wife and daughter. He proposed an uprising to one of his countrymen, Van-ku, who commanded one thousand men. They determined to rise when Kublai and his son had completed their three-month stay and left Achmac in charge of Kanbula.

The two conspirators spread word of their intentions to other leading Chinese and through them to friends in many other cities. A fire was designated the signal for all to rise up and kill those who wore beards. (The Tartars, Saracens and Christians have beards but the Chinese are naturally beardless.)

Understand that because the Grand Khan had obtained the sovereignty of Cathay not by lawful means but by force of arms, he lacked confidence in the people and all the important officers – magistrates and provincial governors – were Tartars, Saracens, Christians and other foreigners who were trusted members of his household. It is true to say that his government was universally hated by the locals, who found themselves treated as slaves by the Tartars and still worse by the Saracens.

When all their plans were laid, Van-ku and Chen-ku made their way into the palace at night in secret, lit the lights and Van-ku settled himself on one of the royal thrones. A bogus message was sent to Achmac who lived across the river, bidding him come to the palace because Genghis had returned.

Achmac was very surprised at the news but, being in awe of the prince, instantly obeyed. Passing into the New City he met a Tartar officer, Kogatai, the commander of a guard of twelve thousand men, who demanded to know where he was going at so late an hour. When Achmac informed him, Kogatai said it was impossible that Genghis could have arrived in secret and without raising any of the guards to attend him.

The Chinese plotters knew nothing of this encounter, of course, and felt sure that once they had finished off Achmac their troubles would be at an end.

Achmac hurried on to the palace leaving Kogatai at the door to the throne room. With the lights blazing in his eyes Achmac mistakenly prostrated himself before the figure on the throne. Hitherto concealed to one side, Chen-ku then stepped out and lopped off his head.

Kogatai saw the whole thing and with a cry of 'Treason!' despatched an arrow which caught Van-ku upon the throne and slew him. His guards captured Chen-ku and then marched into the city with orders to kill everyone they found out of doors. The Chinese, however, realising their plot had failed, stayed inside. The Grand Khan was contacted, informed of what had passed and sent Kogatai an instruction to investigate and punish according to their degree of guilt, those Chinese who were proved to have been involved. Kogatai moved swiftly and by the end of the following day had arrested all the principal conspirators and had them put to death. The same was done in other cities.

Upon his return to the New City, the Grand Khan wanted to know what had caused the rebellion. He quickly established that Achmac and seven of his sons (to a greater or lesser degree) were guilty of the enormous crimes I have described.

Kublai promptly confiscated the family fortune (an incredible treasure) and had it deposited in his own cellars. Achmac's body was taken from its tomb and thrown into the street to be torn to pieces by the dogs. The most guilty of the sons he had flayed alive.

He also read the riot act to the Saracens, calling their sect an 'abomination' which condoned the murder of people of other faiths, and warning them that he regarded them with contempt and guilty of behaviour that made the infamous Achmac and his sons look innocent. Saracen leaders were ordered to appear before him. He banned many of their religious practices such as the blooding of animals by cutting their throats rather than opening the belly and commanded that in future they follow Tartar customs of marriage. I can vouch for all this because I was there when it all happened.

Now let me tell you about the Grand Khan's court. His bodyguard comprises twelve thousand horsemen known as the 'Kastian' which means soldiers devoted to his majesty. Not that Kublai is particularly apprehensive, this guard is a matter of state. Four senior officers command units of three thousand men of the guard with each taking turns to be on duty in the palace for three successive days and nights. The off-duty guards stay in the palace, however, unless they are given leave of absence or are engaged in some other service for the Grand Khan.

When Kublai holds a grand and public court he sits facing south at a table before his elevated throne with the Queen on his left. His sons sit, on seats somewhat lower, on his right hand as do any other relatives of imperial stock. With the exception of his eldest son, Genghis, their heads are about on a level with Kublai's feet.

Other nobles are seated at progressively lower tables, as are wives of sons and grandsons below the Queen on the left-hand side. Essentially everyone is seated at a level representing their status in the royal pecking order.

Most of the officers, including nobles, sit and eat on the carpet. Multitudes of people from different countries wait outside for an audience. They bring with them many rare and curious articles. On feast days or on royal marriages petitioners who have had their possessions taken away appear in the hope of restitution.

Near the Grand Khan's table an odd piece of furniture is placed. A square coffer, it is exquisitely carved and gilded with figures of animals and each side is almost 10 feet long. It contains a huge jar made of precious stones holding about a ton of rice wine. Then there are three smaller vessels filled with mares' milk, camels' milk and a local beverage. They are served in large royal cups and flagons of beautiful gilt plate, sufficient for eight to ten men. Each pair of guests at the tables is given one, together with a kind of ladle shaped like a cup with a handle, which is actually used for drinking. Ladies are served likewise. The quantity and richness of the Grand Khan's gold and silver plate are quite incredible.

Officers of rank wait on the guests. Strangers not familiar with court etiquette are found places and these stewards prowl the hall ensuring everyone has all they want in the way of wine, milk, meat and other delicacies.

Whenever Kublai moves around the hall he is accompanied by two giants with staves. Woe betide anyone who attempts to get too close to the Grand Khan for these guards either confiscate an item of clothing (which can be redeemed for money) or they are ordered to deliver a prescribed number of blows.

Strangers have to be warned of these rules by specially appointed officers. They are, however, strictly observed because it is regarded as a very bad omen if anyone gets too close to the royal presence. I should add that everyone is very merry at the end of an evening and the rule is then not strictly enforced.

The many people who serve the Grand Khan with his food and

drink are required to cover their noses and mouths with beautiful veils of worked silk so that their breath may not affect his victuals. There is a complicated ritual for serving Kublai his drinks. A page presents it then backs off three paces and kneels. The whole hall then prostrates itself in a like manner. On cue the band strikes up and continues to play until Kublai finishes his drink. Then all the guests get up. This happens every time Kublai has a drink!

There is always an excessive abundance of food, then the tables are removed and the guests are entertained by comedians, tumblers, jugglers and lots of musicians. Everyone has a high old time.

The entire Empire celebrates Kublai's birthday on 29 September. Apart from the New Year's Day celebrations, which I will tell you about in a moment, this is their greatest festival. The Grand Khan makes a very grand appearance clad in a superb robe of cloth of gold. He supplies rich silk outfits to some twenty thousand nobles also coloured gold (although not as rich as his) with chamois leather belts and boots delicately worked with gold and silver thread. The closest of his courtiers (Henry of Quiecitari) he rewards with garments embroidered with pearls and precious stones worth thousands. These outfits are also worn for the thirteen festivals commemorating the thirteen lunar months of the year. When the Khan and his court appear in this splendid regalia it is truly a royal spectacle, reflecting the status of the Grand Khan as the ruler of the world.

On his actual birthday all the Tartars and the people of every kingdom and province throughout the Empire send him valuable presents. He also receives presents from people seeking favours and Kublai hands over these decisions to a tribunal of twelve experts in such matters. Upon this day also, Christians, Saracens and idolaters all offer up devout prayers calling on their various gods to bless and keep the Sovereign and give him wealth, health and a long life.

Now let me tell you, as I promised, about the White Feast which takes place on 1 February, the date that marks the start of the year. This time Kublai and his subjects in various countries dress in white, the emblem of good fortune, hopeful of good fortune, pleasure and comfort through the rest of the year.

Silver, gold and precious stones rain down on the Grand Khan from the entire Empire, along with many pieces of white cloth denoting ample love and plenty of money. Nobles, princes and indeed all ranks of society stage festivities at which they also exchange white gifts and wish each other good fortune and embrace joyfully.

Great numbers of white horses are presented to the Grand Khan at this time. Some are not entirely white but white horses are not uncommon in this country.

There is a curious tradition for those rich enough to make up their presents in parcels of 'nine times nine'. Thus if you are sending the Grand Khan horses there should be eighty-one of them. By this means Kublai can receive as many as a hundred thousand horses at the New Year festival. The same equation holds good for, say, gold or cloth.

This is the day when all his elephants, some five thousand, put in an appearance. They form a procession covered in a livery of cloth richly worked in gold and silk with figures of birds and beasts. Each elephant carries two large coffers loaded with vessels of gold and silver plate and other royal necessities. Then follows a train of camels loaded with the royal furniture. They form a splendid spectacle as they pass in battle order before the Grand Khan.

Come the morning of the festival, princes, nobility, courtiers, astrologers, physicians, falconers, public officers, prefects and the officers of the army make their way into the great hall of the palace to appear before the Emperor. Those who cannot get in stand outside but still within view of the Sovereign. Everyone is seated in order of rank, from the King's sons and the imperial family downwards. A senior religious figure then rises and declares: 'Bow down and do reverence.' Whereupon everyone touches his forehead to the floor. 'God bless our Lord, and long preserve him in the enjoyment of felicity.'

The people answer, 'God grant it'. 'May God increase the grandeur and prosperity of his Empire, may he preserve all those who are his subjects in the blessings of peace and contentment and in all their lands may abundance prevail.' 'God grant it,' comes the reply. And they make their protestations four times.

The prelate (he would not be so recognised in our religion) advances to a richly adorned altar bearing a red tablet inscribed with the name of the Grand Khan. He perfumes the tablet and altar with burning incense and the company prostrates itself again.

The gifts are then presented to Kublai and when these have been displayed and he has cast an eye over them the tables are prepared for the feast according to the pecking order I described earlier. Music and merriment follow, and at this feast a full-grown lion is brought in, so tamed it has been taught to lie down at Kublai's feet.

Royal hunting parties are ordered throughout the very cold months of December, January and February. The governors of the surrounding districts are required to provide sport with all manner of large game: wild boar, stags, fallow deer, roebuck and bears. The hunters gather in a designated area where these animals are to be found, and encircle them. The killing is done partly with dogs but mostly with arrows. Large quantities of prepared venison are sent back by carriage for Kublai's enjoyment. If the distance is too far for the meat to travel only the skins are sent back, to be used by the army.

Kublai sometimes hunts deer with leopards, lynxes and even lions (tigers). The latter are larger than the Babylonian lion with fine skins marked lengthwise with white, black and red stripes. These will take boar, wild oxen and asses, bears, stag, roebuck and other sporting game. It is quite a sight to see a lion loosed and in pursuit of its prey and the savagery and speed with which it brings it down.

The big cats are carried about in cages on wagons. Inside with them is a little dog with which the animal is familiar and which seems to keep them calm in the presence of prey animals. They have also to be transported in cases against the wind lest the game scents them and makes off. His majesty actually has eagles which are trained to hunt wolves! Such is the size and strength of these birds, few ever escape their talons.

The Grand Khan enjoys the services of two legendary hunters, the brothers Banyan and Mingan, who are called 'chivichi' or 'masters of the chase' and who look after Kublai's hunting dogs and his pack of mastiffs. The brothers each command a staff of ten thousand huntsmen dressed in their individual livery, one of red the other sky blue. They go into the hunting field with no fewer than five thousand dogs. Each, with his pack, commands a flank and they advance with the Emperor in the middle until they have enclosed a tract of country a day's march across from which nothing can escape.

It is an exciting and exhilarating experience to watch those clever dogs and skilled huntsmen, with Kublai in the middle of it all, energetically covering the ground while bears, stags and other game flee madly in every direction.

The two brothers have a contract to supply the court with a thousand pieces of game daily (quails do not count). Fish – the amount three men might eat at one meal – count as one piece of game and the court takes as much as the brothers can catch.

In March Kublai makes a long journey to the north-east in the direction of the ocean, attended by ten thousand falconers who carry with them a vast number of gerfalcons, peregrine falcons, sakers and vultures with which to hunt the banks of a river. Smaller parties of one or two hundred hunt different areas and send their spoil back to Kublai. With him also are ten thousand men known as taskoal or 'watchers', who spread out across a large tract of land in parties of two or three, each armed with a whistle and a hood. No great distance apart, they are able to call and hood the hawks. When the hawks are loosed they do not have to be followed because one of the 'watchers' will pick them up and assist the birds if necessary.

The falcons all belong to Kublai or to his nobles and carry a silver tag on the leg bearing the owner's name and also the name of the keeper. Lost birds are carried to an officer called *bulangazi*, 'the officer of unclaimed property'. If you find a falcon and do not follow this procedure you are labelled a thief. The *bulangazi* sits under his own flag in an elevated part of the camp so that everyone can find him. Very few birds are lost.

I think nothing rivals falconry as a sport and nothing illustrates this as dramatically as the events that take place when the Grand Khan is out hunting. When the way is very narrow the Grand Khan rides an elephant. Sometimes he uses four, mounting a handsomely carved pavilion the inside of which is padded with cloth of gold, the outside covered with wild-cat skins. Actually he needs this comfort because he is troubled by gout.

In the pavilion he carries with him his twelve best gerfalcons and twelve of his favourite officers to keep him amused. Riders outside warn him of the approach of cranes or other prey birds. The pavilion curtains are raised and the falcons are let fly, bringing down the prey but often only after a long struggle. Everyone finds this hugely enjoyable, the officers in the pavilion, the outriders and of course the Grand Khan who watches it while reclining on a couch.

After several hours of entertaining sport, Kublai retires to a place called Kaksarmodin where a vast camp of the pavilions and tents of his sons, nobles, the royal guard and falconers is pitched. There are more than ten thousand of them and it is quite something to see.

The royal tent, where Kublai gives audiences, is long and wide enough to accommodate ten thousand soldiers, their officers and other persons of rank. Connecting to it is a second tent forming a spacious salon where the Emperor can have more private and intimate meetings. Then behind this is a large and handsome pavilion where he sleeps. All around are tents for other members of the household. All these buildings are of ingenious construction. They are richly carved and gilded and covered on the outside with tiger skins streaked white, black and red so well sewn they are rain and wind proof. Within is a lining of ermine and sable, the latter being the most costly of all furs, the value depending of course on the quality. The Tartars esteem it 'the queen of furs'. Sables, called by the Tartars 'rondes', are about the size of polecats. The tent ropes are all of silk.

Adjoining the royal pavilion are the splendid tents of his ladies. The many gerfalcons and other birds and beasts also have quarters close by.

Incredible, is the only word I can think of to describe the huge number of people housed in the encampment, counting the people from different parts of the Empire. You could be forgiven for thinking you were in the middle of a well-populated city.

The Grand Khan's entire household attends him here, that is, his physicians, astronomers, falconers and all manner of other officials. He is in residence here until Easter, taking a fearful toll of storks, swans, herons and a variety of other birds. His huntsmen in other areas also procure a great deal of fine game.

The excellence of the sport is hard to describe and I honestly think, indeed I have been an eyewitness to it, that Kublai has the time of his life when he is here, and when his time is up he makes his way slowly home, hunting all the way.

Business back at court starts with three days of feasting. The idea is to entertain and amuse the locals and this he does royally. As I have said, Kanbula is vast, greater than the mind can comprehend. In addition to the people of the city there are twelve suburbs (corresponding to the twelve gates) and, if anything, these suburbs are more populated than the city proper. They house mainly merchants who need to be in close contact with the court. Wherever Kublai goes the merchants tend to flock after him. Some of these merchants' houses are as magnificent as those in the city (with the exception of the royal palace, of course).

Special rules apply to the city. No corpses may be buried here and if an idolater dies his body is carried out beyond the suburbs for the traditional cremation. Public executions also take place well outside the city.

Marco's father, Nicolo, and his uncle, Maffeo, leave Venice to set up as merchants in the East. (*Bodleian Library, Oxford*)

Kublai Khan presents the Polos with a golden tablet to guarantee their passage back to the Pope in Italy to ask that he send the Khan '100 learned men' who could prove the claims of the Christian faith. (*Bodleian Library, Oxford*)

The Caliph of Baghdad challenges Christians to prove their faith on pain of death by 'moving a mountain'. *(Bodleian Library, Oxford)*

Genghis Khan does battle with the Christian king, Prester John.
(Bodleian Library, Oxford)

Kublai Khan deployed 100,000 foot-soldiers and 360,000 horse to put down a rebellion by his nephew, Nayan. *(Bodleian Library, Oxford)*

Nayan was put to death by enclosing him in two carpets and shaking it violently until he expired so that 'the sun and the air' would not witness the shedding of the blood of a member of the royal family. *(Bodleian Library, Oxford)*

Kublai's birthday party. Marco claims 'necromancers and sorcerers' caused the refreshments to travel magically across the room at occasions like this, while outside there was a birthday parade of 5,000 elephants. (*Bodleian Library, Oxford*)

Kublai Khan, says Marco, cared for his people well, setting aside grain in special warehouses which he would distribute gratis at times of famine. (*Bodleian Library, Oxford*)

The fabled city of Karakoran with its mighty castle (no trace of which exists today), but Marco claims it was the first settled residence of the Tartars. (*Bodleian Library, Oxford*)

Sin-din-fu, on the borders of Tibet, a city of magnificent bridges (one of which Marco is seen crossing), where 'some of the rivers are half a mile wide'. One and a half million of its inhabitants were said to have been put to the sword when the Tartars occupied it.
(*Bodleian Library, Oxford*)

An attempt to underline religious differences appears to be the object of this picture which shows a shrouded body being burnt by dark-faced Indians while behind the city walls paler faces worship a golden calf.
(*Bodleian Library, Oxford*)

The Chinese city of Sa-yan-fu, which had withstood a siege of three years before it was reduced by the Khan's army using siege-engines (left) designed by the elder Polos – 'greatly increasing their reputation and credit'.
(*Bodleian Library, Oxford*)

The 'celestial' city of Kin-sai in southern China (Manji): 'which it merits from its pre-eminence to all others in the world in points of grandeur and beauty, as well as from its abundant delights, might lead an inhabitant to imagine himself in paradise'. *(Bodleian Library, Oxford)*

The grotesque marvels to be found in India. *(Bodleian Library, Oxford)*

Eight kings offer gifts to a golden idol. Kublai Khan was eclectic on the subject of religion, constantly challenging Nestorian Christians, Muslims, Jews and Buddhists to substantiate their claims to the superior faith. He himself seemed to favour astrology and sorcery as much. *(Bodleian Library, Oxford)*

A meeting of six kings. Kings feature a lot in Marco's book and he tells the story of the Magi in its Eastern form which features a burning well ignited by celestial fire (possibly in the background to this illustration). Burning wells, or caverns, may well have alluded to surface deposits of ignited crude oil which Marco also saw. *(Bodleian Library, Oxford)*

'Ascending mountain after mountain, you eventually arrive at a point of the road where you might suppose the surrounding summits to be the highest in the world.'
(*Photography: Carolyn Horton*)

'Near the banks of this river there are rocky hills and small rocky eminences, upon which are erected idol temples and other edifices.'
(*Photography: Carolyn Horton*)

'Large streams of the purest water precipitate themselves through the fissures of the rocks. In these streams are trout and many other delicate sorts of fish.' *(Photography: Carolyn Horton)*

'So great is the height of these mountains that no birds can be seen near their summits.' *(Photography: Carolyn Horton)*

'Nigh to this city is a valley frequented by a great number of partridges and quails, for whose food the Great Khan causes millet, panicum and other grains suitable to such birds to be planted along the sides of it every season and gives orders that no man may dare to reap the seed in order that they may not want for nourishment . . .'
(Photography: Carolyn Horton)

'Wheat is eaten in the form of vermicelli or pastry . . .' This reference is thought to have introduced Marco Polo's Italy to pasta. *(Photography: Carolyn Horton)*

'Amidst the highest of these mountains there live a race of savages who subsist upon the animals they can destroy and clothe themselves in their skins.'
(*Photography: Carolyn Horton*)

'Here, between two ranges, you perceive a large lake from which flows a handsome river.' (*Photography: Carolyn Horton*)

'However extraordinary it may be thought, it was affirmed that from the keenness of the air, fires when lighted do not give the same heat as in lower situations . . .' *(Photography: Carolyn Horton)*

'Towns and villages, respectable habitations, many fortified posts and also places adapted to hunting and fowling exist along the rivers.' *(Photography: Carolyn Horton)*

'The inhabitants live by trade and manual arts . . . It contains many halls and chambers ornamented with paintings and wooden carvings.' (*Photography: Carolyn Horton*)

'These mountains are extemely lofty, insomuch that it employs a man from morning till night to ascend to the top of them. Between them are wide plains clothed with grass and trees . . .' (*Photography: Carolyn Horton*)

'The idolaters have many religious houses, or monasteries and abbeys, built after the manner of the country . . .' (*Photography: Carolyn Horton*)

'In Kesmur they can compel their idols, although by nature dumb and deaf, to speak.' (*Photography: Carolyn Horton*)

'The people of Bascia worship idols; and are skilled in the art of magic, and the invocation of demons.' *(Photography: Carolyn Horton)*

Prostitutes are supposed to work only in the suburbs although some go into the city secretly. As I have said, there are twenty-five thousand of them. Nor to be frank, in the light of the massive and ever-changing merchant community, does demand exceed supply.

Kanbula attracts everything that is rare and valuable in the way of trade from all over the world. It is especially a major centre for Indian goods such as precious stones, pearls and various medications and spices. Goods from the provinces of China as well as other provinces of the Empire find an insatiable demand from those obliged to maintain a presence close to court. I would say that more merchandise changes hands here than in any other place; no fewer than a thousand carriages and pack horses loaded with raw silk come in daily. They form the raw materials for an immense quantity of gold tissue. Worked silks are also manufactured locally.

There are several towns, some walled, in the vicinity of Kanbula that are entirely dependent upon the trade and manufacturing they do for the court.

Kanbula also houses Kublai's famous mint. At first glance you might think he has mastered the secrets of the alchemists because here he manufactures his own unique form of money! Bark is stripped from mulberry trees (the same as feed silkworms) and the thin inner layer between the bark and the wood carefully harvested. This is soaked then pounded to a pulp in a mortar for making into a paper. It resembles paper made from cotton, but it is black. When dry it is cut into pieces of money.

Notes are almost square (somewhat longer than they are wide) and of different sizes. Of these the smallest is worth a *denier tournois*; the next size a Venetian silver groat; others for 2, 5 and 10 groats; others still for 1, 2, 3 and upwards to 10 besants of gold.

The value of this paper money is authenticated as if it were gold or silver, each note bearing the name and seal of a specially appointed group of officials. The principal officer embosses the note with a vermilion seal, confirming it to be valid, current currency. Counterfeiting is a crime punished by death.

Produced in large quantities, this paper money is circulated throughout the Empire and nobody (on pain of death) dares not accept it. Actually it is accepted without hesitation because it can be used to purchase whatever merchandise is available at the time, such as pearls, jewels, gold or silver – in short, everything!

Several times each year large caravans of merchants bring in these articles as well as gold tissue and it is all laid out before the Grand Khan who calls in twelve skilful, experienced people who, having examined the goods with great care, fix their value. Allowing a reasonable profit the merchants are paid out in paper money. No one objects because, as I have said, they can use it to buy what they want. Merchants from countries where paper money is not in circulation trade it for goods they can sell at home.

If you end up with paper that has been damaged by being too long in circulation you take it to the mint and exchange it for fresh notes. There is a charge for this but it is only 3 per cent. If you are after bullion for manufacturing purposes, you likewise apply to the mint, trading gold and silver for paper. The king pays his army with paper currency and the value is the same for gold or silver. I would say that through the use of this currency Kublai has a much greater command of his economy than does any other sovereign in the universe.

Now let us look at the way the army and the Empire are administered. There is a twelve-man army council which decides troop movements, appointment and transfers of officers and assesses the need for troops for a particular situation. They also decide on the promotion of officers on the basis of individual valour. These must have Kublai's approval and if you get promotion you are awarded a tablet which is a warrant confirming your new post, as well as large presents designed to encourage you to greater things. This tribunal is called the 'Thai' or supreme court, and it answers to no one but the Sovereign.

A similar committee, the 'sing' comprising twelve nobles, presides over the affairs of the thirty-four provinces of the Empire.

They have their own grand palace in Kanbula with many chambers and halls. Each province has its own law-officer and a number of clerks running departments for different affairs, all answerable to the Thai.

The Sing appoints the provincial governors and delivers the tablet warrants confirming these appointments. They collect taxes and customs revenues and decide the disbursement of these funds. Essentially the Sing controls every department of state other than the army and while it is a high court directly responsible to the Grand Khan, it does not quite have the status of the Thai.

Rapid communication between the outlying cities and provinces and the Palace of Kanbula is facilitated by a series of post houses (called 'yamb') with facilities for travellers. They are large, handsome buildings located at 25- or 30-mile intervals on all the main roads out of the capital and furnished with draperies of silk and are good enough for all persons of rank, good enough for kings in fact. For some of them the court makes regular provision, or they are catered for by nearby towns. At each station 400 good horses are kept in a state of high readiness to ensure that Kublai's messengers and all the ambassadors may always be provided with relays of fresh horses.

Even in the mountainous districts, far away from the great roads where there are no villages and the towns are a great distance from each other, Kublai has caused to be erected elegant buildings furnished with all the necessities and many houses. He sends people to live in these remote places, to cultivate the land and mind the posts, and by these means quite large villages are formed and as a consequence messengers and ambassadors pass through the land with great facility. No less than two hundred thousand horses are used in the post service and some ten thousand beautifully furnished houses are maintained. I find it difficult to describe how wonderful and effective the system is.

You may wonder how the country manages to supply sufficient people to staff the service. Indeed, how do you feed so many? Well, you have to remember that Saracens and idolaters keep six, eight or even ten women, depending on their circumstances, and they have a prodigious number of children. Some men have as many as thirty sons. When you compare the way they live to our system where a man has only one wife, with whom he must remain even if she is barren, you will see how inferior our population is to theirs. And there is no shortage of good food as the Chinese and the Tartars subsist for the most part on rice, panicum and millet. The soil here is also very rich and for every three grains planted you get back more than a hundred. You do not, of course, get the same return from wheat, but bread is not on the diet here. It is used for vermicelli and pastry. The paste is boiled in milk or stewed with meat.

Not an inch of cultivable land is left untilled and their livestock multiplies prolifically. Scarcely anyone has less than six horses for his personal use.

Foot messengers who carry the post live in little villages of about forty houses spaced equidistant between the large post houses. Around their waists they wear a girdle hung with a number of small bells. They run about 3 miles and the bells serve to give notice to the next messenger so that he may instantly carry the message forward. So efficient is the system, a message for the Grand Khan that would normally take ten days, is delivered in two days and two nights. At the time of the fruit harvest, produce from Kanbula is conveyed to the Grand Khan at Shan-du in a little over thirty hours. This is generally considered a ten-day journey.

At each of the 3-mile stations a clerk notes the exact day and hour one courier arrives and another leaves; similarly at the post houses. Then there is a monthly visit by an officer to keep the staff on their toes and punish anyone not performing diligently.

The couriers do not pay tax and they receive good allowances from Kublai. The houses used are not his expense; the cities, towns and villages in the neighbourhood are obliged to supply and maintain them.

There is an officer who works out, according to their means, a quota for each of these units. The cost of maintaining the houses is, however, deductible from the revenues they pay to the Grand Khan. The stations have about four hundred horses, of which half are in service at any one time, the others put out to graze. Rivers or lakes that have to be crossed either by horse or foot messengers are serviced by three or four boats which the neighbouring villages are obliged to keep in a state of readiness. Cities on the edge of deserts that would normally take several days to cross and where there is no accommodation are likewise obliged to provide houses for the Grand Khan's ambassadors and to supply them and their suite with provisions (for which they get paid from the royal Exchequer). Post stations remote from the great roads are supplied with horses partly from neighbouring towns and cities and partly by Kublai himself.

The system is at its most effective when used to send news of events such as civil disturbances or rebellions of which Kublai needs to be informed with the utmost despatch. In these circumstances messengers will ride some 200 or even 250 miles in a single day. They carry with them a tablet inscribed with the gerfalcon to confirm the urgency of their mission. To ensure the delivery of these urgent messages, very often two messengers, stripped down to skin-tight clothes and with a cloth bound around their heads, take off together, pushing their horses to the limit until they reach the next relay station 25 miles on. Without a moment's rest they pick up fresh mounts and race on, covering, as I have said, 250 miles by the end of the day.

I have known of really urgent cases where the relay goes right on into the night, when, in the absence of a moon, runners bearing lights precede the messengers. (This goes a bit slower, of course.) Messengers with this kind of stamina are held in very high esteem.

In spite of his fearsome reputation I can tell you that Kublai is capable of great benevolence. Every year he sends commissioners to areas where the people have suffered crop damage from storms, violent rains, locusts, worms or other plagues. He not only refrains from demanding his normal tribute from these poor people, but from his own granaries furnishes them with as much corn as they need to survive and to plant a new crop.

He stockpiles grain during times of plenty and stores it in granaries in several provinces. These granaries are carefully tended to ensure their contents keep for three to four years. They are always kept full to guard against times of famine and when the grain is sold he hands out four measures for the price of one.

Similarly, any heavy mortality of cattle is compensated for from his own herds which are sustained by his one-tenth levy on the national herd. Indeed, all his thoughts are directed to assisting his people in order that they may live well and improve their standing in life.

I also want to mention a peculiarity of the Grand Khan; when there has been an accident caused to domestic stock by lightning – no matter how large the herd may be – he waives his one-tenth tithe for three years. This applies even to ships laden with goods. He waives any customs duty or share of the cargo. The reason is that such incidents are regarded as ill omens. God, he says, has shown himself to be displeased with the owners of the goods and he is reluctant to allow goods bearing the mark of divine wrath to enter his treasury.

On both sides of the public roads the Grand Khan has caused to be planted beautiful dense boulevards of trees. Planted just two paces apart these trees offer shade from the summer heat, and when the road is covered in snow, markers to assist and comfort travellers. These boulevards are planted wherever there is soil to support them. In deserts and over rocky mountains he has caused stones to be placed and columns raised to serve the same purpose. High-ranking officers ensure that the roads are kept in good order. Interestingly, the Grand Khan is following his astrologers when he plants these trees, believing it will bring him long life.

The majority of the people of China drink a wine brewed from rice mixed with a variety of spices and herbs. This is so flavoursome no one could wish for better. It is clear, bright, easy on the palate and because it is drunk hot, gets you drunk quicker than any other wine I know.

In the mountains of this province they mine a sort of black stone. There are big seams of it. When lit it burns like charcoal and gives off much more heat than wood and will burn throughout the night and still be going in the morning. The stones flame a bit when first lit but then glow, giving off considerable heat. Abundant and cheap in a country where admittedly there is also an abundance of wood, these stones make possible the continuous firing of stoves and baths. Warm baths are taken by everyone at least three times a week and daily in winter, if a person can afford it.

As well as providing famine relief for people in the provinces, Kublai also takes care of people in the city. Any family of quality falling on hard times because of illness will receive a year's supply of grain. There is a special palace where officials distribute this largesse after considering a written report on the needs of the claimant. Kublai gets a tenth of the Empire's production of wool, silk and hemp which he has woven into different sorts of cloth in a factory built for that purpose where shifts of workers are obliged to work one day a week in his majesty's service. Garments, both summer and winter items manufactured from these stuffs, are given to the poor families. Wool clothing, paid for from the 'Imperial Tenth', is also prepared for the army at factories in various towns.

I should note that it was not the traditional practice of the Tartars, who had not yet adopted the religion of idolatry, to give alms. They sent beggars packing with the warning: 'God sends bad seasons. Had he loved you as it appears he loves me, you would have prospered like me.' The wise men of the idolaters (particularly the *backsi*) have got to him, however, and these days providing for the poor is seen as 'good work' and much appreciated by their deities.

Essentially no one is denied food and clothing who comes to court asking for it and not a day passes without some twenty thousand containers of rice, millet and panicum being handed out. As a result, the people all regard Kublai as a god.

There are a huge number of astrologers at Kanbula; at least five thousand astrologers and soothsayers among the Saracens, Christians and Chinese for whom Kublai provides food and clothing in the same manner as he does for the deserving poor. They all have astrolabes inscribed with the signs of the planets, the hours based on a calculation of the meridian and their implications for the whole year. The astrologers (also known as almanac makers) are divided into several sects, each making prognoses from the movement of the heavenly bodies and their positions relative to the moon. They can thus forecast the state of the weather, peculiar phenomena of each and every month, for example thunder and storms in one, earthquakes in another; lightning and violent rains, diseases, mortality, wars, discords and conspiracies. They consult their astrolabes and make such predictions but always with the proviso that God, according to his own good pleasure, may do more or less than they have forecast. They write their predictions upon small squares, called *Takuni* and sell them to all who want to peer into the future.

Those making the most accurate predictions, the perfect masters of the art, are the most honoured. Anyone who is contemplating a big project or undertaking a long journey consults an astrologer. The latter demands information about the year, the month and the hour in which he was born and bases his calculations on the relationship of these to ascending stars. From these predictions the astrologer then suggests whether the adventure should be pursued or not.

You should be aware that the Tartars tell time by a cycle of twelve years. The first of these is called lion and subsequently, ox, dragon, dog and so on. When a person is asked his birthday he replies, 'in the year of the dragon' upon such a day and at such an hour and minute. This has been carefully recorded for him by his parents in a book. Upon completion of the twelve-year cycle it starts all over again.

All the people here are now idolaters and their god is represented by a tablet placed high on the wall with his name written on it. They pay homage to this and burn incense, lifting their hands and striking their heads against the floor three times, praying for a sound mind and a healthy body.

On the floor is usually a statue called Natigai which is the god of the earth and terrestrial things. Natigai has a wife and children, and they also worship him as I have described, praying for good weather, abundant crops, children and the like. These people believe themselves to be immortal in the sense that when a person dies the soul enters into another body. If the person has acted virtuously or wickedly in his lifetime he can expect a like host. His future state will thus become progressively better or worse.

A poor man who has lived a worthy and decent life could therefore expect to be reborn from the womb of a gentlewoman and himself become a gentleman, later a nobleman from the womb of a woman of rank and so ever onwards and upwards on the ladder of existence until he is united with the Divinity. On the other hand, if the son of a gentleman behaves unworthily, in the next state he will be a buffoon then a dog, descending each time to a condition ever more vile than the one before.

Everyone treats everyone else courteously and they salute each other politely. They have an air of good breeding, eat their food cleanly and appear well satisfied with life. Parents are treated with respect, in fact if a child acts disrespectfully or neglects his parents he can be tried for filial ingratitude by a public tribunal and may receive a severe punishment.

Criminals guilty of a great variety of crimes are executed by strangling. Prison sentences are limited to three years whereupon the miscreant is released with a mark imprinted on his face so that he may be recognised as such.

The present Grand Khan has banned gambling and other forms of cheating in an edict which affirms, 'I subdued you by the power of my sword. Consequently, everything you possess belongs to me. If you gamble, therefore, you are sporting with my property.' He does not exercise these rights, however. (This law, by the way, has been necessitated by the fact that the people of this country are more addicted to gambling than is anyone else on earth.)

I should note that strict rules apply when you approach the Grand Khan. Come within half a mile of Kublai and you are obliged to adopt a humble, placid and quiet demeanour and not call out or indeed speak. Each man of rank carries a small spittoon which he must use in order to avoid spitting on the floors of the hall of audience. You spit, replace the cover, then make your salutation. It is likewise customary to take with you into the hall handsome slippers – buskins – made of white leather. Just before an audience you change into these (leaving your ordinary shoes in the care of a servant) to avoid soiling the colourful carpets worked with silk and gold.

It is time I moved on to describe parts of the Empire other than northern China and the city of Kanbula. I had by this time been appointed the Grand Khan's ambassador to the West and this involved a journey of four months.

Ten days out of the capital you come to the Pulisangan river which discharges itself into the ocean and carries all manner of merchandise to and from the sea. The most spectacular bridge in the world spans this river. Constructed of stone it is fully 1,000 feet long and 25 feet wide. Ten men can easily ride abreast across it. Twenty-four arches, supported on twenty-five pieces of serpentine stone, all constructed with great skill, span the river. There is a handsome parapet formed in a masterly style of marble slabs and pillars.

You ascend on to the bridge on a slightly wider road but thereafter it runs straight as a die. There is a massive, lofty column resting upon a marble tortoise. Nearby stands the figure of a lion that is echoed by a similar figure atop the column (as the bridge slopes down there is another handsome column with a lion a few feet away from the other one). In the spaces between the pillars along the whole length of the bridge there are curiously carved marbles all surmounted by lions – all in all a beautiful spectacle. These parapets are also designed to prevent accidents to passengers using the bridge.

The next 30 miles of my journey west took me through country rich in fine buildings, vineyards and well cultivated, fertile ground.

Here is the large, impressive city of Goaza where the idolaters have a great number of convents.

The people are in the main traders and manual workers. They make gold tissue and the most beautiful fine gauzes. There are a great number of inns for travellers. A mile from here the road divides, one going to the west across Cathay (Northern China) and the other south-east to Manji (Southern China). If you take the southern route there are many fine cities and strongholds in a kingdom known as Ta-in-fu [Tai-yuen-fu, capital of the modern province of Shan-si], with flourishing manufacturing and commerce and there are more cultivated lands and vineyards. Grapes from here are carried into the interior of China where you do not find them. You also see groves of mulberry trees for silkworms from which the people produce a great deal of silk. These people are reasonably civilised as a result of their cosmopolitan contacts with the numerous towns of the region. There are lots of markets and fairs, one after the other, and the merchants travel round them with their goods.

A further five days on, I am told, there is a city still larger and more impressive than Ta-in-fu called Archbaluch. Kublai's hunting grounds extend as far as this and apart from his family and those on the Grand Falconer's list no one may hunt here. Beyond this anyone of rank may hunt. Kublai rarely takes his sport on this side of the country and as a consequence the game, especially hares, is so prolific it represents a real danger to the province's corn. When this threat becomes too great the Grand Khan and his court come in and take huge multitudes of animals.

The city of Ta-in-fu is famous for the manufacture of arms and military ordnance, very convenient for Kublai's army. The city is large and very beautiful, surrounded by vineyards, and grapes are gathered in vast abundance. Although no vines are found other than in the immediate vicinity of Ta-in-fu, they produce enough grapes to supply the whole of the province. Other fruits are plentiful, as is the mulberry tree for feeding the worms that produce silk.

West again and we arrive at the spectacular fortress of Thai-Gin, which was supposedly built in very ancient times by a king called Dor. Within the walls there is a spacious and finely ornamented palace, the hall of which boasts a superb exhibition of portraits of all the princes who, from ancient times, have reigned here.

There is a remarkable story told about Prince Dor. A powerful ruler, he was waited upon by a vast number of young women of extraordinary beauty. By way of recreation he was drawn in a small carriage about his palace by these beauties. They were entirely devoted to him and provided every convenience and, it has to be said, sexual pleasure.

Notwithstanding, he was an active monarch who ruled with dignity and justice and ran a strong administration from his castle. According to reports I have heard, his castle was all but impregnable. He was, however, the vassal of Unc-Khan, who as I have said was also known as Prester John.

King Dor rebelled against Prester John's rule who, while furiously angry, knew the Dor castle was too strong for him to take, and that any attack on it would probably fail.

This stalemate went on for some time until seven cavaliers of his retinue offered to try and capture King Dor and bring him before Prester John alive. The offer was favourably received and the group was promised a large reward.

Then the seven, purporting to have come from a distant land, moved into King Dor's territory and were soon performing so ably and diligently in the King's service they earned his respect and many royal favours. For example, he always took them with him when he went hunting.

Then one day when the King was engaged in the chase and had put a river between himself and the rest of his party, the seven spotted their chance, drew their swords, surrounded King Dor and took him forcibly to Prester John. None of the King's own people were in a position to help him.

When they arrived at the court of Prester John he gave orders that the prisoner should be humiliated by being dressed in rags and made to work as a cowherd. King Dor remained in this wretched condition for two years, carefully guarded against escape.

Then Prester John summoned him, King Dor trembling with fear that he was going to be put to death. Instead the King delivered a sharp and severe admonition, warning Dor against the pride and arrogance that might tempt him to rebel in future. Then he was dressed in royal apparel and sent back to his principality accompanied by a guard of honour. I am told that thereafter he behaved himself.

Twenty miles from Thai-gin you come to the river called Kara-moran (the Yellow River), which is so incredibly deep and wide that no solid bridge could span it. Along its banks are to be found many important trading cities and castles. Silk and ginger are produced in large quantities. There is a multitude of bird life, especially pheasant costing three to the Venetian groat. They also grow a special kind of large cane here, about 18 inches in circumference, which is employed locally in a number of useful ways.

Cross the river and travel a further three days and you come to Ka-chan-fu where the inhabitants are idolaters. They trade industriously and manufacture a great variety of goods: silk, ginger, galangal (a medicinal root), spikenard (another) and a great many medicinal products all but unknown in our part of the world. They also produce silk and gold tissue.

I then headed west for eight days, through cities and commercial towns, gardens and cultivated lots where they grow an abundance of mulberry trees for silk production, to Ken-zan-fu. Idolaters are in the majority but you also find Nestorian Christians, Turkomans and Saracens. The wildlife of the surrounding country provides excellent sport and it is a fine place to hunt birds.

In ancient times Ken-zan-fu was the capital of an extensive, noble and powerful kingdom, the seat of many kings of venerable ancestry who were distinguished soldiers. At the moment it is governed by a son of the Grand Khan, named Mangalu, who was made King by his father. It is a hive of industry and commerce producing raw silk in large quantities, tissue of gold and worked silks as well as every kind of army ordnance. Food is abundant and cheap.

In a plain some 5 miles distant stands King Mangalu's palace, a beautiful place boasting many fountains and water features both inside and out. There is a fine park of almost 5 acres where all manner of wild animals are kept for sport. It is enclosed behind high battlements.

The symmetry and beauty of the central palace simply cannot be surpassed. Its rooms and halls are decorated with painting of gold, the finest azure and a great profusion of marble. Mangalu, who lives by his father's example when it comes to government and maintains strict equity, is much loved by his people. He is also very keen on hunting and hawking.

It is about time I said something about the two distinctive states of China, Cathay in the north and Manji to the south.

Travel three days from Mangalu through towns and cities whose people subsist on commerce and manufacturing, particularly in silk products, and you come to a region of mountains and valleys which lie within the province of Kun-kin [Szechwan]. The people, mostly farmers, worship idols. They also take much of their food from the wild lands, the area being covered with woodland. Lions [tigers], bears, lynxes, fallow deer, antelope and stags provide exciting and useful sport.

The whole region takes about twenty days to cross through mountains, villages and woods still interspersed with towns where the traveller may find convenient accommodation. Then you arrive at the white city of Ach-baluch Manji. This is set in level country, heavily populated by people who are mostly traders and manual labourers. Ginger is produced in large quantities, which is traded very profitably throughout Cathay. The country also produces great quantities of wheat, rice and other grain, all very reasonably priced.

This plain, which can be crossed in two days, is densely inhabited, after which you again come to high mountains, valleys and forests.

Another twenty days' travel west through country where the inhabitants all worship idols, live off the land and the meat they can hunt (the country has great numbers of the ox from which musk is obtained), you leave the mountains and, descending into the plain, arrive at the province of Sin-din-fu on the confines of Manji.

Here there is a large and noble city (of the same name), the capital of the province and once the seat of many rich and powerful kings. The city once covered some 20 miles but has subsequently been split into three; a division that occurred as a result of a decision made by the late, old king. He had three sons all of whom he was concerned should reign after his death and he had walls built which would partition the city into three, although the whole continued to be surrounded by one big wall. All these rich, extensive lands were later conquered by the Grand Khan, who took them into his Empire.

The city is well watered by many powerful streams flowing from the mountains. Some are half a mile wide and very deep and have been spanned by several large, imposing stone bridges some 8 yards wide depending on the breadth of the river. These bridges have very handsome wooden roofs supported on marble pillars that are painted red and tiled. All manner of trade is conducted from neat apartments and shops along the length of these bridges. From a building larger than the rest officers collect duty on provisions and merchandise and a toll from persons using the bridge. I was told that the Grand Khan receives 100 besants of gold a day in this way. The rivers unite below the city to form the mighty River Kiang which discharges into the ocean, the equivalent of a hundred days' journey away. More of that later.

Numerous vessels loaded with merchandise ply these rivers past many towns and forts bringing goods to and from the city. The people here are all idolaters.

I travelled on from here for four or five days through a plain and several valleys graced with many respectable mansions, castles and small towns to the province of Thebeth. The inhabitants work on the land and in the cities where very fine cloths and crêpes or gauzes are manufactured. The country around here is infested with tigers, bears and other wild beasts.

Thebeth was laid waste by Mangu Khan and in a twenty-day radius of here numerous towns and castles lie in ruins. As a consequence wild beasts, especially tigers, have proliferated to such a degree it is dangerous for commercial travellers to tarry hereabouts at night.

You have to carry with you all the provisions you need and employ draconian measures to ensure that your horses are not eaten. The canes called bamboo are found here (particularly close to rivers), some of them 30 feet high and 9 inches in circumference. In the evening the travellers tie several of these, in their green state, together in bunches and surround them with a hot fire. The action of the heat causes the canes to burst in a tremendous explosion. The noise can be heard up to 2 miles away and this drives the terrifying beasts away. The horses are tethered with iron shackles otherwise the noise would cause them to flee too. Even so, lots of people who have not taken these precautions have lost their livestock.

So it is twenty days through desolate country without sight of an inn and no more than once every three or four days can you replenish your provisions. A few castles and fortified towns finally begin to appear on the rocky heights on the summits of mountains and the country gradually becomes more cultivated and inhabited and the danger from beasts of prey recedes.

There is a frankly scandalous custom prevailing in these idolaters' provinces where the men are disinclined to marry the women if they are virgins. It is their religious conviction that a girl who hasn't been had by lots of men is worthless! Accordingly, when a caravan of travellers arrives and sets up their tents, come nightfall local mothers arrive with their marriageable daughters and entreat the new arrivals to have their way with them for as long as they stay there.

The most beautiful girls, of course, get chosen and the rest return home very disappointed and angry. The women dally with the travellers until they have to move on.

It is accepted that all these girls must be returned to their mothers and there is no attempt to carry them off. The young women take home trinkets, rings and other complimentary tokens of regard. Then, afterwards, when they prepare to be married they wear all these ornaments around their necks and other parts of the body. Those who exhibit the most exotic collection and the greatest numbers are rated with having attracted the greatest number of men and on this count are the most sought-after by young men seeking wives. A good quantity of these gifts is thus very acceptable to an aspiring husband and at her wedding the bride makes a display of them to all the guests. Her husband regards them as proof that their gods have rendered her lovely in the eyes of men and she is also thereafter free of the attention of other men!

I have to say, however, that these idolatrous people are treacherous and cruel, regarding it as no crime to rob others, hence they are the greatest thieves in the world. They subsist on the fruits of the earth, hunting and fowling.

The country is redolent with the smell of musk, the musk ox which produces it existing in such great numbers. The secretion of musk occurs once every month, forming itself into a sort of boil full of blood near the navel of the animal. It appears to me that this blood that is being constantly replenished becomes musk. The natives call the musk ox *gudderi* and they are hunted and killed with dogs.

These people do not have coined money nor the paper money of the Grand Khan but use coral as their currency. Their dress is frankly homely, being of leather, undressed animal skins or rough canvas.

They have a language distinctive to this province of Thebeth which borders on Manji and once upon a time this was a kingdom of such importance it had eight kingdoms and many cities and castles. It has numerous mountains, lakes and rivers and in the latter gold is to be found in large quantities. Coral is used not just as currency but as jewellery by the women. They wear it as necklaces and as ornamentation for their idols. They make camlet, gold cloths and medicines, many of which have never been seen in Europe.

Necromancy is widely practised here, an infernal act by which they perform the most extraordinary deeds of enchantment and delusion. They call up tempests accompanied by lightning and thunderbolts and many other miraculous effects. I found them, nonetheless, altogether a primitive lot.

Their dogs are the size of asses, strong enough to hunt all manner of wild beasts, particularly the wild ox called Beyamini which are extremely large and fierce. Some of the best lanner falcons are bred here. They are very swift in flight and the natives have good sport with them.

This province of Thebeth is subject to the Grand Khan, as are all the other kingdoms and provinces I have mentioned.

To the west is the province of Kain-du which formerly had its own princes but was brought under the dominance of the Grand Khan and is now ruled by his appointed governors. The inhabitants here are idolaters and there are many cities and castles. The capital, positioned as you enter the province, is also called Kain-du. Nearby is a large lake of salt water where can be found an abundance of pearls, white in colour, but not round. So great, indeed, is the quantity that should Kublai allow anyone to gather them, their value would be debased, so he limits the fishing by licence. Similarly he controls the production of turquoise from a nearby mountain.

These people also allow, indeed encourage, travellers through the country to have their way with their wives, daughters and sisters. The visitor will be invited into their home and then all the women of the house are his, indeed the owner will depart, leaving the guest in every sense, as master. He in turn places a signal in the window (his hat or something similar), and while this is on display the owner of the premises stays away. This custom goes on throughout the province. It seems the locals believe their idols will bless them for their kindness and hospitality and endow them with all the fruits of the earth.

These people also trade in interesting currencies, the first being rods of gold cut into different lengths which give different denominations according to weight. They also trade uniquely in salt. The product of salt springs is boiled down in small pans and after about an hour the salt is reduced to a paste and is formed into cakes worth about 2 pence each. Convex on top and flat underneath the tablets are impressed with the stamp of the Grand Khan and placed on hot tiles until they dry rock hard. No one but officers of the Crown may produce them. Eighty of these cakes trade for one Venetian saggio of gold (one sixth of an ounce) although the exchange rate goes down to sixty, fifty or even forty cakes to the saggio when the merchants are trading with the mountain population. These people, though less civilised, always have a market for their musk, other commodities and alluvial gold. Even at the lower rate it is still rather a good deal for them.

This salt currency is traded by merchants throughout the province of Thebeth and their profits are considerable because salt is essential to the people's diet, indeed indispensable. (It is interesting that in the cities the people consume only broken fragments of the cakes, keeping whole ones as a 'hard' currency in common circulation.)

Musk is taken here in great quantities and the lake abounds with a wide variety of good fish. Wild game in the form of tigers, bears, deer, stag, antelope and numerous birds is prolific.

They make an excellent wine here from wheat and rice flavoured with spices and this is a great place for cloves which grow on a small bush whose leaves resemble the laurel but are somewhat larger and narrower. The flowers are white and small as are the cloves themselves, but they darken as they ripen. Ginger, cassia in great abundance and many other medicinal herbs grow here, although none of them ever reaches Europe.

A journey of fifteen days from Kain-du brings one to the opposite boundary of the province, passing respectable dwellings, many forts and places set aside for hunting and fowling. Here the mighty River Brius forms the frontier of the province and flows eventually into the ocean. The river produces great quantities of alluvial gold.

I now want to move westwards to the province of Karaian which is so large it is ruled by seven governments. The Grand Khan's rule prevails here and he has appointed his grandson, Timor Khan, to look after his interests. Timor is a rich, powerful and magnificent prince who is said to rule with consummate wisdom, virtue and great justice.

Five days of travelling west from the river takes one through well-inhabited country and you see lots of castles. The people are all idolaters and live off the land. They have a language of their own which is difficult to learn. Here they breed the best horses in the country.

At the end of the five days you come to the capital Yachi, a large, noble city. There are merchants and artisans of all faiths: idolaters, Nestorian Christians, Saracens and Mahometans, although the idol-worshippers predominate. The land is very fertile producing both wheat and rice. They do not like bread (considering it unwholesome) but from the wheat make a fortified wine flavoured with herbs which is clean and light coloured and a great drink.

Seashells of a white porcelain colour are used both as currency and necklaces. They trade at eighty shells to two Venetian groats. The people also mine salt, paying a large tax to Prince Timor.

And they really do not mind if you have your way with their women, providing the girl is ready and willing!

There is a lake here almost 100 miles in circumference in which a large variety of fish, some of them very large, are caught.

The people eat fowl, sheep, oxen and buffalo which has been cured. They cut the meat into very small pieces and pickle it in brine flavoured with several of their spices. Rich and poor alike eat it but after mincing the poor tend just to steep it in a sauce of garlic.

West again from Yachi and a journey of ten days brings you to the province of Karasan with a capital city of the same name. The country, populated entirely by idolaters, is in the dominion of the Grand Khan and royal functions are in the hands of another of his sons, Kogatin.

There is much gold to be found in the rivers hereabouts, both grains and ingots, and there are veins of it in the mountains. Because of the large quantity of gold it trades only for a saggio of gold to six saggio of silver. They also use the porcelain-like shells as currency (the shells are not actually found here but are brought from India). As I have said before, these people never take virgins as wives.

But let me tell you about the huge serpents to be found here, ten paces in length and ten spans in girth. Near the head they have two short legs with three claws like those of a tiger and glaring eyes larger than a four-penny loaf. Their jaws are wide enough to swallow a man and their teeth are large and sharp. Their whole appearance is so formidable neither man nor beast can approach them without feeling terrified. You come across others of smaller size – four, eight, six or five paces long – and these are hunted. These creatures spend all day avoiding the great heat by lurking in caverns, emerging at night to seek food. Nothing is safe from them. Be it tiger, wolf or beast, all are devoured. Then they drag themselves off to some lake, spring or river to drink.

Due to their great weight they leave a depression in the sands, as if a heavy beam has been dragged along, and this makes them easy for professional hunters to track. The hunter marks out one of these familiar routes and sets a trap of several pieces of wood tipped with sharp iron spikes, which they render invisible with a covering of sand. The serpents are wounded on the spikes and thus easily killed. Screaming crows lead the hunters to the dying animal and they are skinned, great care being taken to secure the gall which is highly prized as a medicine. A pennyweight of gall dissolved in wine is used to treat those bitten by mad dogs and it is also useful in pregnancy, accelerating parturition once the labour pains have started. A small quantity of it cures carbuncles, pustules or other eruptions on the body.

The flesh of serpents fetches a very good price as it is thought to have a stronger flavour than other meats. Everyone regards it as a delicacy.

Horses from around here are big and young are taken to India to be sold. It is a local practice to remove one joint of the tail to prevent them from lashing it from side to side. Whisking about its tail when being ridden is regarded by these people as a bad habit in a horse. They prefer that the tail remains pendant.

Here they ride with long stirrups in the French fashion. The Tartars and most other people wear them short as this makes it easier to use a bow, rising in their stirrups above the horse to shoot their arrows which are always poisoned. They wear complete body armour of buffalo leather and carry lances, shields and crossbows.

I was told as a fact that it is common practice, especially among those who are up to no good, to carry poison about their person. This they will swallow if caught in any delinquency. They would rather kill themselves than suffer the pain of torture. But the rulers are wise to the trick and they keep a supply of dog shit to hand which they oblige the miscreant to swallow causing them to vomit up the poison!

Before Kublai Khan conquered here the people were also addicted to another brutal custom. Strangers, particularly the brave and beautiful, were murdered in their sleep, not for the sake of money but because it was believed that the victim's spirit, endowed with his accomplishments and intelligence, would grace the household and cause it to prosper. You were accounted specially fortunate if you possessed the soul of a noble person and many such lost their lives as a consequence. However, severe punishments inflicted since Kublai took over the running of the country have caused this practice to cease.

We continue west. Five days' journey in that direction brings one to Kardanan, another dominion of the Grand Khan and where the principal city is called Vochang. Again, the currency is gold and the porcelain-like shells. An ounce of gold trades here for 5 ounces of silver, there being no silver mines in the country. They have a lot of gold, however, and consequently merchants who import and take payment in silver make a lot of money.

The men and women of the province cover their teeth with thin plates of gold. The plates are very finely fitted and remain on for life. The men also tattoo dark stripes or bands on their arms and legs. They use a bundle of five needles which is pressed into the flesh until blood is drawn. Dark pigment is then rubbed into the wounds leaving an indelible mark. The marks are considered to be marks of distinction and honour as well as being ornamental.

But they really pay little attention to anything other than horse-manship, hunting and military pursuits. Household management is left entirely to the wives assisted by slaves who have either been bought or are prisoners of war.

They have a peculiar custom when a child is born. As soon as a woman gives birth and has risen from her bed and washed and swaddled the infant, the husband immediately takes the place she has vacated. The wife lays the child beside him and family, friends and relatives visit to pass on their congratulations. The mother meanwhile takes care of the household, carries food and drink to her husband in bed and for forty days suckles the infant at his side.

These people eat their meat raw or pickled as I have described, with rice. They make rice wine flavoured with herbs and it is very good.

There are no temples and no idols worshipped here, instead the people worship their ancestors and their elders, believing they derive their whole existence from them and are indebted to them for all they possess.

They cannot write but this is understandable given the primitive nature of the place. It is mostly a mountainous tract of land covered with the thickest of forests. In summer it is so gloomy and unwholesome the merchants leave, fearing for their health.

When there is a business transaction involving debt or credit, their chief takes a square of wood and divides it into two. Notches are cut into it recording the sums in question and each party is given one. When the term of a loan expires or the debt is paid, the creditor delivers up his wooden counterpart and both parties are satisfied.

There are no doctors here, instead the people rely on sorcerers. When a person falls ill he summons one of them, gives a full account of his complaint and then sacrifices are made to idols. Musicians with loud instruments are also hired to dance and sing in honour and praise of their idols. Eventually the evil spirit takes possession of one of them and the proceedings are brought to a close.

He who has become possessed is then asked the cause of the patient's indisposition and how a cure might be effected. The evil spirit answers, using the voice of the possessed, that the sickness has resulted from an offence to a deity. The sorcerers offer up prayers to that deity, beseeching him to pardon the sinner on condition that, when cured, he will offer up a sacrifice of his own blood. I have noticed, however, that if the demon perceives that there is no prospect of recovery the sorcerer makes it known that there is no sacrifice that can appease him. The sacrifice requires a number of sheep with black heads to be slaughtered by hand by a similar number of sorcerers and their wives.

The relatives of the patient immediately go along with all this and the sheep are slain, their blood sprinkled towards the heavens, and the sorcerers (men and women) burn perfumed incense all over the house of the sick person and make a smoke of the wood of aloes. They cast it into the broth in which the sheep meat has been seethed, along with some of the wine brewed with spices, and everyone laughs and sings and dances about in honour of their idol or the Divinity. The possessed person is then asked whether the idol is satisfied and if the answer is yes, the sorcerers, male and female, sit down and feast on the sacrificial meat and the spiced liquor, all in the highest of spirits.

The sorcerers are paid and return home. The idol gets the credit if the patient lives. If he or she dies, the sorcerers declare that their rites have been rendered ineffective by the people who had prepared the meat and tasted it before presenting it to the deity. I should add that these ceremonies, which happen a couple of times a month only, are reserved for nobles and the very rich. They occur, however, throughout the whole of Cathay and Manji, where the presence of a proper physician is very rare. As far as I am concerned this is all a case of demons sporting blindly with these deluded and wretched people.

A very famous battle was fought here in the Kingdom of Vochang. In 1272 the Grand Khan sent an army into the countries of Vochang and Karazan to protect them from foreign invasion. At this time he had not yet appointed his sons to rule the provinces, as he would later do. (Cen-temur became the prince here.)

King Mein and Bagala in India, who ruled a great number of subjects and was very rich, decided to oppose this incursion. He assembled a huge army spearheaded by a multitude of elephants (in which this country abounds) equipped like moving castles with battlemented wooden structures on their backs each accommodating twelve to sixteen soldiers. Led by these elephants and a vast host of horse and foot soldiers, King Mein took the road to Vochang where the Grand Khan's army lay encamped close by.

The Grand Khan's troops were led by Nestardin, a brave and able soldier who was greatly alarmed by the size of the force from Mein, he himself having a mere 12,000 men under his command. (They were admittedly battle-hardened troops.) The Mein army he estimated at 60,000, not counting the elephants. But Nestardin did not show apprehension, descending into the plain of Vochang and positioning himself so that his flank was protected by a thick wood of large trees into which, in the event of a ferocious charge by the elephants which his troops could not withstand, he could hurriedly retire and from there counter the attack with arrows.

He called his officers together, urged them to be brave and reminded them that victory depended not on the number of men but upon courage and discipline. He pointed out that the troops of Mein and Bangala were raw and inexperienced. 'Feel confident in your own valour which has so often been put to the test,' Nestardin urged them. 'Let your name be the subject of terror not merely to the enemy before you but to the whole world.' He concluded by promising to lead them to certain victory.

The King of Mein set his own army into motion about a mile from the enemy and took up a position with his elephants in front and his horse and foot soldiers formed into two wings a considerable distance to the rear. He too encouraged his troops to fight valiantly, pointing out that they had a four to one advantage not counting the elephants, which the enemy would find overwhelming as they had never faced elephants before. Giving orders to sound a prodigious number of warlike instruments, he advanced the whole army towards the Tartars – who stood firm.

In true Tartar fashion they then rushed out but found that their horses, totally unused to the size of huge animals like elephants with their castles, were terrified and wheeled about attempting to flee. Their riders could do nothing to control them and the main body of the King's army was getting closer every moment. Nestardin observed the chaos of his cavalry and with great presence of mind, ordered his men to dismount and lead their horses into the wood where they were fastened to the trees.

The cavalry returned as a regiment of archers firing a barrage of arrows at the elephants. This fire was hotly returned but the advantage was with the Tartars who were the stronger bowmen. The Tartar commanders ordered their men to concentrate their fire power on the elephants and soon these were stuck all over with arrows and began to fall back, causing great confusion to their troops in the rear. It soon became impossible for the mahouts to manage the frenzied elephants and they flailed about in the wood, breaking the castles from their backs and killing the men in them.

Seeing the state of the elephants, the Tartars took courage, regrouped in perfect order into their original detachments, remounted their horses and, rejoining their divisions, began the last dreadful phase of the battle.

The King's troops were certainly not lacking in valour and he himself went among them urging them not to be alarmed by the beserk elephants and to stand firm. But the Tartars' consummate archery was too strong for him and his men were depressed at not having the same body armour as their opponents. When all the arrows had been expended violent hand-to-hand fighting followed, with both sides employing swords and iron maces. Horrible wounds were inflicted, limbs dismembered and thousands fell to the ground maimed and dying. The sight of so much blood was terrible to behold and the cries and shrieks of the wounded, coupled with the clash of weapons, ascended to the heavens.

The King of Mein, acting like the valiant chieftain he was, was present wherever the greatest danger manifested itself; inspiring his soldiers and urging them to hold their ground against every assault. Fresh squadrons from his reserve were sent to reinforce those exhausted in the front line. With the bulk of his troops either killed or wounded, the field covered with the carcasses of men and horses and surviving troops beginning to give way, it became evident that he could no longer stand against the Tartars and he fled the field taking the battered remnants of his army with him. A great number of them were slain in the retreat.

Victory was later judged to have been largely the result of the troops of Mein and Bangala lacking body armour as strong as the Tartars'. Likewise the elephants had been unable to withstand the Tartar arrows and thus to break through their ranks and throw them into disorder. The King was also deemed to have been in error when he attacked the Tartar force whose flank was protected by the wood. He should instead have endeavoured to draw the Tartars out into open country where they could not have resisted the advance charge of armed elephants. Also, had he extended his cavalry on the two wings he might have surrounded the Tartars.

Returning to the wood, the Tartars found enemy soldiers chopping down trees to block their way, but these barricades were soon demolished and many of the defenders killed. The Tartars also captured the King's mahouts and with their help caught two hundred elephants or more. Since then the Grand Khan has always employed elephants in his armies and has annexed all the lands of the King of Mein and Bangala into his domains.

Leaving Kardanan you descend very steeply for about two and a half days through deserted country. This brings you to a great plain where, three days a week, a great trading fair assembles to which people bring gold to exchange for silver from the neighbouring mountains. One saggio of gold fetches five of silver. The gold comes from high and very strong mountain reaches that are very difficult to approach and to which only the natives have access. But the inhabitants must trade their gold, hence the existence of this market in the plain.

If you continue south towards India, you reach the city of Mein after a journey of fifteen days through largely depopulated country which abounds with elephants, rhinoceros and other wild animals. I did not see a sign of people anywhere.

Mein itself is the large and magnificent capital of the kingdom. The people hereabouts are all idolaters with their own unique language. A former rich and powerful monarch whose death was drawing near ordered the building of a sepulchre flanked by two marble pyramids, thirty feet high and capped with a ball. One of these pyramids was plated with gold an inch thick so that you saw nothing but the gold. The other was similarly plated but with silver. The balls supported small bells of silver and gold that sounded in the wind. The tomb was also of silver and gold. It was all very splendid! The whole thing was designed as a memorial for the king and an honourable place for his soul.

Kublai had his eye on the place, however, and pretty soon despatched an army led by a valiant officer, who took with him from the Grand Khan's court a number of the sorcerers. You could always find great numbers of them there. When they entered Mein they saw the great gold and silver tomb but were nervous of meddling with it until Kublai's pleasure was known. On learning that it had been erected in pious memory of a once great king, Kublai insisted it should not be violated, not to the smallest degree. (The Tartars generally regarded the removal of anything to do with the dead as a heinous sin.)

In the vicinity of Mein we saw many elephants, large and handsome wild oxen, fallow deer and other game.

A note about the province of Bangala [Bengal] which is in the southern confines of India which, when I was living at Kublai's court, had not yet fallen under the thrall of the Grand Khan, although his armies had been engaged there for a long time. The province has its own peculiar language. The people worship idols and they have schools for instruction in the principles of the idolatrous religion and of necromancy. The religion prevails through all ranks of society, including the nobles and chiefs of the country.

Oxen are to be found here almost as tall but not as bulky as elephants. The people live on meat, milk and rice, of which there are no shortages.

Herbal medicines like spikenard, galangal, ginger and sugar are grown here and merchants come from other parts of India to buy them. They also buy eunuchs as slaves. These prisoners, taken in war, are emasculated and there is not a prince or person of rank hereabouts who does not want one to look after their women. Merchants make large profits from this trade.

It takes thirty days to cross Bangala where, in the extreme east, you find a country named Kangigu that has its own king but has voluntarily submitted to the Grand Khan and pays him an annual tribute.

The king is so devoted to sensual pleasures he has some four hundred wives and is reputed, when he hears of a beautiful woman, to send for her and add her to his collection.

Gold is found here in great abundance and valuable herbal medicines, but because the country is so far from the sea these are hard to bring to market. Elephants and other beasts abound and the diet consists of meat, rice and milk. They make a good wine, fortified with herbs, from rice.

Both males and females have their bodies tattooed all over with figures of birds and beasts. It is the sole employment of many people to tattoo hands, legs and breasts using a needle, a black pigment then being rubbed into the punctured skin. It is utterly impossible to get the marks out. Among the women, those with the most tattoos are regarded as the most beautiful.

You also find the province of Amu over towards the east but here the inhabitants are subjects of the Grand Khan. They are all idolaters and live off the land and their cattle.

Itinerant merchants come here to buy horses and oxen for the rest of India. Because of the rich pasture there are also numerous buffalos. The men and women wear lots of gold and silver rings on their wrists, arms and legs, with those adorning the women being much the most costly.

It is a twenty-five day journey to Kangigu and another twenty days to Bangala. Eight days further on to the east is the province of Tholoman. Here again they have their own language, are idolaters and are subjects of the Grand Khan. The people are tall with dusky complexions and very good looking. They are reported to be just in war and peace. They have a fair number of cities and a multitude of villages situated in the high mountains. To these mountains are carried, in little wooden caskets, the bones of the dead after they have been burned and then they are concealed in vast caves in the rocks where no wild animals can get to them.

An abundance of gold is to be found here, but for ordinary currency, as they do also in Kangigu and Amu, they use the porcelain-like cowrie shells from India.

Let us head back into China by continuing for twelve days to the east via a river on each side of which lie many towns and castles.

You come eventually to the large and handsome city of Chintigui where the inhabitants are idolaters and all subjects of the Grand Khan. This is a city of traders and artisans who make a good-looking cloth, which is worn by all the ordinary people in the summer, from the bark of certain trees. They have a reputation for being brave warriors. We are also back to the use of Kublai's stamped paper as the standard currency.

The tigers are so numerous in these parts the people do not dare sleep outside their towns at night and it is not even safe to moor close to the bank of the river as these monsters have been known to plunge into the water, swim to the boat and drag their victims out. Everyone anchors well out in the stream where they feel safe.

The largest and fiercest dogs I have ever encountered are also from here; so courageous and powerful that a man with a couple of them may overcome a tiger. A hunter will set a pair of these dogs upon a tiger the moment the beast is encountered. The tiger immediately seeks a tree to protect his rear, making for it slowly, showing no signs of fear. The dogs attack at this time and the hunter looses his arrows. The tiger tries to bite the dogs but they are too nimble for him and stand at bay. His retreat is slow and deliberate but in time he is bitten so often and has received so many arrows that he collapses from weakness and loss of blood and is eventually taken.

Silks for sale to other parts are extensively manufactured in Chintigui and exported by the river which continues for a long way through towns and castles. The people live entirely by trade.

I travelled from this area to Sin-din-fu mentioned earlier, twenty days to Gin-gui, and a further four days to Pazan-fu which is to the south and belongs to Cathay. Here there are some Christians and they have their own church. All are still subjects of the Grand Khan and his paper money is in circulation here. Trade and manufacturing again provide the population with their living, in particular silk, of which there is an abundance, tissues of silk mixed with gold and also very fine scarves.

Pazan-fu has many towns and castles under its jurisdiction and the great river to Kanbula, by which the merchants ship large quantities of merchandise, flows past it.

Going on into Cathay (North China), a journey of three days brings one to the large city of Chan-glu. The inhabitants worship idols, burn their dead and use the Grand Khan's paper money. Great quantities of salt are made here. In the surrounding countryside salty earth is picked up in large heaps and water is poured through it. The water is collected into channels and from there into huge salt pans where the salt crystallises in the sun. It is very white and of good quality and is widely exported. The Grand Khan derives considerable revenue from the rich profits of the manufacturers of salt. Fantastic peaches, weighing as much as 2lb, are also a speciality of the region.

Head further south into Cathay and after five days you come to the city of Chan-gli. The currency remains Kublai's paper and everyone worships idols, and this is another important centre of commerce from which the Grand Khan receives considerable customs revenue. Likewise the towns and cities, many of great importance, encountered on a further journey six days south to the city of Tudin-fu. This was formerly a magnificent capital but the Grand Khan sacked it. It remains a delightful place to live thanks to beautiful gardens with handsome shrubs and superb fruit trees. Silk is produced here in extraordinarily large quantities.

Eleven cities and several towns are administered from here and it was ruled by its own king until Kublai conquered it. As is his wont, Kublai, in 1272, appointed an officer of the highest rank, named Lucansor, to the governorship and garrisoned an army of seventy thousands horse to hold the place. But Lucansor, finding himself master of so rich and highly productive an area and in command of so large an army, became drunk with power and plotted rebellion against his sovereign. Leaders of the community were roped into these evil schemes and persuaded to stage a revolt which encompassed the whole province.

Kublai reacted instantly, sending an army of one hundred thousand men under two of his nobles, Angul and Mongatai.

Lucansor reinforced his forces to match them and went straight into the fight. There was great slaughter on both sides and Lucansor was killed, which caused his troops to take flight. Many were killed or made prisoners. The principal conspirators were put to death but Kublai pardoned the rest and took them into his service and they have remained faithful to him ever since.

All of this region houses cities with flourishing commerce and manufacturing, and another journey to the south brings one to Singui-matu, a truly large, noble and handsome city. On its southern side a deep river has been divided by the inhabitants into two, one runs through Cathay, the other, taking a westerly course, flows towards the province of Manji. The river traffic is incredible and is the conduit for every kind of consumable. It actually takes the breath away when you see the multitude of huge vessels, continually plying back and forth, laden to the gunwales with the richest merchandise.

If you leave Singui-matu and travel six days to the south through a ceaseless procession of commercial towns and castles you will reach Lingui where the people are idolaters, burn their dead, are subjects of the Grand Khan and use his paper money. This is a city of noble traditions whose menfolk are famously warlike. The city of Pingui follows three days later where they have all the necessities of life. The city pays Kublai a great amount of revenue from its commerce and manufacturing. On again, for two days, to Cingui which is huge, prosperous in commerce and manufacturing. This is wheat-growing country and they also have very handsome and useful dogs.

And so you come eventually to the mighty River Kara-moran (the Yellow River) which has its source in the countries belonging to Prester John. It is a mile wide. Its great depth allows large ships to navigate it fully laden. Large fish are caught in considerable quantities. About a day's distance from the sea there is a port on the river that provides anchorage for fifteen thousand vessels, each capable of carrying fifteen horses and twenty men besides the crew, stores and provisions. They are kept in a constant state of readiness allowing Kublai to carry an army to any of the islands in the neighbouring ocean that might be in revolt. The port is close to a large city called Koi-gan-zu.

Cross the river and you enter the noble province of Manji. I must confess that I have only given you a cursory account of Cathay, indeed I have only described about one-twentieth of it, dealing simply with cities that were on my route. To have described all the cities would have made this book far too long and boring.

Manji is the richest and most magnificent province of the Eastern world. In about 1269 it was the kingdom of a prince called Facfur who, for at least a century, was the wealthiest and most powerful monarch that had every reigned. He was of a peaceable and benevolent disposition, so beloved of his people and so protected by huge rivers and the power of his kingdom that invasion from outside, indeed by anyone on earth, was considered impossible. As a result he and his people were very complacent about the military threat, declining, for example, to keep up any cavalry. That said, his cities were remarkably well fortified, being surrounded by deep moats a bow-shot wide.

His main pursuit was that of erotic pleasure, keeping at the court, very close to his person and whose company he greatly enjoyed, about a thousand beautiful women. He was famous for his strict enforcement of the law, indeed it was said that shopkeepers could leave their premises open and no one dared rob them. Travellers passed through the country without fear of molestation. He looked after the poor and needy and famously took care of twenty thousand foundlings a year. The boys were instructed in some trade when they grew up and married the young women the King had had raised in like fashion. He could not have been more different to Kublai Khan! As I have told you this grand emperor of the Tartars delighted in war, the conquest of countries and extending his power, and now he turned his attention to Manji.

Under the command of General Chin-san-bay-an (which means the Hundred-Eyed) Kublai assembled a vast army of horse and foot soldiers. The invasion was launched from ships. The inhabitants of the city of Koi-gan-zu were the first to be ordered to surrender and, when they refused, instead of launching a siege Hundred-Eyes moved on to the next town. They too refused to surrender so the army moved on again until four towns had called his bluff. But it was not bluff. Aware that reinforcements were on the way he skilfully turned one of these cities and put every one of its inhabitants to the sword. The news spread to the other recalcitrant cities and they promptly surrendered!

Hundred-Eyes waited for Kublai's second army to arrive then moved on to King Facfur's royal city of Kin-sai. The King, who had essentially never been involved in any kind of warfare, reacted as you might expect. He made his escape to a fleet of vessels which had been readied for that purpose and, with most of his treasure and valuable effects, left the city in the charge of his Queen, with orders to defend it to the last man, believing that as a woman she would be safe if the city fell to the enemy. For his part, the King made out to sea and reached some well-fortified island and there he remained until his death.

In the meantime, the Queen heard from some astrologers that the King had been told that he would never be deposed other than by 'a chief who would have a hundred eyes'. At first this persuaded her that Kin-sai, although by now gravely weakened, would never fall because it seemed impossible that any mortal could have that number of eyes. But enquiring as to the name of the general commanding the siege and being told he was Chin-san-bay-an she grew convinced that this must be the person to drive her husband from his throne. She no longer attempted to resist but immediately surrendered. Once they had captured the capital, the Tartars soon brought the rest of Manji under their domination. The Queen was brought in person before Kublai Khan, who received her with due honours and arranged for her to receive an allowance that enabled her to retain the honour and dignity of her rank.

Moving on south and east you reach a very wealthy and handsome city, Kolgan-zu, which lies at the entrance to Manji 5 miles from the river of Kara-moran to which it is connected by a grand canal. This waterway runs through an area of marshy lakes and, as I have said, is deep and carries a prodigious amount of traffic. It is effectively the only road into Manji. Salt is produced here in great quantities for local consumption and for export; a trade from which Kublai derives ample tax revenues.

A handsome stone causeway through other marshy lakes provides the only road on into Manji. These lakes are deep and can be navigated and it was by this method that the Grand Khan's generals invaded, using ships to land an entire army. A day's journey down this causeway, which also forms the bank of the canal, you reach the large town of Pau-ghin where everyone worships idols and gains their living in manufacture and trade, particularly silk and woven gold tissues. Everyone lives pretty well here. In nearby Kain, just a day away, a great variety of fish is available; also game. Pheasants in particular are so plentiful that for a piece of silver equivalent to a Venetian groat you get three of these birds the size of a pea fowl. Four days on, through the city of Tin-gui, you reach the sea. All the fields around here are much tilled and again there is a flourishing salt industry. From the town of Chin-gui the salt is exported to supply all the provinces around and from this trade the Grand Khan derives so much revenue it can hardly be credited, all of it in paper money.

We come now to Yan-gui, an important city with twenty-four towns under its jurisdiction and where I was to be the governor. This is a place of considerable consequence where they specialise in the manufacture of arms and all sorts of military ordnance to meet the needs of the great number of troops who are stationed around here. I took up my post in a room in a palace of one of Kublai's nobles and was to preside here for three years.

Nan-gin, situated to the west, is renowned for its hunting, especially tigers. The people produce much corn and cattle.

Nearby is the considerable city of Sa-yan-fu, having under its jurisdiction twelve large and wealthy towns. My father, my uncle and I played no small part in the conquest of this city by the forces of the Grand Khan in the following manner.

San-yan-fu is amply appointed with everything you would expect of a great city and had withstood a siege of three years even though by then Kublai had already conquered the rest of Manji. The army was having difficulties largely because the city was surrounded by water on three sides. Only the northern side was approachable.

Kublai was furious that San-yan-fu was still holding out and my father and uncle, who were then living at the royal court, went to him and proposed that they should build siege engines like those used in the West which could hurl stones weighing 300lb and destroy the city and its inhabitants. The Grand Khan warmly welcomed the scheme and gave orders that the finest smiths and carpenters should be placed at my father and uncle's service, among whom were some Nestorian Christians who proved to be the most able engineers.

As a result these mangonels were completed in a matter of days and Kublai and his whole court came to watch their trials. They were then sent by ship to the army outside San-yan-fu. The very first stone hurled by them hit a building with such force that the greater part of it was smashed and collapsed. The terrified inhabitants of the city thought they were suffering thunderbolts from heaven and they met to consider a surrender. Emissaries were sent to court to sue for peace and San-yan-fu made its submission on the same terms and conditions as had been granted to the rest of the province. Needless to say, a surrender brought about by such ingenuity greatly increased my father and uncle's reputation at court.

Fifteen days to the south-east is the city of Sin-gui which although not that large a place is a tremendous commercial hub. It is close to the River Kiang, the largest river in the world, and its traders own a prodigious number of ships. The Kiang at this point is about 8 to 10 miles wide as a result of a vast number of rivers, which rise in other countries, emptying into it. It is upwards of a hundred days' journey to travel the whole length of the Kiang until it discharges into the sea. Numerous large cities and towns are situated on its banks and more than two hundred, in sixteen provinces, take advantage of the shipping that plies up and down it. The transport of merchandise is frankly incredible.

The length of the river, travelling as it does through so many places, also means that the quantity and value of the trade are virtually incalculable. The principal commodity is, however, salt and the river is used to transport it to the far corners of the country.

On one occasion when I was in Sin-gui I saw at least fifteen thousand vessels and there are other towns along the river where they have even more! All these vessels are decked, have one sail and a carrying capacity of between 200 and 600 tons. The mast and sail are supported by hemp ropes, but they also commonly use canes, split lengthwise into very thin pieces and then twisted together. The canes employed can be 90 feet long and can be made up into 'ropes' 900 feet in length. These cane ropes, harnessed to ten or twelve horses, are used to tow barges down the river. They can even handle the up-river pull against the current. On many hills and rocky bluffs you see a lot of temples and other religious buildings, and the progression of towns and villages along the riverbanks is virtually continuous.

Most of the wheat and rice for Kublai's court comes by water from Kayn-gui, a small town on the southern bank of the river. It is shipped down via rivers and lakes and then along a deep, wide canal which the Grand Khan has had dug. Vessels can go all the way to Kanbula without having to go to sea. I admire this magnificent piece of engineering not so much for its vast length or the way it winds cleverly through the country as for the great benefits and convenience it has brought to the cities lying along its course.

The river's sides comprise a strong embankment and a terrace that make for easy passage on land. In the middle of the river, opposite the city of Kayn-gui, there is a rocky island with a grand temple where two hundred monks live and perform services to their idols. This place is the spiritual centre for many other temples and monasteries.

Tin-gui-gui is another large and handsome town occupied entirely by idolaters living by the arts and commerce, who all use Kublai's paper money. It is a centre of raw silk production from which beautiful tissues in many patterns are woven. All the good things of life are to be found here including a variety of game providing excellent sport.

Sadly, the inhabitants are vile. You will remember my describing how Chin-san-bay-an ('Hundred Eyes') conquered all these provinces of Manji. Well, in the case of this city he sent a group of Albanian Christians accompanied by some of his army to receive the surrender of Tin-gui-gui. They were allowed to enter the city without resistance.

Tin-gui-gui has a double protective wall and Kublai's emissaries set up their camp inside the outer wall. Tired and thirsty they quenched their thirst with a large quantity of wine which they found there; drinking far too much of it in fact and, intoxicated, they eventually fell deeply asleep. However, inside the second enclosure the people of Tin-gui-gui waited until they were all asleep, then sprang on the visitors and murdered them to a man.

You can imagine Hundred Eyes's reaction when he heard what had happened. His fury knew no bounds. He sent his whole army to attack the city and gave orders that everyone, girls and boys, young and old, should be put to the sword.

Sin-gui is another magnificent city to the south-east with an astonishingly vast population sharing both the same idolatrous religious practices and the use of paper money. They produce vast quantities of raw silk, clothe themselves in silk and export it to other markets. There are some very rich merchants but generally they are a mean bunch devoted entirely to manufacturing and trade. I have to say that there are so many of them that if you consider their prodigious output, manliness and warlike temperament they could, should they so desire, take over the whole of Manji, indeed beyond.

They have excellent physicians who can establish the nature of a disorder and know how to apply the proper remedies.

There are distinguished professors of learning, or more accurately philosophers and others who should be termed magicians or sorcerers.

On the mountains near the city superb rhubarb is grown and distributed throughout the province. Ginger is also produced in large quantities and sold very cheaply, 40lb of fresh root for one Venetian silver groat. Sixteen wealthy and respectable cities come under the jurisdiction of Sin-gui and trade from the arts flourishes in these cities as well. 'Sin-gui' in fact translates as 'city of the earth'.

The principal city of Manji, Kin-sai lies three days away via a town called Va-gui (one day) where they trade a vast amount of raw silk. Kin-sai means 'celestial city' and its grandeur and beauty well deserve that name, indeed it is the greatest city in the world. The abundant delights it has to offer the traveller lead one to think one might be in Paradise. I went there regularly and took copious notes of which the following are a small selection.

Including the suburbs the city is 100 miles in circumference, with perfectly proportioned streets, squares, marketplaces and canals serving the needs of a prodigious population. It lies between a freshwater lake of very clear water on the one side and a huge river on the other. The city is criss-crossed by canals large and small. Water from the river flows through this canal system into the lake taking all the filth of the city with it, then on into the sea.

The system purifies the air and provides an ideal method of communication to all parts of the town. I was told that there are twelve thousand bridges. Those bridging the principal canals are so high and skilfully constructed that a full-masted vessel can pass beneath. Carts and horses, of course, pass overhead. Actually you need this many bridges to get from one part of the city to the other.

Beyond the city, enclosing it on one side, is a dam erected many years ago by the old kings, both as a line of defence and to take the overflow from the river when it floods. The excavated earth forms a series of hillocks around one side of the dam.

Within the city limits there are ten principal squares or marketplaces housing innumerable shops. Each side of these squares is half a mile in length and in front of them is the main street more than 100 feet wide, passing right through the city from end to end. Each square (each 2 miles across) is 4 miles from the next and constructed in a line parallel to the square.

Capacious warehouses have been built of stone for the merchants from India and elsewhere who come here with goods to trade in the many squares. Something in the order of forty to fifty thousand people come, three days a week, to markets. Everything one might desire may be purchased: a vast quantity of game, such as roebuck, stags, fallow deer, hares and rabbits, together with partridge, pheasant, francolin, quail, chickens, capons and many ducks for just one Venetian silver groat. Butchers slaughter fresh oxen, calves, kids and lambs for the table of the rich and the great magistrates. The ordinary people eat everything that is left over, however unclean.

All year round the markets offer a great variety of herbs and fruit, pears of an extraordinary size weighing 10lb each that have a white, paste-like inside and are very fragrant with a delicious flavour. Dried grapes which are also very good are brought from elsewhere and wine, which admittedly the locals do not rate, preferring their fortified rice wines.

The sea is only 15 miles away so there is a daily supply of fish in vast quantities. The lake also supplies local fishermen with steady employment. These lake fish actually grow very fat and tasty from the offal carried down the canals. It is surprising to think that so much fish can be sold, but in fact it is all gone in a few hours.

Each of the ten market squares is surrounded by dwellings several storeys high. Shops take up the ground floor manufacturing and selling among other things trinkets, pearls, herbs and spices. Wine shops brew all the time and the wine is moderately priced. The side streets offer bathhouses where cold baths may be obtained. The people here are used from childhood to bathe in cold water, believing it to be very good for them. They wash every day, particularly before meals.

Other streets house brothels frankly too numerous to list. The girls prefer to live near the great squares where they find most of their trade, but are also to be found in every part of the city. Their houses are well furnished and the girls themselves, highly perfumed, are decked out in the most exquisite finery and attended by many female servants. These girls are masters of the art of love but they also posture charmingly and once you have tasted these fruits the fascination stays with you for ever. I have known men so intoxicated by the courtesans of Kin-sai that they return to their homes telling stories of the 'celestial city' and literally pant to get back to this paradise.

Other streets, usually close to the squares, house the premises of physicians and astrologers, who also teach reading and writing and many other, darker, arts.

On opposite sides of each of the squares there are two large 'courts' where Kublai's officers are stationed to deal with any trouble that might arise, mostly between the locals and the foreign merchants. It is their job also to see that the huge number of bridges are guarded; they punish any delinquents at their discretion.

Grand houses of great size, all with gardens, are to be found from one end of the city to the other. Nearby are the dwellings of the artisan class who work in their shops at their several trades. Day and night a multitude of people pass by, so numerous you would think it impossible to feed so many hungry mouths. In truth there are so many provisions on sale on the market days, brought in by carts and boats, that there is an abundance of food for everyone.

Let us take pepper as an example. I was told by one of Kublai's customs officials that almost 1,000lb of it was sold every day and this was probably only the amount on which tax was being paid.

Paper money is used exclusively hereabouts and all the people worship idols. The men and women are light-skinned and handsome. Usually they wear silk which is produced here in huge quantities. There is also a lot of silk imported.

There are twelve handicrafts practised here, so superior in their execution as to be worthy of mention. For each of them there are at least a thousand workshops with each shop employing between ten and fifteen craftsmen. Some places have as many as forty. The owners of these premises do not, of course, get their own hands dirty but, on the contrary, parade about in opulent dress affecting an air of gentility. Their wives do not work either. As I have already said, these women are very beautiful and they display a languid air of refinement. You would not believe how much they spend on jewels and clothes.

Under an ancient royal edict each citizen is required to follow in his father's profession but the way this works in practice is that once you have made your money you can give up manual labour provided you continue to keep the family business staffed.

Their houses are very well built and richly ornamented with carved wood. They spend an enormous amount on interior decorations; carvings, paintings and fancy buildings.

The famously gentle demeanour of Kin-sai's kings has dictated the nature and behaviour of the people. They are pacifist and tranquil. They do not carry arms nor do they keep them in their houses. You rarely hear rows and they conduct their mercantile and manufacturing businesses in an atmosphere of perfect equanimity and probity. They are very friendly towards each other and you see people who live in the same street, men and women alike, acting like one family. In their domestic life they are seemingly free of jealousy or suspicion of their wives to whom great respect is shown. Indeed, any man who used indecent language to these women would be very seriously frowned upon. Traders visiting the city are invited freely into their houses and given much hospitality and advice on how best to go about their business.

That said, these people really resent the presence of Kublai's soldiers because it reminds them of the time when their own kings and rulers were deposed.

All around the lake are many fine spacious homes belonging to the highest in the land. Likewise there are many monasteries whose monks do obeisance to their idols. In the middle of the lake are two islands on which stand some superb buildings; an incredible number of apartments and separate pavilions. When the inhabitants of Kin-sai stage a wedding or some other sumptuous event they retire to one of these islands. Everything they need is provided: vessels, napkins, table linen and the like. Moreover, these are all paid for by a charge upon the people for whom the buildings were erected. You can get as many as a hundred parties going on at the same time, weddings or other festivals all so judiciously arranged in the rooms and pavilions that they do not interfere with each other.

On the lake itself a large number of pleasure boats, 15 to 25 feet long and capable of accommodating between ten and twenty people, ply their trade. These vessels are very wide and do not keel over as they move through the water. You hire one of them for pure enjoyment; men with women or just with their male companions. The boats are always kept in pristine condition with proper seats and tables and all the furniture you might need for entertaining. They have cabins with a flat-roofed upper deck where the boatmen, with long poles (the lake is nowhere more than 2 metres deep), thrust the barges along to various designated destinations. The cabins are decorated inside in a variety of colours and with figures, as indeed are other parts of the vessel.

On either side of the boat, the windows open wide to allow the guests to feast their eyes on the lovely views on all sides while they sit at table. There is nothing on land to compare with the feeling of gratification you get out here on the water.

The lake extends along one whole side of the city so, standing in a boat, you get a real feeling for its grandeur and beauty, its palaces, temples, convents and gardens with large trees growing to the water's edge. All around are other boats full of people enjoying themselves.

In fact, the people here think nothing of devoting themselves to pleasure once their day's work is done. With their wives and their mistresses they go out in the boats, or in marvellous carriages (which deserve a special note). Remember that the streets of Kin-sai are all paved with either stone or brick as indeed are all the principal roads the length and breadth of Manji. So passengers can travel everywhere without even soiling their feet. One side of the road is left unpaved just so the royal couriers can travel along them on horseback at great speed.

In the city itself the main road is paved for 30 yards either side of a trench filled with gravel that, with a number of arched drains, ensures the bad water from the adjoining canals is carried off and the road remains dry. Carriages use this gravel lane, continually passing and repassing, and these are very fine vehicles indeed, trimmed with curtains and cushions of silk. They hold six people. So you get men (and women) seeking a pleasurable outing hiring one of these splendid carriages as a result of which, at any hour, you will see vast numbers of them travelling up and down the middle part of the street. They visit various gardens where attendants introduce them to shady spots created by the gardeners for that purpose and here the men – how shall I put it – 'indulge' themselves with the ladies, returning home by a similar method when the day is done.

There is an intriguing custom practised by the people of Kin-sai when a baby is born. They make an immediate note of the day, hour and minute of the delivery and take the information to an astrologer. He gives them the child's star sign and this is also carefully noted down. When the child grows up and is about to go into business, or upon a journey or a voyage, this document is again presented to an astrologer for his appraisal. He then weighs up all the circumstances and makes certain forecasts in which the people place great trust. Great numbers of these astrologers or, if you like, magicians, can be found in the marketplaces every day. They also make pronouncements about marriages and no nuptials are ever celebrated without them.

When a rich person dies here the relatives dress themselves in coarse clothing and accompany the body to where it is to be burnt.

Various musical instruments are played as the procession moves along while prayers to the idol are chanted. On to the pyre they throw many pieces of cotton paper upon which are painted representations of the deceased's male and female servants, their horses, camels and also silk wrought in gold, also gold and silver coins. They believe that this will allow the deceased to enjoy their servants, silks and money in the next world. When the body has been consumed all the instruments are played at once, producing a loud and continuous noise. It is believed that this cacophony induces the idols to receive the soul of the person whose body has been reduced to ashes and results in his reincarnation.

In every street of the city there are stone fire watchtowers, a necessary precaution because most of the houses are made of wood and serious fires are very common. By order of the Grand Khan there are teams of ten watchmen stationed under the principal bridges, five of whom watch by day and the other five by night. They also sound the hours, based on readings from a water clock (known as a clepsydra), using loud instruments of wood and iron. The first hour of the night is sounded by a watchman, first with a stroke on the wooden instrument, then with one on a metal gong. Then on the second hour, two sets of strokes sound and so on through the night. The guards are not allowed to sleep and are always on the alert. As soon as the sun rises in the morning they go back to a single stroke and then progress throughout the day.

There is a curfew on open fires and the guards patrol the streets to ensure that it is kept. If someone is delinquent they mark his front door and in the morning he is taken before a magistrate for punishment. Similarly, if they find anyone wandering about late at night they arrest and confine them and take them before the magistrates in the morning. These patrolmen are also responsible for taking to hospital anyone they find who is infirm. There are several of these hospices founded by the old kings in various parts of the city and they are richly endowed. When a patient gets better he is obliged to return to work.

When a fire is spotted, the watchmen raise the alarm by beating on a sort of wooden gong. These sounding boards comprise a wooden frame raised on mounds of earth a mile apart. On hearing the gong the watchmen from the other bridges converge on the conflagration to extinguish it and to save the goods of merchants by taking them to store towers. Sometimes they put the goods on boats and take them to the safety of the lake. And the night curfew even applies when a fire is in progress. Only those whose property or possessions are threatened are allowed out. But this, together with the watchmen, usually adds up to one or two thousand men.

Kublai's militia comes into its own in the event of a riot or an insurrection, but he also keeps a large force of infantry and cavalry commanded by his ablest officers on call in the city. This is only to be expected when you consider the importance of this province and especially its great capital which is in grandeur and wealth undoubtedly the greatest city in the world.

When Kublai conquered the province of Manji and commanded its obedience, he divided the old single kingdom into nine parts, each under a king or viceroy who were charged with dispensing good government and justice. They, in turn, make an annual report to a commissioner on all matters within their jurisdiction, particularly revenue. All these public officers are changed every three years.

The Viceroy of Kin-sai has authority over more than 140 cities and towns, all very large and rich. This is not a number to be wondered at because, remember, in the whole of Manji there are no fewer than one thousand two hundred, each housing large populations of industrious and wealthy people. In each of these centres Kublai maintains garrisons of at least one thousand, sometimes ten thousand or twenty thousand according to its importance. Not all of these are Tartars, most of them are Chinese. The Tartars are traditionally horsemen forming units of cavalry and many of these cities are on low marshy ground where it would be difficult for them to operate. So in such places, Kublai stations his Chinese troops and people from the south who are of a military bent. Every year Kublai selects from his subjects those best able to bear arms and enrols them into the various garrisons. In fact they make up several large armies.

Very astutely, Kublai does not allow recruits from Cathay and Manji to be garrisoned in their native cities. They are stationed at least twenty days' march away and there they stay for four to five years. The greater part of the revenues raised in the cities is used to pay for these garrisons.

Rebellions are not uncommon in the cities. Governors are often murdered, usually as a result of anger or drunkenness. Retribution is immediate. Garrison troops from neighbouring cities are moved in to destroy the rebels, rendering unnecessary the despatch of the main army from another province. For this purpose, the city of Kin-sai supports a permanent garrison of thirty thousand soldiers.

The former King, Facfur, built a marvellous palace enclosing between high walls some 10 miles of land which he divided into three parts. The centre part is entered through a lofty portal, on each side of which, on a flat terrace, are magnificent colonnades supporting a roof highly ornamented with the most beautiful azure and gold. On the other side of the entrance the colonnades are even bigger, supporting a richly ornamented roof and gilt columns. Inside, the walls are hung with exquisite paintings depicting the history of the old kings.

Here, on feast days, King Facfur held court and staged a feast for his principal nobles, the chief magistrates and rich citizens, a gathering of some ten thousand people. The festival went on for ten to twelve days and the magnificence of the spectacle, the silks, gold and precious stones, was beyond imagining as every guest sought to outdo the others in the opulence of their dress.

Inside the colonnaded grand portico there is a kind of pillared cloister separating the inner court from the outer, from which the royal apartments lead off. The pillars and walls are very richly ornamented. A covered passage six paces wide leads from here all the way to the lake. On each side there are entrances to ten courts again surrounded by porticoed cloisters, with each court having fifty apartments with gardens. These are the apartments of one thousand young women who were kept by the King. Accompanied sometimes by his Queen and often by a party of these females, it was the King's custom to take his amusement on the lake in barges ornate with silk and to visit the temples and idols.

The royal seraglio also enclosed two other sections laid out to groves of trees, stretches of water, beautiful gardens with fruit trees and enclosures for all sorts of animals (such as antelope, deer, stag, hare and rabbits) kept for hunting.

Here the King sported himself, often with a bevy of his concubines, some in carriages, some on horseback. No other men were allowed at these gatherings but the girls were practised in the art of coursing with dogs and hunting animals. When they grew weary of these activities they retired into the groves of trees beside the lake, shed their clothes and rushed naked into the water where they would swim energetically about while the King watched.

Sometimes he took a meal in these groves where the foliage of lofty trees afforded thick shade, waited upon by his girls. He was in fact so worn out by their devotions he had little thought for the defence of his kingdom and was no match for Kublai Khan who deprived him of all these splendid possessions and expelled him with ignominy.

I was told about all this by a rich merchant of Kin-sai, when I personally visited the city. Then very old, he had been a confidential servant of King Facfur and knew everything about the King's life. He had known the palace in all its former glory and was anxious to show me around. The palace is now occupied by the Grand Khan's viceroy and while the colonnades have been preserved, the court-yards where the women lived have been left to go to ruin, indeed only the foundations are still visible. The great wall enclosing the park and gardens has also fallen into decay and the groves of trees and the animals have all gone.

Let us now leave Kin-sai and head towards the north-east where, at a distance of 25 miles, you come to the sea and a fine port called

Gan-pu used by ships trading with India. The port is at the mouth of the river that flows past Kin-sai and a huge fleet of boats plies up and down this waterway with the downstream traffic carrying exports for Cathay and India.

I was in Kin-sai when his majesty's commissioners were making an annual tally of revenues and a census, and had the chance to see some of the results. In the latter were registered one hundred and sixty 'tomans' of fireplaces (families dwelling under the same roof). As a toman represents a thousand souls, it follows that the population of the city is one hundred and sixty thousand families! Every head of a family, or the housekeeper, is required to put a notice on his front door giving the names of each member of the family, whether male or female, and the number of houses they have. When someone dies their name is struck off and when a child is born its name is added. The great officers of a province and the governors of the cities are thus able to keep an exact check on the inhabitants. This same system applies in Cathay as well as Manji. All the keepers of inns and hostelries are likewise required to keep a register of their guests, noting the day and hour of their arrival, and this is posted daily with the city magistrates. There is just one church for Nestorian Christians here.

In Manji I also found it a custom among the ordinary people to sell their children to the rich in order that they might be brought up in a better manner.

Here is an indication of the kind of revenues Kublai can expect from Kin-sai, and the places within its jurisdiction, which constitutes the ninth division (or kingdom) of Manji. From salt (the most productive item) he levies a yearly duty of 80 tomans of gold, each toman being 80,000 saggi. Each saggi is equal to a gold florin, so the total adds up to 6,400,000 ducats.

This vast output of salt may be accounted for by the huge number of salty lakes and marshes near the sea where, in the heat of the summer, the salt forms crystals sufficient to meet the needs of five other divisions of the country.

They also cultivate large quantities of sugar from which Kublai takes duty, as he does on the production of rice wine. Artisans, merchants, importers and exporters pay a duty of 3.5 per cent. On goods coming by sea from distant lands like India, you pay 10 per cent. Cattle, agricultural produce and silk all attract a tithe for the Grand Khan and I personally saw an annual account (excluding the revenues from salt) of royal duty amounting to 210 tomans or 16,800,000 ducats.

A day's journey to the south-east of Kin-sai, through a countryside rich in houses, villas and delightful gardens producing an abundance of vegetables, brings one to the very large and handsome city of Ta-pin-zu. It is under the jurisdiction of Kin-sai, the people are all idolaters, burn their dead and use paper money, but otherwise it is of no special interest. Travelling in these parts you are continually passing through towns, seeing castles and other habitations so extensive that they give the appearance of being one continuous city. Everything required for the good life is produced in great abundance and they have bamboo canes here a foot or so thick and some 45 feet long.

If you continue to the south-east again, you pass through densely populated agricultural land. These provinces of Manji do not have many sheep but there are oxen, cows, buffalo, goats and a huge number of pigs. A further three days of travel brings one to the pretty city of Zen Gian built upon a hill in the middle of the river, embraced, as it were, by two streams, one of which branches to the north-west the other to the south-east. All these cities pay allegiance to the Grand Khan and are dependent upon Kin-sai. This is a country of abundant game, both birds and beasts.

Three days more on the road brings one to the large and noble city of Gie-za which is the limit of Kin-sai's authority, and after that you enter another kingdom (or vice-royalty) of Manji, known as Kon-cha, where the principal city is Fu-jiu.

I travelled on from here for six days through hills and valleys, never out of sight of towns and villages where food is abundant and there is much field sport, particularly birding. You have to be very careful of tigers of great size and strength. It is a centre for the production of medicinal plants like ginger, galangal and tea. A Venetian silver groat buys you 80lb weight of fresh ginger! There is also a plant here that has the colour, smell and properties of saffron but which it is not. It is used extensively in the local cooking and as such fetches a high price.

But what makes this part of the country unique is the appetite of the local inhabitants for human flesh. They regard it as of a more delicate flavour than all other, provided, of course, that the person has not died of some foul disease.

You should also see them go into battle! They loosen their long hair so that it falls about their ears and paint their faces bright blue. Armed with lances and spears they make their assault on foot, all except the chief who is on horseback. They have a reputation for appalling savagery for, having slain their enemy, they eat their flesh and drink the blood.

At the end of the six days you reach the large city of Kue-lin-fu which features three spectacular bridges upwards of 300 feet long and 24 feet wide.

The women here are very beautiful and live lives of ultimate ease. Raw silk is produced and manufactured into a variety of silk cloths. Cotton is also woven and dyed into coloured clothes exported all over Manji. There is also lots of ginger and galangal. I was told of an extraordinary domestic fowl here which has no feathers but is covered in black hair like a cat. Nevertheless it lays eggs and is very good to eat. This is also tiger country, of which there are such a multitude that travelling can be quite dangerous – in fact it is best to go in company.

This whole area is rich in castles and towns where silk is produced in abundance by an essentially idolatrous population. A centre for the production of sugar, Un-guen is three days further on. Almost all its output is sent to Kanbula to supply the royal court.

Before Un-guen was conquered by the armies of the Grand Khan the manufacture of fine quality sugar was unknown and they never produced anything better than a boiled dark brown paste. In

Kublai's court at the time, however, there were some people from Babylon who were sent to Un-guen to teach the locals how to refine sugar using the ashes of certain woods.

Fifteen miles further on is Kan-gui, the headquarters of a large army charged with the protection (and the suppression in the event of rebellion) of all the cities in Kon-cha. A river a mile wide flows through the city flanked by extensive, imposing buildings. A great number of ships are berthed here, loading various merchandise, especially sugar. It is also a port for large numbers of vessels from India bringing rich cargos of jewels and pearls, all sold at a considerable profit. The ships are able to navigate up the river from the sea which is no great distance away. It is a beautiful place, rich in all the good things of life and with delightful gardens producing exquisite fruits.

Cross the river and travel five days to the south-east, all the time past numerous towns, castle and substantial houses, you will arrive at noble, handsome Zai-tun with its busy port on the coast. This is a journey over hills, across plains and through woods in which are found many plants from which camphor is produced. Zai-tun is a very busy port through which imports are sent to all parts of Manji. I would estimate that the well-known trade in pepper, which travels from here to Alexandria to supply the Western world, amounts to no more than a hundredth part of that which is imported through Zai-tun. In fact, it is impossible for anyone to convey the extent and variety of the merchandise that flows through this, one of the largest and most commodious ports in the world.

The Grand Khan derives vast revenues from this trade as every merchant is obliged to pay customs duty of 10 per cent. In addition there are their shipping costs: about 30 per cent for every boatload of fine goods, 44 per cent for pepper and 40 per cent for lignum, aloes, sandalwood, medicinal drugs and trade in general. Nevertheless, even though the charges, customs and freight can amount to half the value of a cargo, their profit is still considerable. They are very happy to return to this market with further stocks of merchandise.

The countryside around here is delightful. Although the people are idolaters they have goods aplenty and they are by nature peaceable and very fond of the easy, indulgent life. Many people come to this city to get tattooed and the artists who engage in this work are much celebrated.

The large river that runs by Zai-tun, which is actually a branch of the river passing Kin-sai, is very swift. Where the river divides you find the city of Tin-gui, famous for the manufacture of porcelain bowls, dishes and cups. Porcelain is made as follows. A certain kind of earth is dug up from what might be termed a mine and is then left in heaps to be weathered by the sun, wind and rain for between forty or fifty years, during all of which time it must not be disturbed. The process refines it to a material suitable for shaping into the vessels I have mentioned. Colours are then laid on the clay and afterwards it is baked in an oven or furnace. Great quantities of porcelain ware are sold in the city and for a Venetian groat you can get eight cups.

There is one other place in the kingdom of Manji from which the Grand Khan draws as much revenue as Kin-sai and that is the vice-royalty of Kon-cha. I should just note here that while the people of Manji speak one language there is a great diversity of dialects, just as there is between Genoese, Milanese and Florentines.

But it is time I brought this account of Cathay and Manji, the two great fiefdoms of China, to a close and moved on to mighty India which may be divided into Greater, Lesser and Middle India and which I was fortunate to be able to visit in the service of the Grand Khan. I went there on the King's business on a number of occasions and also with my father and uncle when Kublai, although reluctant to use us, charged us with the task of providing a safe escort for a princess betrothed to King Argon of Persia. Needless to say, this was a journey of many extraordinary adventures but you shall also hear some of the stories I was told along the way by reliable people and some privileged information I was given about charts to the Indian coastline.

BOOK THREE

Introduction

We come now to the Third Book, in which Marco Polo, after seventeen (or possibly eighteen) years in the service of Kublai Khan, tells the incredible story of how he beguiled Kublai, now an ageing and cantankerous absolute dictator, into allowing him and his family to go home to Venice.

Marco was about forty years old and had survived several Tartar wars, serious illnesses (from one of which he took a year to recover), attacks by robbers on the roads he travelled as Kublai's ambassador, murderers who believed their religion would be served by killing strangers, battles in the van of the Grand Khan's final assault on China, lethal enemies made at court and immense natural hazards such as he encountered during the first climb by a Westerner on to the 'Roof of the World' (the Pamir Plateau) and crossing the Gobi Desert on foot. Moreover, Kublai Khan was bitterly opposed to his going. And the Grand Khan was not at this time a man to be argued with!

From the way this altercation is described in the introductory material in Book One, I actually wonder whether Marco himself wanted that much to leave Kublai's court. The account of the row is briefly told (in the third person), some believe by Rustichello, Marco's ghostwriter. Marco never actually records this seminal event himself. Instead, Nicolo Polo, Marco's father, is recorded as one day 'taking the opportunity when he observed him [Kublai] to be more than usually cheerful, of throwing himself at his feet and soliciting on behalf of himself and of his family to be indulged with his majesty's gracious permission for their departure'. The request went down like a lead brick!

'He appeared hurt at the application,' Nicolo records. In fact, Kublai went so far as to question their sanity, doubting whether they would survive the dangers of the return trip. He also tried to bribe them out of going, offering to double their salaries and grant them any honours they desired. Then, when all that failed, he simply said no 'positively' (as the text politely puts it). There the matter rested – you argued with Kublai Khan at your extreme peril – and had fate not intervened, the Polos would simply have been three more merchants lost to Asia.

What seems to have shifted Marco's opinion about leaving and his involvement in the escape plot was Kublai's age – he was about eighty, a very old man for the times. It is understandable that his father and uncle, also ageing, and who appear to have remained simply merchants throughout their time in Asia, would have wanted to go home and enjoy their well-earned, immense wealth in civilised Venice.

Not so much Marco. He had left the place as a teenager and he now enjoyed a rich and extraordinarily influential role at the court of the most powerful monarch on earth, the ruler of three-quarters of the world. If he went back to Venice his status would be that of merchant, albeit rather a rich one. He must also have had severe doubts that anyone would believe his incredible story because almost three years were to elapse before he thought of writing it down, and he would do so then only because he was in gaol with nothing better to do. As we now know, these fears were well founded. He would be Marco Millione, the grand liar, and was still protesting – 'I have not told half of what I saw' – on his deathbed.

But Marco was persuaded by his family that in the light of Kublai's extreme old age they'd best get out while they could. Again the text politely presents their difficulties as: 'His death, if it should happen previously to their departure, might deprive them of that public assistance by which alone they could expect to surmount the innumerable difficulties of so long a journey.' This, frankly, is the one and only grand understatement in the whole book. Without Kublai's golden passport these three were as good as dead, or at best trapped, in a court and country where they had made many enemies. As it was, and in spite of the Grand Khan's blessing, it still took them some four years to fight their way home.

Interestingly, it fell to Marco to obtain Kublai's blessing and that gives us one of the few clear pointers to the unique nature of Marco's 'special relationship' with the Grand Khan; certainly a much closer relationship than that enjoyed by his father and uncle who, on the grounds of their senior status alone, one would assume would have had much more in common with Kublai.

The plot runs as follows. Kublai has been exercised by the last wish of the late Queen of Persia, Bologna, the mighty King Argon's late Queen, who insisted on her deathbed that her place should only be taken by one of her relatives from Cathay in the dominions of the Grand Khan.

Kublai's problem was the same as that worrying the Polos. Between his court and the Persian capital a number of Tartar wars were raging. In fact, so fraught with danger was their route that the ambassadors returning to King Argon to tell him that a suitable new bride had been chosen had eventually been forced, after travelling for eight months, to turn back to Kublai's court.

Marco, just home from a long sea voyage to the East Indies in command of a fleet of ships, saw his chance. He went to Kublai and told him that he knew the way to get the princess safely back to Persia by sea. Word of this offer reached Argon's ambassadors, who had now been away from Persia for three years and could see no hope of getting home overland. They held a meeting with the Polos and afterwards had an audience with Kublai, at which they urged him to honour his commitment to the King of Persia. They took the beautiful young Queen-elect along with them to help persuade him. The journey by sea, they said, would be shorter and cheaper than a land journey but could only be safely commanded by Marco Polo and his relatives because of his recent experience of navigating these waters.

Kublai really did not want the Polos to go – as the text puts it: '[he] showed by his countenance that it was exceedingly displeasing to him' – but he knew there was little alternative as Argon was his most powerful ally. In the end he accepted their offer graciously, extracting a promise from the Polos that when they had stayed a while with their families they would return to him. As things turned out, this was not a promise they needed to keep because by the time they got back to Venice, Kublai had died.

The key to their escape was Marco's managing to convince Kublai Khan that he had somehow acquired the skills of an oceanic navigator in waters he'd never been near. When did he pick up this knowledge? How did he get away with so outrageous a claim? True, he had recently returned from a sea journey, but this voyage is unlikely to have taken him through the uncharted islands of the Far East where he was now proposing to sail with the princess.

His essential ignorance of Eastern oceans and their landmasses is quickly revealed in Book Three. He takes a stab at describing the vast number of islands and actually puts a figure on them – 7,440! How he came by so exact a count can only be guessed at, indeed I am sure it was a guess.

He's fascinated, as were all Europeans of the time, by Japan – Zipangu – which virtually no one from the West had visited by this time. He reports on the spectacular disaster that overtook Kublai Khan's expedition to conquer Japan, surely the Grand Khan's greatest failure, but this simply adds to his vicarious fascination with the ferocity and brutality of the Japanese, not least that they prefer the flavour of human flesh to all other. Japan is also reported to be layered in gold and enormously rich.

But while stretching credibility with descriptions of islands and landfalls he never visited, unlike most early travel writers he is meticulous about informing his readers when his reports rely on hearsay. The truthfulness of much of his material can also be judged by the small detail. For example, in this book he makes it clear that black and white pepper are 'products' (white pepper is produced by blanching the ripe peppercorns) when, right up to the twentieth century, black and white pepper were thought to come from different plants.

Elsewhere his detailed description of whaling in the Indian Ocean, using harpoons tied to heavy lines, reveals that the techniques of whaling did not change for the next six hundred years. Reflecting his deep interest in natural history (the whole manuscript is interspersed with descriptions of natural phenomena) we hear of the 'great white bear', sometimes 10 feet long, of the far north; the first Western description of the polar bear.

There are a number of intriguing references, utterly fantastical at first glance, where Marco creates a story out of what is probably just a grain of truth. The best of these is the tale of the strange islands near 'Succotera' off the coast of Africa where men and women each have their own island and the men take the women as wives for three months each year. The children are looked after by their mothers until aged twelve when the boys go to the men's island and the girls enter the marriage market. Marco was ridiculed when he claimed that the inhabitants of these islands at the mouth of the Gulf of Aden were Christians worshipping the Old Testament and part of the 'See of Succotera', but yet again he may have been right.

He may even have mistaken the Succotera islands for the Comoros further south, as all this information is admitted hearsay. The exact whereabouts of the islands is ill-defined, indeed the name has been badly mutilated in the translations. (In the Basle edition it is *Sciora*, in the older Latin, *Scoyran* and in the early Italian epitomes, *Scorsia*.) And it was revealed about thirty years ago that the Comoros, entirely surrounded by Muslims, houses a sect practising a very early form of Solomonic Old Testament Christianity. They believe that they are descended from the ancient Jews.

The Comoros are also a short distance from Madagascar and Madagascar is the next important landmass Marco describes, although he does not claim ever to have been there. Nonetheless his descriptions are quite detailed and he certainly could have picked up his knowledge of the place from the natives of Comoros.

Ships from India and the Persian Gulf visited Madagascar fairly regularly, indeed nearby Zanzibar was ruled by Omani sheiks. It is almost certain that Marco got much of his information from Indian and Arabian mariners who he probably employed to help him pilot his battered fleet across the Indian Ocean and up the Persian Gulf.

Almost certainly because they are hearsay the stories Marco Millione tells of Madagascar are among the most fantastical in the book. But as is so often the case with this remarkable manuscript, time and the work of modern scientists have come out in support of what seem like the most ludicrous of tall tales. For example, arguably his most unreal description of an animal is that of the legendary great auk (or *rukh*) of Madagascar, which has a wingspan of some 40 yards and can lift an elephant. Pure fantasy? Well, for hundreds of years this particular yarn certainly did Marco's reputation little good. Yet early in the twentieth century in the jungles of Madagascar ornithologists found fossilised eggs the size of footballs of a gigantic extinct bird.

And Marco Polo notes observantly that Madagascar has a unique and distinctive fauna. He records the existence of 'camelopards and wild asses'. More scientifically informed observers such as Gerald Durrell and David Attenborough would demonstrate (but some 700 years later) that Madagascar's early separation from the ancient continent of Gondwanaland produced singular evolutionary paths here, not least the development of a distinctive primate, the lemur.

When describing the natives of the nearby island of Zanzibar Marco Polo, who has seen so many disparate peoples of so many colours, surprisingly lapses into blatant racism. It may have been his first actual contact with Negroes (although it's hard to believe he had never seen a Negro slave), 'whose hair is sort of crisp and even when wetted stays tightly curled . . . their noses turn up towards the forehead, their ears are long and their eyes are so large and scary they have the appearance of demons. The women are equally ugly with heads that are large and out of proportion. They are the most ugly women in the world with large mouths, thick noses and ugly breasts four times as large as other women's.' A few paragraphs later, however, he commends these people as being very brave in battle, which they fight from the backs of elephants, showing a complete contempt for death. I have worked on conservation projects in Madagascar and I did not know there were ever elephants there, but who knows, there may have been some once.

Marco Polo can be excused all this hearsay because he was compiling a book which he knew would be read by aspiring Western explorers, traders and mariners who at the time had little or no knowledge of these waters. We know that Christopher Columbus took a heavily annotated copy of Marco's book on all his famous voyages and Marco is very good when it comes to detail vital to navigation under sail. He accurately describes in this book the trade, or monsoon, winds that blow, reversing direction summer and winter, between India and the Gulf, and so far as I know his is the first Western description of this extremely useful natural pheno-menon, which since the dawn of recorded time has stimulated trade between Africa and India. Indeed, it was probably on the strength of information about how these winds behaved, or the knowledge that Arab and Indian mariners were safely making the voyage to and from Persia, that he got up the courage to offer to take Argon's seventeen-year-old bride-to-be home by sea.

Book Three has its fair share of the salacious tittle-tattle we have come to expect from this red-blooded young Italian. There's an eyewitness account of the virgins of Ziambu who are not allowed to marry until the king has tried them out, and another of the dusky lotharios of Maabar who have 'sensual natures', go about virtually naked and marry their brothers' widows and their widowed mothers-in-law.

We also meet, for the first time in Western literature, the Sumatran rhino which has a single horn. The one Marco Polo met apparently fought with a tongue armed with sharp spikes. They are not, he warns seriously, to be confused with unicorns. Marco apparently believes in the unicorn as much as this rhino and reminds us in all seriousness that a unicorn can only be tamed by a virgin clasping its head to her bosom.

Marco's (or Rustichello's) imagination runs away with him in other places. He tells a wonderful story of natives collecting fabulous diamonds by tempting wild eagles with scraps of meat, afterwards invading their nest on the high peaks to collect the stones which have attached to these scraps. Later researchers found this story, told almost identically, as one of the adventures of Sinbad the Sailor in the Arabian Nights. It is further evidence of Marco's habit of collecting juicy snippets to titillate the jaded appetite of the Grand Khan or his readers.

At the end of Book Three our hero then goes on a worldwide ramble as he attempts to tidy up a number of stories told elsewhere and which results, sadly, in a rather anti-climactic end to his tale. Be that as it may, in my view Book Three is the most exciting section of manuscript – some six hundred members of the expedition died on the voyage back to Persia – and it begins aptly enough with a description of the ships of the time, his initial journey overland to Java and then the incredible voyage halfway round the world.

BOOK THREE

The Journey Home

Let me start with ships, as in this book I shall be spending a lot of time in them. Built of pine they have a single deck, below which the space is divided into about sixty or more small cabins. Each of these spaces is allocated to a merchant.

These ships have good rudders and four masts each carrying a sail. There are also some two-masted vessels whose masts can be raised or lowered as circumstances demand. I've seen large ships which as well as the cabins have a hold divided into thirteen sections by thick mortised planks. These bulkheads are designed to keep the ship afloat in the event of an accident such as striking a rock or being hit by a whale. The latter occurs quite frequently because, when sailing at night, these vessels make a foaming white bow wave which appears to attract hungry whales. Hoping for food, the leviathan charges violently at the ship striking a blow that quite often caves in her bottom planks.

There is a kind of well in the ship that is always kept clear into which water can flow if the ship springs a leak. Goods likely to be damaged by the water are removed and because the bulkheads are so well built the water is kept from spreading. The ships are all doubled-planked, the inner hull being sheathed with a second skin held on with iron nails. Inside and out they are well caulked with oakum. They don't have pitch here so the hulls are coated with a mixture of quicklime and chopped hemp which is mixed with oil from a particular tree. A kind of unguent, it actually retains its viscous properties and sticks better than pitch.

Some of the larger ships have a crew of three hundred!

They can carry five to six thousand baskets (or woven bags) of pepper. In former times, I'm told, the ships were even bigger but the violence of the seas hereabouts has broken up the islands and silted up some of the principal ports. Vessels of shallower draught have been built in recent times to handle this want of water. These vessels are rowed by banks of four oarsmen.

The larger ships are often accompanied by quite large barques each capable of carrying a thousand baskets of pepper and with crews of up to a hundred. They are often employed to tow the larger vessels, sometimes with oars but also under sail. You have to be careful where the wind is coming from. If it is directly aft, the sails of the larger vessels will becalm and the smaller vessels run them down.

Each ship is equipped with as many as ten small boats for putting out anchors, fishing and a variety of other chores. They are slung on the sides of the ships.

Ships that have been at sea so long they're in need of repair are often sheathed over, giving them a third skin of planking. The process can be repeated as many as six times with the new boards fitting as snugly as the originals.

The part of the world to which I now found myself directed has a great many islands of which the most intriguing is Zipangu [Japan], some fifteen hundred 'li' [Chinese miles] from the coast of southern China. You find gold here in great abundance, in fact the supply is said to be inexhaustible. But few merchants visit the place as the king does not allow the wealth to be exported, nor is Zipangu frequented by much shipping from other parts of the world.

The sovereign's palace, according to all reports, is extraordinarily opulent. Its entire roof is plated with gold in much the same way as we would roof a building or a church with lead. The ceilings of the royal halls are of the same precious metal. These apartments have small tables of solid gold of a considerable thickness and the windows are also ornamented with gold. To be quite honest, it's really impossible for me adequately to convey the richness of these royal apartments.

Pearls of a red [pink] colour, round in shape and of a great size are to be found here in large quantities. They are equal in value or even exceed that of white pearls. Some of the inhabitants – those who bury rather than burn their dead – place one of these pearls in the mouth of the corpse. A number of other precious stones are also to be found here.

The island of Zipangu was so famously rich it excited a desire in the Grand Khan to conquer it and annex it to his possessions. To this end he fitted out an extensive fleet and embarked a large body of troops under the command of two of his principal officers, Abbacatan and Vonsancin, and a Chinese Mongul general. The expedition sailed from Zai-tun and Kin-sai, managed the voyage safely and arrived in Zipangu in good order.

Jealousy between the two commanders, however, caused each to treat the plans of the other with contempt, as a result of which they failed to gain possession of a single city or fortification bar one, which was carried by assault but only after the garrison refused to surrender. The entire city was put to the sword, in fact they were beheaded. Just eight people survived thanks to the working of a diabolical charm, a jewel inserted in their right arms between the skin and the flesh. No iron weapon could either kill or indeed wound them. So they were beaten to death with heavy wooden clubs.

Kublai's fleet was anchored near the shore of Zipangu when a strong north wind began to blow, causing the Tartar ships to foul each other. The troops were quickly re-embarked and the fleet put to sea. The gale, however, became so violent that a number of ships foundered. Fortunately many of the people aboard these vessels managed to save themselves by floating on pieces of wood to an island about 4 miles off Zipangu.

The plight of these Tartars – some thirty thousand of them – was now desperate. Abandoned by their generals and having neither arms nor provisions, they fully expected to be taken captive or perish, especially as the island offered nothing in the way of sustenance or shelter. And as soon as the storm ceased and the seas calmed a large force of people from Zipangu came over with the aim of imprisoning the shipwrecked Tartars.

The Tartars had concealed themselves on high ground and the search for them was conducted in a somewhat disorderly fashion. They were able to observe the movements of the Japanese and, by another road, made their way round the coast to the Japanese boats. Keeping the Japanese colours flying the Tartars set a course for the principal city of Zipangu where, thanks to the flags, they managed to enter the port undetected and unmolested. They found few men there. The women – how shall I put it? – were retained for their own use, the others being driven out.

The king of Zipangu was enraged by all this and immediately ordered the city to be blockaded. For six months no one entered or left the city. At the end of this time the Tartars, convinced that no one was coming to their rescue, surrendered on condition that their lives would be spared.

All these events took place in the year 1284. Some years later the Grand Khan, having learned that his expedition had suffered these disasters as a result of the discord of his commanders, had the head of one of them cut off and exiled the other to the savage island of Zarza where prisoners suffer execution in the following manner: they are sewn up tight round both arms in the hide of a freshly killed buffalo. As the skin dries the victim is squeezed until he perishes miserably.

The people of Zipangu and its various islands worship idols with the heads of animals: oxen, pigs, dogs, goats and many others. Some are single heads displaying two faces, others have three, one in the proper place, the others on each shoulder. Then there are those with fourteen and sometimes even a hundred arms. The more arms the more power and the more devotedly they are worshipped.

Asked by Christians why they give their deities these many forms, the natives answer that their fathers did it before them and it is their duty to preserve the tradition for all time. I should add that the various rites practised before these idols are so wicked and diabolical it would be an inexcusable abomination to repeat them here.

You need to know this, however. When these idolaters make a prisoner of some enemy who is unable to pay ransom they invite all their relatives to the house and put the prisoner to death. They then prepare his flesh tastily and eat it with great relish, declaring that there's nothing to rival human flesh for flavour.

The ocean in which Zipangu is located is called the Sea of Chin [China]; so extensive is this eastern sea I am told by experienced pilots and mariners who have sailed there and obviously know it well, that it contains no less than 7,440 islands, most of them inhabited. I've also heard it reported that all the trees that grow on them give off sweet smells.

They produce many spices and medicinal plants, particularly lignum-aloes and pepper, both white and black, in great quantities. It's impossible to put a value on the gold and other goods to be found on all these islands but their distance from the mainland is so great and so troublesome is the navigation that vessels trading from Zai-tun and Kin-sai don't reap large profits. Sailing in summer and returning in winter, a voyage can consume a whole year, for in this region you only get two shifts of wind, in one direction in winter and the other way in summer.

That's about all I can say about these very remote islands and countries as they do not come within the dominion of the Grand Khan and thus I did not have occasion to visit them in person.

So let me turn to the Gulf of Kei-nan [Hai-nan] which involves a voyage of some 1,500 miles to the south-west and took me two months. It's located off the coast of southern Manji [China] and bounds the countries of Ania, Tolomon [Kochin China] and many others I've already mentioned, including Burma.

Within the Gulf are a multitude of islands, for the most part well inhabited. Along the coasts of these islands much gold dust is collected from places where rivers discharge into the sea. Copper is also found and a lively trade goes on between the islands, one supplying what another lacks. There is also a rich exchange with the people of the mainland, gold and copper being traded for such necessities as the islanders may require, although most of the islands raise grain in abundance.

To be honest, the Gulf is so extensive and the inhabitants so numerous, it is in every sense another world.

At the end of my long voyage across the Gulf of Kei-nan I arrived in the huge, rich country of Ziambu [Kochin China]. It is governed by its own king and has a distinctive language of its own. A tribute of elephants and lignum-aloes is paid annually to the Grand Khan. This came about as follows.

In about 1268, Kublai heard of the vast wealth of the kingdom and set about conquering it with a large and powerful army under the command of General Sogatu. The king of the time, Accabale, was elderly and did not feel up to engaging Kublai's forces in the field, so he retired to a stronghold and there proceeded to defend himself valiantly. Kublai quickly overran and laid waste the undefended towns, cities and the inhabitants of the plains until the king grew fearful that he and his entire country would be destroyed. He sent ambassadors to the Grand Khan offering to pay an annual tribute if he would withdraw his army and leave the country in the state of peace and tranquillity which had prevailed for so long previously.

Kublai, moved to compassion, immediately sent word to Sogatu to pull his army out and campaign elsewhere. The King, for his part, agreed to pay the tribute in the form of a very large quantity of sweet-scented wood and twenty of the largest and most handsome elephants to be found in his kingdom.

I went to this kingdom in the year 1280 and can thus bear witness to some of its singular customs. As a start no young woman can be given in marriage until she has been tried out by the King! Those whom he likes he keeps for some time and when they are retired they are given a dowry which allows them to make advantageous marriages. When I was there the King had three hundred and twenty-six children. Most of his sons had distinguished themselves as daring soldiers.

This countryside [Malaya] abounds with elephants, lignum-aloes and forests of fine black ebony which is made into fine furniture.

Voyaging south by south-east for another 1,500 miles brings one to Java, another island of great size. According to reports I was given by well-informed navigators, it is the largest in the world, some 3,000 miles in circumference. It has a single king and it pays tribute to nobody. The people all worship idols.

Its produce includes pepper, nutmeg, spikenard, galangal, cubebs, cloves and all the other valuable spices and efficacious plant materials. More spices are traded from here than from anywhere else in the world. The only reason the Grand Khan hasn't brought Java into his domains is the length of the voyage to get there and the dangers of navigation.

Seven hundred miles south, or rather south-west, of Java Major you encounter the islands of Sondur and Kondur, both uninhabited. Then on a south-easterly heading you reach a rich province, Lochac, forming part of the mainland, with an independent king who discourages visits from strangers in order that his treasure and other secrets of his realm may be as little known to the rest of the world as possible. The country is wild and mountainous and gold is abundant in quantities scarcely credible. Sappan, or brazilwood, is logged in large quantities and there are vast numbers of elephants and other game. From here are exported all the cowrie shells which other countries use as currency. They have a delicious fruit about the size of a lemon called *berchi*.

Holding course due south for another 500 miles brings you to the island of Pentan (near the eastern mouth of the Straits of Malacca), which is a wild and uncultivated place but where the forests abound with sweet-scented woods. For 60 miles around the island the sea is nowhere more than 4 fathoms deep, obliging ships to lift their rudders or risk running aground. After sailing another 60 miles in a south-easterly direction you reach an island, in itself a kingdom, named Malaive [Malaya], which is also the name of the principal town. The town is large and well built and a considerable trade is carried on here in spices and medicinal plants.

Still sailing to the south-east for about 100 miles you arrive at the island of Lesser Java [Sumatra]. Small by comparison with Java Major, it is still 2,000 miles in circumference. It is divided into eight kingdoms, each with its own distinctive language. The people, all idolaters, engage in a brisk trade in all manner of spices, lignum-aloes, various kinds of medicinal plants and sappan wood used for dyeing. This produce finds its way to Cathay and Manji but rarely to Europe because of the long and dangerous voyage involved.

One observation of interest: these islands lie so far to the south that the North Star is no longer visible.

I personally visited six of the eight kingdoms and had some strange experiences. First there is the Kingdom of Felech of which not much can be said, especially of the natives, who live like beasts in the mountains eating human flesh and all other forms of flesh, clean or unclean. They have a peculiar form of worship, each individual revering the first thing he sees upon rising in the morning. The people who live in the seaside towns are mostly idolaters but a good number of them have been converted to follow Mahomet by the Saracens who come here all the time.

Next is Basman which is independent of all the other kingdoms and has its own language. The people profess obedience to the Grand Khan but render no tribute, as it is too far for him to send an army to enforce payment. Ships that pass this way often bring him rare and curious gifts such as a particular breed of falcon.

There are many elephants and a type of monster beast called a rhinoceros which is smaller than an elephant but has similar feet. Their hide is like that of the buffalo and in the middle of the forehead they have a single horn. They do not, however, use this to attack, relying instead on the tongue, which is armed with long sharp spikes. They also use their knees and feet. They have heads like wild boars, which they carry low to the ground, and they are filthy in their habits, mostly frequenting muddy pools. (I should point out that these are not unicorns which can be tamed by a virgin standing close to one and clasping its head to her bosom.) You also find a lot of monkeys in this district and large, savage vultures black as crows.

I should also correct the myth that this is where you get the dried bodies of diminutive humans, or pygmies, which one often sees for sale in India. It's an idle tale, in fact they are fashioned from a monkey of some size with features resembling those of a human. They shave off the hair other than on the chin and the genital areas then dry and preserve the body with camphor and other preparations. Having thus ensured that they have the appearance of little old men, they put them in boxes and sell them as curios to traders who carry them to all parts of the world.

My next move was to Samara, indeed I was obliged to spend some five months there because of unfavourable and contrary winds. Here, where neither the North Star nor the Great Bear can be seen, the king is a vassal of the Grand Khan and I soon became established ashore, admittedly with a party of some 2,000 men to guard me from the savage natives who will happily kill and eat unwary strangers.

I arranged for a deep, wide moat to be dug round our encampment on the land side, the arms of which led round the port in which our ships were moored. The ditch was guarded from a number of wooden redoubts constructed of the abundant local wood and behind this fortification our party lived securely for some five months. In fact, we got on so well with the natives there was no difficulty obtaining food and other necessities.

The finest fish in the world are to be found here and while the people do not grow wheat there is plenty of rice. Nor do they make proper wine but produce an excellent beverage from the sap of a tree that resembles the date palm. They cut off a branch and under the cut place a bowl which fills in about a day and a night. So wholesome is this liquor it gives relief from such complaints as the dropsy as well as those of the lungs and spleen. When the flow of sap ceases they bring water from the river via channels or pipes and after copious watering the flow comes from the trees again. Some trees yield a reddish sap, others a paler colour.

You also get Indian nuts [coconuts] here the size of a man's head with an edible flesh that is as sweet and pleasant and white as milk. In the cavity of the nut is a liquor as cool as water, cooler and better flavoured than any kind of wine or any other drink you can find anywhere. That said, the natives feed upon flesh of every kind, good or bad, without distinction.

The fourth kingdom has a ruler who recognises the authority of the Grand Khan but the inhabitants are uncivilised and they all worship idols. They have one particularly repugnant custom. When a person falls sick the relatives send for sorcerers to establish whether he will recover or not. If it is decided that he won't, they call in another team who with great dexterity, being very experienced, stop up the mouth of the poor victim until he suffocates. The body is then cut into pieces, cooked to make it more appetising, then eaten by all the relatives in an atmosphere of great conviviality. They eat everything, right down to the marrow of the bones!

I asked about this custom and got the reply that if any part of the body were left over vermin would breed on it and when the vermin died they would wreak grievous punishment on the soul of the departed. Afterwards, however, the bones are collected, deposited in a small neat box and carried to a cavern in the mountains where they will be safe from disturbance by wild animals.

There is a lot of eating of people going on around here. In a nearby district they eat people who are captured and cannot pay ransom.

The fifth kingdom is called Lambri and like the others its inhabitants acknowledge the Grand Khan, worship idols and speak their own distinctive language. It was on Lambri, where they grow sappan wood in great quantities, that I obtained the seed of a vegetable which resembles the sappan. When the plant throws roots they transplant it to another spot and leave it for three years. I took the seeds home with me to Venice and sowed them but they didn't find the climate sufficiently warm and none of them came up.

In the mountains, well away from the towns, you find men with tails a metre long like those of a dog but without hair [orangutans – the name translates as 'wild man']. There are lots of them!

The sixth kingdom, Fanfur, is likewise ruled by a king who pays allegiance to the Grand Khan and the people worship idols. They grow a type of camphor wood here much superior to all others. It actually sells for its equivalent weight in gold.

They also have a tree from which they produce a kind of meal [sago]. It has a large, thick stem – two men could only just span it – and a skin about 3 inches thick. Inside is the pith which yields a flour similar to that from acorns. The pith is put in pots of water and stirred with a stick causing the fibres and other impurities to rise to the top while the farinaceous meal sinks to the bottom. The water is poured off and the resulting flour made into all kinds of cakes and pastries. The bread made from it resembles barley bread in appearance and flavour. I ate a good deal of this bread and brought some of it home to Venice.

The outside bark of the tree which, as I said, is first stripped back, is as hard as iron and when thrown into water immediately sinks. It can be split like a bamboo cane and of this the natives make short lances (larger ones would be too heavy) sharpened at one end and, after being hardened in a fire, capable of piercing any kind of armour. In many respects they are superior to iron weapons.

I left Java Minor and the kingdom of Lambri and sailed 150 miles to two islands, Nocuern and Angaman [the Nicobar and Andaman Islands]. The people here, who admittedly have a king, all worship idols yet are only one step removed from beasts. Males and females all go naked. But their woods abound with splendid, very valuable trees such as white and red sandalwood, Indian nut, clove, sappan and a variety of medicinal plants.

The other island, Angaman, is very large, has no king and the people are a primitive, bestial race having heads, eyes and teeth resembling those of dogs or wolves. They live off the land, eating rice, milk and flesh of every description, including, it has to be said, any person not of their own tribe whom they can lay their hands on. The island has many plants unknown in the West, including medicinal plants and Apples of Paradise.

Our next landfall was the island of Zeilan [Ceylon/Sri Lanka] just a little south of west. It is said that Zeilan, which has a circumference of about 2,400 miles, was in ancient times much larger, in fact the largest island in the world. The *Mappa Mundi* [map of the world] records it as being 3,600 miles in circumference but the northern gales, which are prodigiously violent, have eroded the mountains and caused them in places to fall away and sink into the sea, greatly reducing the island's original size.

Zeilan is ruled by a king called Sender-Naz who answers to no one. These people worship idols and, apart from a cloth wrapped round their waists, go about naked. There is no grain here apart from rice, and sesame from which they make oil. The people subsist on milk, rice and meat and a wine made from the date palm-like tree I described earlier. The best sappan wood of all is found here and the island also produces the most beautiful and valuable rubies in the world; likewise sapphires, topazes, amethysts, garnets and many other precious stones.

I was told that the king possesses a grand ruby, the largest ever seen, thick as a man's arm and a hand-span in length. In appearance it is like a glowing fire and, in truth, it is priceless. The Grand Khan heard about this gem and he sent ambassadors to the king offering to trade wealth equivalent to a city for it! The king replied that he would not sell it for all the treasure in the universe and, as it had been bequeathed him by his ancestors, he would never allow it to leave his kingdom. So Kublai failed this time to get his way, this in spite of the fact that the people of Zeilan are of a very timid disposition and not at all inclined to fight. If they ever have a need for soldiers they hire mercenaries from Muslim countries.

Our next port of call was Columbo in the province of Maabar,

60 miles to the west of the continent of India which, as I have already said, is the noblest and richest country in the world. It is governed by four kings of whom the principal is Sender-Bandi.

In the gulf between Zeilan and Maabar, where the water is no more than 10 to 12 feet deep, there is a pearl fishery. The trade operates as follows. A number of merchants form independent companies and hire a good number of boats large and small which are securely anchored over the fishing grounds. Skilled divers work off the boats bringing up in bags or nets tied to their bodies the oysters in which the pearls are enclosed. They dive until they are out of breath then return to the surface and, after a short interval, dive again. They keep this up all day. In the course of a season they bring up enough pearls to supply the demands of all the countries of the world.

The pearls taken from this fishery are round and of a good colour. The oysters are processed at Betala on the mainland. From there the pearl fishery extends some 60 miles to the south.

Because the gulf is infested with a kind of large fish [sharks] that often take divers, they employ magicians of a class of Brahmins so skilled in the diabolic arts that they are able to repel and stupefy these hunting fish and thus prevent them from doing mischief. And here's an interesting twist: legal pearl fishing only goes on in the day time, so the magicians call off their magic in the evenings, leaving the ravaging fish to guard the beds from any diver attempting to steal oysters by night. These magicians are also adept at enchanting all manner of other birds and beasts.

Pearl fishing goes on from April to the middle of May and the privilege of working the beds is in the gift of the king who gets a tenth of the returns. The magicians receive a twentieth part but that still leaves a considerable profit for the merchants.

When the Betala oyster beds have been exhausted the fleet moves on some 300 miles and there they fish from September and through October. As well as having his tenth share of all the crop the king reserves the right to choose all the large and well-shaped pearls. He pays liberally for them, however, so the merchants are quite happy with the arrangement.

This king wears hardly any more clothes than the rest of the population except that he is distinguished by various ornaments such as a collar set with jewels: sapphires, emeralds and rubies of immense value. Round his neck on a fine silken string he wears a necklace of a hundred and four very large and handsome rubies. He wears this necklace because every day his religion requires him to repeat a prayer in honour of his gods a hundred and four times. (The prayer actually consists of repeating the words 'pacauca, pacauca, pacauca' exactly that number of times.)

On each arm the king wears three gold bracelets adorned with pearls and jewels, and on three different parts of his legs are golden bands ornamented in the same manner. His fingers and the toes of his feet bear rings of inestimable value. To this king it is an everyday affair to wear such riches, especially as the precious stones and pearls are all the produce of his dominions.

And the king has at least one thousand wives and concubines. If he sees a young woman he fancies he has only to indicate that he wants to possess her – indeed, this was all that was required for him to have the wife of his brother. Discretion being the better part of valour the brother decided not to have a row about it, but I've heard that he repeatedly contemplated taking up arms against his brother. Their mother intervened, reportedly baring her breasts and warning: 'If you my children disgrace yourselves with acts of hostility towards each other I shall immediately sever from this body the breasts from which you drew nourishment.' In the face of this threat the row subsided.

The king is closely attended by many knights who go by the title 'Devoted Servant of his Majesty in this Life and the Next'. They attend him at court and on all other occasions and ride at his side in processions. They exercise considerable influence in every part of the realm – but this has its price. When the king dies and the ceremony of burning his body takes place, they all throw themselves in the same fire to be consumed with the royal corpse and thus accompany the king into the next life.

The following intriguing custom also applies here. When the

king dies his heir does not meddle with his treasure as this is judged to have been amassed by another. The son and heir is expected, on pain of being judged unable to govern, to show himself as capable of enriching the country as his father was. As a result of this tradition it's rumoured that vast wealth has been accumulated by successive generations.

No horses are bred in this country so the king and his three royal brothers import them annually from merchants in the Middle East at huge cost. The merchants bring in about five thousand a year and charge 500 saggi of gold per animal and they thus get very rich from the trade. In reality there is no one here vaguely qualified to look after them properly (administer medicines and the like) so no more than three hundred live the year out and they have to be replaced annually.

I think the climate here really does not suit the Arabian horse hence the problems of breeding and keeping them alive. Also they feed them on prepared meats and rice as there is no wheat grown here. I saw a large mare which had been well covered by a handsome stallion but her foal was small and sickly with distorted legs and completely unfit to be trained for riding.

Let me tell you about a custom they have here when a man has been tried for a crime and condemned to death. The condemned man has the right to declare that he will sacrifice himself to his idol! His relatives and friends gather round, place him in chains and hand him twelve strong, sharp knives. He is then carried into the city while the relatives proclaim loudly that here is a brave man about to die voluntarily for the love and devotion he bears his idol. When they arrive at the place where he would have been executed the condemned man cries out: 'I devote myself to death' (for such and such an idol) and quickly thrusts home the knives; one in each thigh, one into each of his arms, two in the stomach and two into the chest and the last into his heart which of course kills him. Thereafter, and with a great deal of rejoicing, his relatives burn the body and as a gesture of love for her husband a wife will throw herself on the fire and be consumed with him. Women who go through with this are much applauded by the community whereas women who shrink from it are despised and reviled.

Most people never kill oxen and no one will eat the meat. A particular caste of people, called *gaui*, do eat the meat but won't kill the animal. They seek out carcasses of animals that have died of natural or other causes. All the houses are daubed with cowdung.

It's the tradition to sit on the floor on carpets, the people believing that to sit on the ground is honourable as that's where we all come from and whither we will return. The *gaui* are the descendants of the tribe that slew St Thomas the Apostle and as a result no *gaui* may enter the building where his blessed body rests. Even if ten men were to use their strength to attempt to carry one of them there, the supernatural powers of the holy corpse would repel them.

These people are a very unwarlike race. They fight naked carrying only lances and shields. When they desire to eat the meat of sheep, other beasts and birds they get Saracens, who are not bound by the same religious laws, to do the killing for them.

Both men and women wash their whole bodies twice a day, in the morning and evening, and they do not eat or drink until they have performed their ablutions. To do so would be regarded as heresy.

I also observed that only the right hand is used for eating, the other being reserved for the more basic bodily functions. They each have their own cup and would never think of using someone else's. This cup is held above the head and the liquid poured into the mouth to ensure that on no account does the cup touch the lips. If they give a drink to a stranger it is never from their cup, instead they pour the wine or other beverage into his hands and he drinks that way.

Any offence in this country is punished with strict and exemplary justice, and they have an interesting law for dealing with debtors. Should a man renege on his debts by lying and evasion, the creditor may attach his person by drawing a ring round him. From this he dare not escape until he has paid off his debt or offered adequate security. Escape the ring and you are liable to the death penalty!

On my homeward journey I happened to witness a remarkable application of the law. The king owed some money to a foreign merchant who asked for payment repeatedly but for a long time was given nothing but vain assurances. One day when the king was out on horseback the merchant drew a ring around him and his horse. As soon as he realised what had happened the king stopped and did not dare leave the circle until the merchant had been paid what he was owed. The bystanders much admired the king's behaviour and pronounced him just for having so carefully observed the laws of the country.

They do not drink wine made from grapes here. Anyone who did would be regarded as untrustworthy. A similar prejudice applies to sailors, who are thought to be so hard up they are not to be trusted anyway!

They do not, however, regard fornication as a crime because it's so hot that everyone goes around naked. In fact the heat is so strong during June, July and August that were it not for the occasional falls of rain life would be insupportable.

Adepts in the science of physiognomy – the judgement of men as good or evil – abound here and these people can quickly spot the truth simply from a man's appearance. They also forecast events by observing certain beasts and birds, indeed they pay more attention to the flight of birds than anyone else in the world and will predict good or bad fortune from these movements.

In each and every day of the week there is an hour which they regard as unlucky and is called *choiach*. On these hours they refrain from making purchases or doing any kind of business, believing it would not be a success. These inauspicious hours are worked out for every year and recorded in books. When an infant is born the parents make a careful note of the day upon which the birth took place, also the phase of the moon, the name of the month, and the hour. It certainly seemed to me that astrology ruled their entire lives.

At the age of thirteen a son is put out of his father's home and with a small sum of money (about 20 groats) is expected to go his own way and find work to support himself. You see boys running about throughout the day attempting to turn a profit on some item or other. When it is the season for pearl fishing they trade with the fishermen for half a dozen or so small pearls which they then carry to the merchants who are too lazy to go out in the heat of the day. The merchants usually give them a little more than they paid for the pearls and in this way, dealing in many different articles, they soon become excellent traders. The money they earn is carried home and given to their mothers who at no cost to the family still provide them with their dinners.

In this country and throughout India the animals and birds are completely unlike our own, except for quails. There are bats as large as vultures and black as crows. They fly at great speed and never fail to catch their prey.

In the temples there are many idols to which the parents dedicate their daughters. Once dedicated these girls are expected to attend the temple and do whatever the priests demand of them to gratify the idol. Large bands of young women attend the temple to sing, play instruments and generally enhance the festivals of worship. Several times a week they carry food to the idol and believe it is consumed. The food is placed on a special table and left there for an hour while the girls sit around it singing and gesticulating in a very wanton fashion. After the idol has had time to take a meal – about an hour – they then proceed to eat the meal and they all go home.

I'm told that the justification for all these temple girls behaving in so lewd a manner is that the priests put it about that the male idols are out of favour with the female idols who won't sleep with them or even talk to them. If measures weren't taken to restore peace and harmony it would be the ruin of the temple. So the girls all dance naked with just a cloth round their waists chanting seductively to the idols in the hope of restoring good relations. It goes without saying that in this culture, gods and goddesses are assumed to sleep together.

The natives sleep on a kind of bedstead with draperies so ingeniously contrived they only have to pull a string to close the fine gauze curtains. Such screens are very necessary because there are tarantula spiders here with an awful bite; also fleas and other small vermin. The curtains still let in enough air for you to be able to sleep in this extreme heat, although only well-off people of rank can afford such luxuries. Everyone else sleeps on the open streets.

As I have said, St Thomas the Apostle was martyred in Maabar in this part of India. His body is kept in a small city which few merchants have cause to visit. But vast numbers of Christians and Saracens go there. Saracens worship him by the name of Ananias, meaning holy person, and he is regarded as a great prophet.

The Christians who make the pilgrimage collect earth of a red colour from the spot where he was slain and reverently carry it away with them in the belief that miracles can be performed with it. They also dilute it in water and give it to the sick as a cure for all kinds of disorders.

It's reported that in the year 1288 a fine rice harvest had resulted in a powerful local prince accumulating so large a portion of the crop that he needed somewhere to store it. Much against the wishes of its guardians he decided to commandeer a building reserved for pilgrims belonging to the Church of St Thomas. In spite of their protests the prince insisted on taking over the building. The following night the Holy Apostle appeared before him in a vision holding in his hand a small spear which he pointed at the throat of the prince and warned: 'If you do not immediately quit my house I shall put thee to a miserable death.'

The prince awoke in a state of desperate alarm, declared publicly that he had seen St Thomas in a vision, and immediately gave orders for the Saint's wishes to be complied with. I'm told that several miracles involving the Blessed Saint are now performed here daily.

The Christians in charge of the church possess a grove of trees producing Indian nuts from which they make a living. They have to pay the King's brother a tax of a groat per tree.

The death of St Thomas is said to have taken place in the following manner. He had retired to a hermitage where there were a number of peacocks (in which the country abounds) and was there engaged in prayer when an idolater of the tribe of the *gaui*, not seeing the holy man, shot an arrow at one of the birds which struck Thomas in the side. Mortally wounded, the Saint thanked the Lord for all his mercies, offered up his spirit, and died.

Strangely, the people of this province are not born as black as they appear. They regard black as the perfect skin colour and artificially dye themselves and their children by rubbing themselves with oil of sesame three times every day. They present all of their gods as jet black and the devil they paint white and believe all his demons are also of that colour.

Those of them who revere the ox take with them into battle some of the hair of a wild bull. This is attached to the manes of their horses and they believe it protects them from all manner of dangers. As you may imagine, wild ox hair sells for a high price in these countries.

I want now to take you on a journey 500 miles to the north to the kingdom of Murphili or Mosul. Diamonds are found in the mountains of this country and the people, all idolaters, live on rice, meat, fish and fruit. During the rainy seasons water pours down the rocks and valleys in violent torrents and when these have subsided the people go in search of diamonds and find lots.

I was told that in the summer also, when the heat is extreme and the mountains infested with snakes, they make a very tiring, dangerous journey into the mountains. Near the summits where there are deep valleys full of caverns they find yet more diamonds. Many eagles and white storks make their nests here feeding on the snakes. The diamond-hunters take up positions near the mouths of caverns and throw bits of meat down into the valleys. The eagles and storks swoop down after this bait and carry it off to their eyries in the high rocks. The natives climb up, drive the fierce birds off and recover the scraps of meat which quite often have diamonds stuck to them. Should the eagles have had time to eat the meat the natives note where they roost and in the morning find diamonds among their excreta.

Unfortunately, the local Christians never get their hands on these fine stones. They are taken directly to the Grand Khan or to the kings and chiefs of the country. The finest cotton in the whole of India is manufactured here and they also raise the largest sheep I have ever seen in the whole world. Everywhere there is a great abundance of food.

Leaving the place where the Blessed Saint Thomas rests and proceeding in a westerly direction you eventually enter the province of Lar where the Brahmins, who have spread throughout India, originated. They are without doubt the best and most honourable of merchants to be found anywhere. There is literally no way they can be induced to tell anything other than the truth even if their life depends upon it. They hate robbery and theft and, being content with just one wife, are remarkably virtuous. A foreign merchant, unfamiliar with practices of this country, can with confidence place himself in their hands. The Brahmin will manage his business, dispose of the goods and faithfully account for everything. Even should the foreigner fail to pay the usual gratuity it will never be demanded.

Brahmins eat and drink the wine of their country but do not kill animals themselves but get Mahometans to do it for them. You can recognise a Brahmin by a kind of a badge which consists of a thick cotton cord that passes over the shoulder and is tied under the arm in such a way that the cord spans the breast and the back.

They have an extremely rich and powerful king who loves pearls and valuable stones. When a merchant of Maabar presents one such to the king, the king simply takes their word as to its value and gives them twice the sum they claim to have paid for it. In the circumstances, you can imagine how many fine gems he gets offered!

The people, idolaters all, love sorcery and divination. Before making a purchase they first consult the shadow cast by their own body, only proceeding if their shadow is as large as they think it ought to be. If they are making a purchase in a shop and they see a tarantula (of which there are many), they note the direction it came from and regulate their business accordingly. If they are out and hear someone sneeze they go home and stay in! A certain vegetable [betel] is chewed to keep their teeth clean, promote digestion and is generally beneficial to health.

Among them is one caste, the Tingui [yogis], who devote themselves to the religious life and live very austerely. They go about completely naked believing that this is how they first came into the world and there is thus no shame in it. This even applies to their privates which, not being organs of sin for them, they have no need to be embarrassed at exposing.

They revere the ox and have a small figure of one, in gilt or brass, attached to their foreheads. They also make a paste from the burnt, ground-down bones of oxen with which they reverentially mark various parts of their body. They also put this paste on the foreheads of people with whom they are on cordial terms. They have extreme rules about what they eat. Fruit, vegetables, herbs or roots are not consumed until they become dry as they believe they all have souls. They make no use of spoons or plates, spreading their food instead on the dried leaves of Adam's Apples, also known as the Apples of Paradise. When they need to defecate they go to a beach by the sea, do their business then immediately scatter it in all directions in order that vermin should not breed in it, believing that if such vermin were later to starve to death it would be on their conscience and a grievous fault.

But these people do seem to live to a great age, some say to 150, and even though they sleep on the bare earth they enjoy good health and vigour.

I would like for a moment to refer back to the island of Zeilan with more details which I picked up when I visited the island on my homeward journey. It boasts a very high mountain so steep and rocky you can only climb it with the aid of iron chains fixed for that purpose to the rock face. By such means people do attain the summit and here the Saracens believe you may find the tomb of Adam. Idolaters, on the other hand, say this tomb contains the body of Sogomonbarchan [Buddha], who founded their religious faith and is their most holy person. He was the son of a king of the island who devoted himself to the aesthetic life, refusing to accept the kingdoms and other worldly possessions offered by the sovereign even though the king tried, using alluring women and every imaginable offer of gratification, to turn him from his resolve. Every one of these attempts at seduction proved to be in vain, however, until finally he fled alone to a mountain top where in celibacy and abstinence he eventually quit this mortal life. He is regarded by all idolaters as their saint.

His father, distraught and afflicted with the most desperate grief, caused an image to be created of gold and precious stones and ordered all the inhabitants of the island to worship it as a god. The worship of idols in these parts stems from that event, with Sogomonbarchan still regarded as the most superior of them all. People from many different parts of the island flock on pilgrimages to the mountain top on which he is said to be buried. Some of his teeth, hair and the bowl he used are preserved there. Similar pilgrimages are made by Saracens who, as I said, hold this to be Adam's burial place.

In 1281 Kublai heard from the Saracens that these relics existed and he sent ambassadors to demand them from the king of Zeilan. After a long and tedious journey these envoys obtained from the king two large back teeth, some hair and a handsome porcelain vessel. When the news reached Kublai that his men were returning with such valuables he ordered the people of Kabala to march out of the city to meet them and they were carried into his presence with great pomp and ceremony.

I'll now return to my account of the kingdom of Maabar. Its four kings are brothers. One of them, Astiar, rich in gold and jewels, ruled from the large city of Kael and always maintained a state of profound peace. As a result it is the favourite port for foreign merchants. Ships laden with merchandise and horses from places like Ormuz, Christie, Adem [Aden] and various parts of Arabia make this their favoured port of call.

The King maintains a splendid harem of at least 300 women!

All the people of these parts are addicted to chewing *tembul* leaf and they seem to get much gratification from the habit. Chewing produces a lot of saliva and they are forever spitting. Rich people have the leaf prepared with camphor, others with aromatic ingredients and quicklime. I've been told it's very good for you – but if you should seriously insult someone, they'll spit in your face! I'm not joking. This often results in the injured party going to the King and demanding the satisfaction of a duel. The King ensures the aggrieved parties are supplied with swords and small shields and they go at each other until one lies dead. Interestingly, they are forbidden to wound with the point of the sword.

Leaving Maabar and travelling 500 miles in a south-westerly direction you arrive in the kingdom of Koulam where there are a great number of Jews and Christians who still speak their own language. The king here is not subject to anyone.

Much good sappan wood is grown and in the wooded and also open part of the country there is pepper in great abundance. It is harvested in May, June and July and the vines which produce it are cultivated in plantations. Indigo dye of excellent quality is also produced here in large quantities. They take the indigo herb up by the roots and place it into tubs of water until the fibres rot and the pigmented juice is pressed out. This is then dried in the sun leaving a kind of paste which is cut into the small tablets of dye you see at home.

The summer heat is awful, almost intolerable, yet the merchants gather here from all parts of the world (especially south China and Arabia), so great are the profits to be made from imports and exports.

The kingdom has unique wildlife. There are tigers entirely black [panthers], various birds of the parrot species, some of them as white as snow, some with red feet and beaks, others of mixed red and azure hue. Even the domestic fowl have a peculiar appearance. You can say the same for the fruits that grow here. It's all thought to be the result of the intense heat.

Wine is made from the sugary sap of palms. It's exceedingly good and you get drunk a lot quicker on it than you do on wine made from grapes. The only grain is rice but there's a vast amount of it, in fact these people lack for nothing when it comes to food.

They have skilled astrologers and physicians.

All the people are very black and apart from a little cloth strung round their middles, go about stark naked. They're of a sensual nature and they marry their blood relatives, their mothers-in-law upon the death of their fathers and the widows of their deceased brothers. But I should make the point that such morality is common to all of India.

From Komori [Cape Cormorin], the most southern promontory of India, part of the Great Bear, invisible in China, can be seen just a cubit above the horizon. The country, largely uncultivated, is covered in forests in which live apes with the size, shape and appearance of men. There are also smaller, long-tailed monkeys, tigers and lynxes in great abundance.

Leaving this province and proceeding westwards for 300 miles you reach the kingdom of Deli where the king is not subject to anyone, the people are all idolaters and have their own distinctive language. There is no harbour for shipping but the place is served by a large river with a safe entrance and this also renders invasion by an enemy almost impossible. This is a great place for spices, particularly pepper and ginger. There is, however, a danger. If a ship is driven accidentally into the river mouth when it had not intended to dock, all the goods on board are seized. The authorities argue that as it was the merchant's intention to go elsewhere, the gods have driven them into the harbour in order that their property should be forfeited!

The vessels from Manji, which arrive before the end of the fine-weather season, try to get their cargoes shipped in a week or even less as these are very unsafe moorings. The sandbanks along the coast won't hold a ship in a heavy gale even when large wooden anchors are deployed.

The countryside is absolutely infested with tigers and other ferocious beasts.

Malabar on the Indian mainland is an extensive kingdom to the west with an independent king and a singular language. The North Star may be seen here about 6 feet above the horizon. Here and in the kingdom of Guzzerat [Gujarat], which is no great distance, numerous pirates operating a fleet of almost a hundred small boats plague the shipping lanes, seizing and plundering the ships that pass this way. The pirates take their wives and children with them for the whole of the summer and string their boats out in a line 5 miles apart. Thus twenty boats will prey from a line 100 miles long and nothing escapes them. Whenever a merchant ship hoves in sight of one of them, they signal to each other with smoke and then converge to capture the vessel. The crews of these plundered ships are rarely injured, in fact the pirates let them go back ashore in the hope that they will enrich themselves a second time.

There is a vast abundance of pepper, cubebs and Indian nuts in this kingdom and they make the most beautiful cotton stuffs to be found anywhere in the world. The ships from Manji come in here ballasted with copper and cargoes of gold brocades, silks, gauzes, gold, silver and bullion, together with many kinds of herbs not produced in Malabar. There are even merchants here who buy these goods for export to Adem from where they ship them on to Alexandria.

I should make the point that I don't have space to describe all the cities of India. They are too numerous and the account would prove tiresome. A last word on the pirates of Guzzerat who really are desperate characters. When these fellows come across a voyaging merchant they force him to drink sea water which has the effect of opening his bowels, as the pirates know that when a merchant sees them he will often attempt to conceal pearls or jewels by swallowing them.

Along with the abundance of ginger, pepper and indigo, cotton is harvested in large quantities from trees some 18 feet high. This cotton [kapok] is used for quilting rather than spinning. There are also trees of about twelve years of age which produce a cotton that may be spun into fine muslins and other stuffs of great delicacy.

Vast numbers of goat, buffalo, wild ox, rhinoceros and other hides are processed here and huge bundles of them shipped to different parts of Arabia. Coverlets are made from extremely soft, delicate leather dyed blue and gold and sewn with silver and gold thread. These are very popular with Mahometans. Cushions ornamented with gold wire in the form of birds and beasts originate here and you can pay as much as six silver marks for them. I think this is the best embroidery in the world.

Moving ever westwards you come to the large and noble kingdom of Kanan (when I speak of the west I am describing countries as I found them on a journey that began in the east). Again, they have an independent king and their own distinctive language. A great quantity of incense of a dark colour is produced and trading vessels in large numbers come here for it. Horses are also shipped from here for sale in other parts of India.

Travelling ever westwards, next is the kingdom of Kambaia, rich in indigo, cotton stuffs, wool and hides. You have to pay for these in gold, silver, copper or *tutty* (a metal made in Persia of zinc or antimony). Then west again to the kingdom of Servenath. I was warned that the priests in the temples here are the most perfidious and cruel in the world.

The last and very extensive kingdom in south India is Kesmorcan, again with its own independent king and language, but here the people are mostly Saracens who make their living from trade and manufacturing. It's a popular place for merchants who come by land and sea to trade here for the abundant meat and milk products.

We take to the sea again sailing southwards for about 500 miles to two islands 30 miles apart, one of which is inhabited by men, the other by women. These people are baptised Christians and practise the laws of the Old Testament.

The men visit the women's island and cohabit with them from March through April and May, each man occupying a separate house with his 'wife'. The rest of their year is spent on the Island of Men. The allocation of their offspring is complicated; sons stay with their mothers until they are twelve and are then sent to the fathers. Daughters remain on the women's island until they reach marriage-able age, whereupon they are offered to the visiting men. (I was told that this mode of living is occasioned by the peculiarities of the climate of the islands which would kill off any man – he would quite literally be sacrificing his life – if he attempted to live on the Island of Women all year round.)

These people have their own bishop who is subordinate to the see of Succotera. The men support their wives by planting grain, but the women prepare the soil and bring in the harvest. The islands have bountiful fruit and the men are expert fishermen, bringing home immense catches. Much fresh and salted fish is sold to traders who regularly visit the islands primarily for the large amount of ambergris on offer.

The island of Succotera (we are now off the East Coast of Africa) 500 miles to the south is huge and rich in all the necessities of life. Much ambergris, a substance voided from the gut of whales, is found on the beaches here. The substance is so valuable people hunt these fish using a barbed iron which they strike into the whale so firmly it cannot be drawn out. The harpoon has a long line that enables the fish to be found when it is dead. The whale is dragged to the shore, the ambergris extracted from the belly and several barrels of oil taken from the head.

The natives here, both male and female, all go about naked apart from a scrap of cloth round their waists. Their diet is rice, meat and milk. They are all Christians, having been duly baptised but their bishop, who has powers both temporal and spiritual, is not subject to the Church of Rome. Their patriarch resides in Baghdad and he appoints their bishop, or the bishop can be appointed by the people themselves subject to the confirmation of the patriarch.

This is a haven for pirates, who come here with their plunder knowing that it will be purchased without scruple (it having been taken from idolaters and Saracens) by the islanders.

Every ship bound for Adem calls here to buy large quantities of fish as well as a variety of cotton goods.

Succotera is a hotbed of sorcery and witchcraft, more so than anywhere else around, and this in spite of the fact that the archbishop has anathematised such practices and will excommunicate anyone who engages in them. Little account is taken of this interdict, however, and if a pirate ship should damage a local craft they put the pirates under a spell which makes it impossible for them to go on their way until they have put right the damage. The sorcerers also have the ability to change fair winds causing fleeing miscreants to be blown back to the island, and they can calm the sea or raise tempests at will as well as bring about shipwrecks. Honestly, this is just a small part of what they can do.

We turn now to the great island of Madagascar. Leaving Succotera and steering in a south to south-west direction for 1,000 miles will bring you to this huge, fertile island some 3,000 miles in circumference. The inhabitants are Saracens or Mohametans and they are ruled by four sheiks or more accurately 'elders' who divide the government between them.

Here are sold a vast number of elephants' teeth [ivory tusks] as the country abounds with elephants, as too does the island of Zenzibar [Zanzibar], where they are similarly exploited.

The principal food of the people is camel meat which is eaten all year round. Cattle are also raised, but camel meat is preferred as it is judged to be the most wholesome and palatable of any meat found in this part of the world. Red sandalwood grows plentifully and is cheap.

The natives collect ambergris from the beaches where it is washed up in huge quantities. They also have lynxes, tigers and a variety of other animals. Fine sport is also to be had from hunting antelope, stags, fallow deer and many birds which are quite different to the ones we get at home. Ships from many ports of the world come here laden with brocades and patterned silks, and there are fat profits for the merchants.

The only other island in these waters that is able to handle such shipping is Zenzibar. This is a result of a current that runs with prodigious velocity in the direction of the island. Vessels sailing from the coast of India can make Zenzibar in anything from twenty to twenty-five days but, as a result of the current running so strongly and constantly southwards, they struggle for three months on the return journey.

The people of Madagascar tell stories of an incredible bird that they call a *rukh* or *roc*, which makes its appearance at a certain time of year from the wild southern regions of the island. It is shaped like an eagle but is vastly larger. They are, in fact, so large and strong they can lift an elephant in their talons, dropping it to the ground from a great height in order to prey on the carcass. People who have seen the bird assert that it has a wingspan of almost 50 feet and feathers that are 24 feet in length and proportionately as thick.

When Kublai Khan heard of this extraordinary bird he sent envoys to the island (on the pretext of demanding the release of an ambassador who had been detained there) to investigate the wonderful tale. I am told that when they returned they were able to present the Grand Khan with the feather of a *rukh* said to measure some 43 feet with the quill a foot round! The Grand Khan was very pleased with this curio and the envoys were rewarded with valuable gifts. They also brought him the tusk of a wild boar, weighing 14lb, from an animal the size of a buffalo. Truly, Madagascar has a great deal of unique wildlife, such as the camelopard and wild ass.

Zenzibar island was reported to me to be 2,000 miles in circumference. Here the people are idolaters, have a distinctive language and pay tribute to no foreign sovereign. But I have to say they are the most ugly people in the world. They are large but strangely built with limbs disproportionate to their bodies, otherwise they would appear gigantic. They are very strong, one of them being capable of carrying the load of four or five ordinary people. Admittedly, he'd also require the food of five.

These people are black and apart from a cloth to hide their private parts go about naked. Their hair is sort of crisp and even when wetted stays tightly curled. They have large mouths, their noses turn up, their ears are long and their eyes are large and scary. They literally have the appearance of demons. The women are especially ugly having wide mouths, thick noses and large eyes. Their hands and heads are large and out of proportion and they have ugly breasts four times as large as other women's. These are in fact the most ugly women in the world.

Their diet consists of milk, meat, rice and dates. They have no grape vines but make a sort of wine from rice and sugar flavoured with spicy herbs. Actually, it's delicious and you can get drunk on it as easily as from the grape.

Elephants are found here in vast numbers and their teeth are an important item of trade. Did you know that because of the position of the female organs elephants copulate just like humans?

You find giraffes as well as the camelopard which is a very handsome creature. Gentle in manner with long high front legs and short hind legs, the neck is very long and the head small. They are a light colour with circular reddish spots, standing about 9 feet tall to the top of the head.

They have sheep very different to ours with white bodies and black heads, and dogs of a similar colour that are different in appearance to ours.

The trading ships come here all the time for the ivory and the ambergris, for the sea abounds with whales and a huge amount of it is washed up on the beaches.

The natives are actually very brave people, showing a complete contempt for death when they occasionally engage in battle. There are no horses on the island but they fight on camels and elephants, mounting wooden castles housing fifteen to twenty men armed with swords, lances and stones. Before going into battle the elephants are given copious draughts of wine which they say makes them more spirited and furious when they charge.

Just as I was obliged to describe only the main cities of India so also I must deal with the islands of the Indian sea, the number of which is frankly incredible. Merchants and pilots plying these waters have told me that there are no fewer than 12,700, a figure confirmed by the records of those who have navigated the Indian sea. This figure includes, of course, all the uninhabited as well as inhabited islands.

What I have termed Greater India extends from Maabar to Kesmacoram and comprises thirteen kingdoms of which I have described ten. Lesser India [in this era, eastern Africa] comprises eight kingdoms as well as those in the numerous islands.

Abascia [Abyssinia/Ethiopia] is a large country known as the Second India. The principal king is Christian and there are six others: three more Christians and three Saracens. I have been told that Christians imprint three marks with a hot iron on the face to distinguish themselves, one on each cheek and one on the forehead, a sort of second baptism by fire! The other religions mark themselves as well. Saracens have a mark on the forehead reaching down to the nose while the Jews, who are also numerous, have a mark on each cheek.

The capital of the principal Christian king is in the interior (at Aksum) while the dominions of the Saracens are towards the province of Adem. The people of Abascia were converted to Christianity by the glorious Apostle, St Thomas, who performed a number of miracles. He came to Abascia from Nubia where he also preached and converted the people. You will recall that he subsequently went on to Maabar in Greater India where, after making a host of converts, he was martyred and buried.

The Abascians are very good, brave soldiers as a result of endless wars with the Sultan of Adem, the Nubians and many others with whom they share a border. In fact, as a result of waging these ceaseless conflicts they are regarded as the best soldiers in this part of the world.

In the year 1288 the great Abascian Christian prince (Menelik) decided to make a personal visit to the Holy Sepulchre of Christ in Jerusalem, a pilgrimage also made each year by thousands of his subjects. But Menelik was talked out of making the journey by his ministers who decided it was too dangerous for him to travel through so many Saracen countries. Instead he sent a bishop, a man of great piety, who duly went to Jerusalem and said the prayers and made the offerings as Menelik had directed.

On his way home, however, the bishop was kidnapped by the Sultan of Adem who, when the bishop absolutely refused to embrace Islam, had him circumcised before sending him home. Upon hearing of the violent indignities that had been inflicted on his bishop, the King determined to exterminate the Sultan, assembled a great army and rode out at its head. The Sultan called up two neighbouring Saracen princes who put together a considerable opposing force, but to no avail. Menelik's army prevailed and he sacked and pillaged Adem in revenge for the insults he had suffered through the treatment of his bishop.

The province of Adem is ruled by a Sultan and the inhabitants here are all Saracens and detest Christians.

There are many towns and castles and it enjoys the advantages of a fine port to which come ships from India loaded with many spices and medicinal herbs. Merchants then ship these goods overland to Alexandria, or up the Gulf in smaller craft, a voyage of some twenty days.

Camels are used to carry the goods all the way overland to the

River Nile from the various ports of call where they are again put aboard small vessels, called *jerms*, which go to Cairo and then via an artificial canal known as the Kalizene to Alexandria. This is the shortest route from Cairo to Alexandria. It's from Adem that the merchants ship a great number of Arabian horses to all the islands and kingdoms of India. They fetch high prices and earn the merchants fat profits.

The Sultan of Adem is immensely rich from the import and export duties he levies on the India trade. Adem is in fact the main centre for all the commodity trade in the area and its port is the most popular.

I was told that the Saracens so loathe the Christians that the first time the Sultan besieged the city of Acre [then in Venetian hands] and took it, the town of Adem supplied him with 30,000 horses and 40,000 camels. The Sultan also controls (I should say with exemplary justice) the city of Escier 45 miles away to the south-east. Here the people are Mahometans. Within the city's administrative control are a great number of towns and castles and it has a good port also used by many ships from India. The trade in excellent horses is also carried on here very profitably, with these horses commanding considerable prices in India.

In this district white frankincense of the highest quality is produced, distilled drop by drop from a small tree that resembles a fir. A tree is 'tapped' by paring away the bark to allow the frankincense to seep slowly out and afterwards become hard. As a result of the extreme heat of the climate, trees seep even when you don't cut them.

Dates are produced in abundance from groves of palm trees but no grain apart from rice and millet is cultivated in this country. They have to import all their wheat. There is no wine made here from grapes but they produce a delicious beverage from rice, sugar and dates.

They have a small breed of sheep with ears unlike those of other sheep; they have small horns where you would expect the ears to be. Lower down towards the nose are two small orifices that serve the purpose of ears. The countryside is dry, sun-scorched and arid and produces virtually no vegetables, but they have accustomed their sheep, cattle and horses to eat dried fish which is consumed with relish.

The town of Kalayati, some 50 miles from Dafar to the south-east is a substantial place on the Gulf. The people are Mahometans and subjects of the Regent of Melik. Melik has the reputation of being so strong and well situated for defence it has never been successfully invaded. Its harbour is good and many trading ships from India come here to sell piece-goods and spices to great advantage, as there are a number of towns and castles within range creating a steady demand. The ships return to India laden with thoroughbred horses.

There is a fortress so well positioned at the entrance to the Gulf of Kalatu no vessel may come in without permission. Every so often the Regent, who gives allegiance to the King of Kermain, reneges on his dues when he thinks the King has made unreasonable demands on him. An army is then routinely despatched to enforce the demands, but the Regent simply quits Ormuz and makes his stand at Kalatu secure in the knowledge that no ships may come or go without his say-so. This restriction of considerable revenues and duties usually has the effect of bringing the King to heel.

The heat is so awful here that all the houses have been cunningly fitted with means of ventilation which let in air to the various floors of the apartments. I can't tell you what relief these provide, in fact without them it would be impossible to live here.

We are nearly home. Before bringing this account to a close, however, I think I should reflect further on some of the places and people I frankly overlooked earlier.

As you now know, in the northern parts of the world there are many Tartars under a chief named Kaidu who is a descendant of Genghis Khan and a distant relative of Kublai. I've mentioned him before. He rules very independently and his people are genuine

Tartars and retain the Tartar language, and observe the customs and traditions of their ancestors. They worship a god, Naagai, the god of the earth and all things born of it. Images and idols are made of this god of the material called felt.

These Tartars do not shut themselves away in forts and towns but live all the while on the open plains, in the valleys and the woods in which their country abounds. As no cereals are grown they subsist solely on a diet of milk and meat and they live in perfect harmony, following the orders of their king to the letter. He in turn holds two things dear: the preservation of peace, and unity among his subjects. I personally regard these as the essential duties of a sovereign.

True to the Tartar tradition they keep huge herds of horses, sheep and other domestic animals.

In the far northern districts are found white bears of prodigious size, some almost 10 feet long. There are also black foxes, wild asses in great numbers and a small animal having the most delicate of fur which they call *rodes* and we know as sable. Then you have 'Pharaoh's mice' [marmots], which are small beasts of the marten or weasel family. There are incredible swarms of these but the Tartars, using ingenious traps, catch them easily.

To reach these latitudes involves a fourteen-day journey across an uninhabited plain featuring innumerable lakes and streams. It is in fact a huge marsh. The long winter here means that apart from a few months when the sun melts the ice and reduces everything to mud, it is entirely frozen over and thus much easier to cross in winter. To encourage merchants to come and buy their furs (the only item of trade) the Tartars have built wooden houses high above the marsh at the end of each day's travel. These are staffed by people whose job it is to accommodate the weary traveller and see him safely on his way. Without these hostelries I very much doubt you could cross this region.

The natives themselves travel in a vehicle that is an invention of the mountain people of the region. Called a *tragula* it is a kind of sledge with curved runners ideally adapted to crossing the ice. They are pulled by animals that look like dogs (they could well be dogs), but are as large as ponies. They are exceptionally strong and used to towing such loads. Six of them in pairs can pull a driver, a merchant and all his goods. The dog teams are replaced daily. The merchant, this time loaded with furs for sale in the West, returns in the same way.

I should now like to return briefly to those countries that go by the name 'The Heart of Darkness'.

Beyond the most distant reaches of the domains of the Tartars there are lands stretching to the utmost boundaries of the north and are described thus because for most of the long winter the sun is invisible. Conditions resemble those of our dawn, a time, if you think of it, when you can see and yet not be seen.

The men of the lands of darkness are tall but have very pallid complexions. They have no society governed by a king or a prince and live without laws or customs as brutishly as nature made them. They are slow and stupid and the Tartars often plunder their stock and possessions. These raids are undertaken without fear of detection in the dark time and the raiders then employ a remarkable method of finding their way home through the gloom. They ride only mares with young foals!

The foals accompany their dams to the edge of the Tartar lands and there are left in the charge of grooms while the raiders push on into the gloom. When the work of darkness has been accomplished and the Tartars need to find their way back to the land of light, they lay their bridles on their mares' necks and simply rely on them to find their way home. Guided by the maternal instinct the mares make their way unerringly back to their foals, thus carrying the Tartars safely home.

Vast numbers of ermine, martens, arcolini, foxes and other furry creatures with more delicate coats (like sable) are hunted by the polar tribes in the continual daylight of the summer months. The raiding I have just described results from one not being able to find these finer furs in Tartar lands. The furs are sold very profitably in neighbouring countries and some, I'm told, even find their way to Russia.

A word about Russia which I have been told by people who have been there. It's vast, is divided into many provinces and borders on that region which I have just described as the Heart of Darkness. There are also Christians in Russia who follow the rituals of the Greek branch of Mother Church.

The men are well put together, tall and fair, while the womenfolk have light complexions, wear their hair long and are also nicely proportioned.

The eastern side of Russia borders the Kingdom of the Western Tartars and pays tribute to them. The fur trade is based in Russia and within its borders you find vast quantities of ermine, arcolini, sable, marten, fox and other skins. There is also a considerable trade in wax.

My information is that Russia extends as far as the Northern Ocean and is a very cold place indeed. Gerfalcons and peregrines, as mentioned before, are taken from here in huge numbers for trade elsewhere in the world.

Returning now to our homeward journey. We arrived eventually in Greater Turkey which is the kingdom ruled by Kaidu, the mighty great-grandnephew of the Grand Khan, and is a land of numerous cities and castles. Kaidu is a very grand lord indeed. The people are superb Tartar warriors, which is no wonder considering that they are all men raised to war. I tell you, this Kaidu has never given an inch to the Grand Khan without putting up a fierce fight.

Their troubles began with Kaidu demanding a share of the territories of Cathay and Manji that Kaidu and Kublai had obtained by conquest. The Grand Khan said he was quite willing to give Kaidu his share as he had done with his other sons if he, Kaidu, would attend court whenever he was sent for, take his counsel and generally obey him like his other sons and barons. Kaidu, who did not trust the Grand Khan, rejected these conditions and said he would gladly promise his obedience at home but would not go to court for anything because he was afraid of being murdered. This impasse led to some almighty wars. In the end the Grand Khan mounted a military blockade of

Kaidu ostensibly to stop Kaidu attacking his people, whereupon Kaidu retaliated with the first of many attacks on the Grand Khan's forces.

Kaidu could readily call up a hundred thousand cavalry, expert horsemen and all battle-hardened. Also he had under his command many barons of the lineage of Genghis Khan, the founder of the Tartar empire.

Let me tell you something about the fighting methods of these people. When they go to war every man carries sixty arrows, thirty small ones for long-range work and thirty large ones with a broad-bladed tip which are used at close range to strike the foe in the face or arms, to cut the strings of their bows and generally do the utmost damage. Once having discharged all their arrows they go into the attack with swords and heavy maces in what can be a very bloody exchange.

So, in the year 1266, we have King Kaidu and his cousin Jesudar attacking in this fashion two of the Grand Khan's barons (who were also Kaidu's cousins) with a vast army. One of the barons, Tabai or Ciban, was the son of Ciagatai, a brother of Kublai Khan, who had been baptised a Christian. The barons were also able to field a large army, bringing the total of Kaidu's horsemen in the field to about two hundred thousand. The battle was hard fought and many were killed on both sides. Finally, however, the army of Kaidu was victorious and a considerable slaughter followed. Kaidu's cousins, thanks to their superior horses, escaped unharmed.

Kaidu's pride and arrogance now knew no bounds and although he took his army home and kept the peace for some years he was soon assembling another large force. He had also received intelligence that Kublai's son, Nomogan, was at Carcorum and with him was George, the son of Prester John, at the head of a great army of horsemen. Kaidu immediately marched on Carcorum.

So here we had two mighty armies, led on the one side by the formidable Kaidu and on the other by two men from a great fighting tradition. Their army numbered no less than sixty thousand horse, neither were they lacking in courage and determination. Nomogan and George advanced and pitched their camp in a plain about 10 miles from Kaidu's position and there they remained preparing for the coming battle for three days. The armies were about equal, with each man armed with a bow and arrows, a sword, shield and mace.

The armies were split into six squadrons of ten thousand men, each with its own commander. When the time came to do battle they all sang and sounded instruments – it was wonderful to hear – until a loud cymbal clash. The troops seem to draw great solace from the custom of singing and playing on two stringed instruments, but as soon as the cymbal, the *nacar*, sounds they immediately enter the fray. In an instant the air is filled, just like rain, with arrows, and many men and horses are struck down dead. The very thunder of the gods could not have been heard above such shouting and noise of battle!

They fought as if they were mortal foes, every man no sooner having loosed one arrow than he prepared to fire the next, until they had none left; then they stowed their bows back in their cases and went at each other savagely with swords and maces. The ground was soon covered with bodies and this fierce and dreadful encounter turned into a slaughter. And the outcome? Complete stalemate!

Kaidu especially performed great feats of arms, indeed but for his personal involvement in the battle his army would have lost its nerve and been routed. Similarly, on the other side the heirs of Kublai and Prester John fought with great bravery. The battle lasted until nightfall and in spite of all their efforts neither army could drive the other from the field. There were corpses everywhere and many a wife was that day made a widow and many a child orphaned.

When the sun went down both sides quit fighting and went back to camp to sleep. The following morning at daybreak, having heard that Kublai had despatched a vast army to reinforce his opponents, Kaidu called his remaining men to arms and hurried home. Their opponents were so weary from the previous day's encounter that they could make no attempt to follow, so Kaidu left unmolested. They retired to Samarcand in Greater Turkey.

The Grand Khan was now furious with Kaidu for continuously invading his territory and injuring so many of his people. Only the fact that he was his nephew saved Kaidu from an unpleasant death. Eventually, however, they were obliged to settle for another uneasy peace.

Let me now tell you about Kaidu's remarkable daughter, Aigiarm, which means 'shining moon', who was reputed to be immensely strong and fierce. In fact there was not a young man in the kingdom who could subdue her, indeed she took pride in beating up all her would-be suitors. Of course, her father the King was anxious that she should marry but she declined, saying she could never love a man who could not overcome her by force. The King ended up giving her written permission to marry whomsoever she wished.

So Aigiarm caused it to be proclaimed in different parts of the Tartar world that if any suitor fancied wrestling with her and could defeat her she would accept him as her husband. Many came to try their luck from all parts of the land and these trials of strength were staged with great ceremony. The King took his seat in the principal hall of the palace together with a large company of eminent citizens of the land, both men and women. Then came in the King's daughter in a richly adorned dress of *cendal* and stood in the centre of the hall. The terms were that if the contender could throw the Princess to the floor he could have her; if he failed he had to give her one hundred horses. I'm told that in this way the girl built up a collection of one thousand horses!

People came to think of her as a giantess because she was so tall and strong. At last in the year 1280 a very beautiful young man, the son of a rich king, accompanied by a rich retinue and one hundred horsemen, came to King Kaidu's court to try his luck with the lady. The King was delighted, seeing the prince as an ideal son-in-law (he was the son of the King of Parma) and the King told his daughter that this might be the occasion to 'take a dive'. Aigiarm replied that nothing in the world would persuade her to do such a thing. So Kaidu and his Queen were obliged to take their places in the great hall surrounded by their most influential friends and courtiers. In came the Prince boasting that if he lost he would forfeit all of his one thousand horses – and was then soundly trounced!

After this the King accepted the inevitable and took his daughter with him into battle and there was not a soldier in the land who could equal her bravery. The story also has a happy ending. One day in the heat of battle, the Princess spotted a horseman she fancied, carried him off to her own people and, so far as I know, lived happily ever after.

The lands to the east of Kaidu, comprising many provinces, were commanded by Abaga, known as the Lord of the East. His extensive domains extended east as far as the famous forest, the 'Arbor Secco', which is mentioned by Alexander the Great in his book on the wonders he saw on his eastern conquests. This land had been much ravaged by Kaidu and eventually Abaga sent his son Argon with a great army of horsemen as far as the River Ion to the region of the Arbor Secco and there they remained to protect it from Kaidu's raiders.

Across the whole of the plain of the Arbor Secco they garrisoned many cities and towns. King Kaidu could not countenance this, so he in turn deployed his own large mounted army under the command of a wise and prudent man, his brother Barac. A long march brought him to the Ion where his troops went immediately into battle and a very fierce engagement resulted which ended in his defeat. In the rout, which involved retreating over the river, a great slaughter ensued.

Soon after these events Argon heard that his father Abaga had died and he left immediately with his army for court, a journey of some forty days, to claim the sovereignty. But there was another contender for the throne, Abaga's brother, Acomet Soldan, and when he heard that Argon was on his way to claim his inheritance he resolved to get to the court first and take over the throne. This he duly did, finding an enormous amount of treasure which he distributed so lavishly among Abaga's barons and knights that he completely bought their loyalty and they all swore allegiance to him. It has also to be said that Acomet Soldan turned out to be a very good ruler and was soon loved by everyone.

Apart from Argon, of course! When finally he arrived at court at the head of a vast army Acomet Soldan was ready for him, having assembled a huge number of cavalry all of whom declared they would march on Argon and put him swiftly to death.

At the head of an army of sixty thousand Acomet Soldan marched for ten days to confront Argon and his troops. When intelligence reached him that Argon was just five days' away with an army of equal size, Acomet picked a place in the great plain which he thought would give him the military advantage and addressed his men as follows:

Lords. As I think you know I sought to be liege lord of Abaga's kingdom because I was the son of his father and I assisted in the conquest of all the lands and territories he possessed. True, Argon was my dead brother's son and some say the succession is rightfully his, but with due respect I say that's wrong. My generosity alone allowed Abaga to hold the whole kingdom when I was entitled to half of it and it's only right that I should retain the whole now. So pray for our victory. I promise you that all I want from this battle is fame and honour. You may have the profits and the goods from all the lands and provinces. I know that you are all wise, just men and you act from honour and the good of us all.

To a man they declared that they would not desert him and would stand by him while they had life in their bodies. They further promised to deliver Argon into his hands.

In Argon's camp the news that his uncle was waiting with so large an army met with considerable alarm, but Argon felt he had no choice but to show courage and determination before his men. He said to them:

Fair brothers and friends, you know how tenderly my father loved you, treated you as brothers and sons, and how you conquered and gave him the lands he possessed. You know that I am the son of he who loved you so much and also loved you as though you were his own body. It is just and right, therefore, that you should support me against one who seeks to disinherit us all. He is not even of our Law – he has abandoned it to become a Saracen worshipping Mahomet – and it ill becomes us to let Saracens rule over Tartars. You should draw courage and resolve from all this and do your utmost to prevent it happening. Be valiant and make every effort to win this battle so that the sovereignty may belong to you and not to Saracens. Justice is on our side and we will prevail. Our enemies are in the wrong. Do your duty.

Argon's barons and knights heard his words and said they would prefer death in battle to defeat. One of them rose and replied:

Fair Sir Argon, I will be spokesman for the men and assure you that we know you speak the truth and that we will not fail you for as long as there is life in our bodies. We would rather die than not be victorious. We have confidence in our ability to conquer the enemy because of the justice of your cause and the wrongs which have been done to you. So let's go against them right away and so acquit ourselves in battle all the world will talk of our deeds.

The entire army clamoured to go into battle right away and first thing the next morning they marched to within 10 miles of Acomet's camp. From there Argon sent two trusted emissaries of very advanced age to Acomet; they went to his tent where they found him surrounded by a great company of his barons. Acomet knew these two elders and received them courteously, bade them welcome and invited them to be seated.

The message they brought to Acomet went as follows:

Your nephew questions your conduct in depriving him of the sovereignty and that you have come to meet him in mortal combat. This is not the way an uncle ought to act towards his nephew. So he pleads with you, as a good uncle and father, to restore to him that which is rightfully his. There is no need for this battle. He will honour you and you will be lord of all the land, under him.

But Acomet's reply was uncompromising.

What my nephew says amounts to nothing. The land is mine not his. I conquered it with his father. Go and tell my nephew that if he so desires, I'll make him a great lord with more than enough land. He'll be like my son, the highest in the land, after me. Otherwise – and be sure he gets this message – I'll do all in my power to put him to death and that's my final word on the subject.

The emissaries insisted on knowing that this was really Acomet's final word on the matter. He said it was and there would be no other as long as he lived.

When Argon heard this he was enraged and made it clear to everyone that he believed he had been injured and insulted by his uncle and vowed never to hold a scrap of land until he had taken vengeance in a manner the whole world would hear about. 'Let us go out tomorrow,' he declared, 'and put these faithless traitors to the sword.' And so it came to pass. Argon arranged his troops in good battle order, advanced the following morning and soon met Acomet, his forces similarly well disposed.

The battle began in the traditional way with a shower of arrows, so thick they seemed like rain from heaven. Everywhere men were thrown from their horses and the cries and groans of the fallen were dreadful to hear. Then the swords and maces were brought into bloody play. The slaughter on both sides was huge and although Argon himself displayed extraordinary bravery, an example to all his men, it was all in vain. The day went against him and he was forced to flee, closely pursued by Acomet's army who slaughtered many more in the rout. And Argon himself was soon captured, whereupon the chase was abandoned and the exultant victors returned to their camp.

Now came a great turn of fate! Acomet, a man who liked his sensual pleasures, ordered Argon to be locked away and guarded while he returned to court to celebrate his victory in the company of the many fair ladies he had there. The command of the army was left to a grand *melic* or chieftain under strict orders to follow him back to court in short marches that would not tax his exhausted troops.

In the camp, however, was a great Tartar baron, an older man, who took pity on Argon, regarded all that had happened as an act of wicked disloyalty, and vowed to do his utmost to set him free. He began by personally influencing many of the other barons to see things his way and, because of his great age and a reputation for justice and wisdom, soon had them on his side and accepting his orders.

The gentleman's name was Boga and the other conspirators in the enterprise were Elcidai, Togan, Tegana, Taga, Tiar Oulatai and Samagar. Accompanied by them, Boga went to the tent where Argon was confined, told him that they had repented, and that they intended to set him free and recognise him as their lord.

At first, Argon was very angry, thinking that they'd come to mock him.

'Fair lords,' he said, 'you sin greatly in making me the object of your mockery. Be satisfied with the wrong you have already done me, your rightful lord. Go away!'

'Lord, we're not here to mock you,' Boga protested, and there and then took an oath affirming him as their rightful lord and master. For his part Argon swore to forgive them. With these mutual oaths properly sworn, they freed Argon who took them to the tent of the *melik* and ordered Boga and his men to riddle it with arrows, killing him.

Confident of his sovereignty, Argon now gave orders for the army to march on the court. Acomet was still partying when a messenger brought him the news that Argon was on his way with the whole force. He announced that the *melik* was dead and he was sure the same fate awaited Acomet.

Acomet was taken totally by surprise and knew not what to do or say. But he gathered his wits, ordered the messenger not to repeat the news to anyone, at the same time ordering his most trusted followers to arm themselves and saddle up. Telling no one where he was going, he took the road to the Sultan of Babylon believing that there he would be safe.

His objective could only be gained by way of a pass, but when six days later he tried to cross it, the men guarding it recognised him and realised he was fleeing for his life. The guards, loyal to Argon, outnumbered Acomet's party and they decided to arrest Acomet even though he tried to buy them off with offers of a great deal of treasure.

Acomet was placed under a strong guard and marched for three days back to court where he was handed over to Argon. Acomet's capture brought Argon the greatest joy imaginable. He immediately called his army to gather and there, before everybody, Acomet was cut down. Argon ordered that Acomet's body be disposed of in such a way as to ensure that it would never be seen again. Indeed, no one has seen or heard of it since.

Argon recovered his crown in 1286 and ruled for six years, when, I'm reliably advised, he was poisoned. An uncle called Quiacatu then took over the throne, Argon's son, Casan, being judged to be too far away in Arbor Secco, but his uncle making it clear he ruled only in a caretaker role to keep the kingdom safe from its enemies. As his father before him, Casan declared he would return as soon as he could. Quiacatu, fond of sensual pleasures, took Argon's wife and made her his own as well as a great number of other women. He too was then poisoned!

In 1294 Argon's brother Baidu snatched the throne and this time Casan was really furious and decided it was time he abandoned the lands of the Arbor Secco and went home to claim his heritage. Baidu and Casan's armies met after ten days of forced marches and after a fierce battle Baidu was killed and his army routed. So in 1294 Casan became king and rules the Eastern Tartars to this day.

The founder of the Western Tartar empire was the great king Sain who conquered Russia and Comania, followed by Alania, Lac, Mengier, Zic, Gucia and Gazaria who united the Western Tartars under one government. He was succeeded by Patu, Berca, Mongotimur, Totamangu and Toctai who is the reigning monarch.

In the year 1261 the most savage war in the history of the Tartars erupted between the Tartars of the west, ruled by King Berca, and of the east where King Alau was on the throne. This dispute was, inevitably, over border territory.

Both declared their intention of occupying the land, each daring the other to stop him. Within six months they had vast armies, approaching three hundred thousand men, all very well equipped for war, indeed there had never been an assembly of troops to equal this. Alau now set out for the disputed lands with his vast army, riding for many days without meeting any opposition until they entered a great plain between the areas known as the 'Iron Gates' and the Sea of Serain, where they encamped in good order with many a rich pavilion and tent.

Alau waited for Berca to make the first move. He was now occupying the disputed border area and waited to see what would happen. Berca arrived with some three hundred and fifty thousand men and in his traditional battle speech he emphasised this advantage of numbers and promised them victory.

Alau was aware of the odds against him but told his men they were more experienced and would prevail. Intelligence had also been received by Alau that the attack would be launched three days hence and he urged his vast assembly of Eastern Tartars to be ready to die rather than dishonour themselves. On the morning of the battle Alau rose very early and showed great skill in the disposition of his mighty army, dividing them into thirty squadrons of one thousand horsemen, each very well led. Then they advanced half the distance to the other camp.

King Berca had also arranged his men into squadrons of one thousand but he had thirty-five of them. These advanced to within half a mile of the enemy. This was fine fighting ground and these were impressive armies commanded by the two most powerful warriors in the world. They were also related, both being of the lineage of Genghis Khan.

Then the *nacar* gongs sounded and the arrows flew so that you could hardly see the sky and many were slain, both man and horse. Hand-to-hand fighting with maces and swords followed in a battle that was so fierce the noise was louder than the thunder of heaven. The ground became covered with corpses and red with blood. Both the kings fought very bravely and their men followed their example, keeping on till dusk until Berca began to give way. Alau's men pursued the fleeing enemy, furiously cutting them down without mercy.

After a short chase Alau recalled his men and they returned to their encampment, laid down their arms, dressed their wounds and were so weary they sought their tents and slept. Next morning Alau caused the dead to be buried, friend and foe alike. The losses were so huge it is beyond my ability even to estimate them.

Similar difficulties to these also plagued the succession of a powerful King of the Western Tartars called Mongotimur. His natural successor, Prince Tolobunga, was murdered by a chieftain known as Totamangu with the assistance of another Tartar king, Nogai. Totomangu ruled for a short time until a very able and prudent man by the name of Toctai was chosen king.

When the two sons of Tolobunga grew to maturity they assembled a fair-sized army and presented themselves at King Toctai's court demanding that Nogai, the last living conspirator in the murder of their father, be brought to justice. Toctai agreed with them and Nogai was summoned to court.

Nogai laughed at the two messengers from the court of King Toctai and said he would not go. Enraged, Toctai told Tolobunga's sons that if Nogai didn't come to him, he would raise an army and destroy Nogai. Back went the two messengers to Nogai and related this ultimatum, again to no avail. Nogai put together a huge army, albeit not as large as the army Toctai could field (it numbered over two hundred thousand) because he was not so powerful a king. Tolobunga's sons, with a fair-sized company of horsemen, joined him.

When battle commenced it soon became apparent that Nogai's men, who numbered only one hundred and fifty thousand were much the more experienced and the army of Toctai was routed with a terrible slaughter of some sixty thousand of his men. Toctai and the two sons of Tolobunga, who had fought very valiantly, escaped.

Postscript

And there, patently exhausted by the never-ending Tartar wars, Marco Polo brings the story of his incredible journey to a close. Many translators share my view that this is a poor way to end so epic a tale. There is even a short epilogue in a Tuscan version dating from the early fourteenth century which excuses Marco's abrupt ending by having him say:

> I refrain from telling you of this (the Black Sea and the Provinces which lie around it) because it would be tedious to recount what is daily recounted by others . . . Venetians, Genoese and Pisans who sail these waters every day.

There is a similar, arguably as dubious, final chapter that closes the famous Marsden translation, which runs as follows:

> And now you have heard all that I can tell you about the Tartars and the Saracens and their customs, and likewise about the other countries of the world as far as my travels and knowledge extend. Only we have said nothing whatever about the Greater Sea and the provinces that lie round it, although we know it thoroughly. But it seems to me needless to speak about places that are visited by other people every day. For there are so many who sail all about the world constantly.
>
> Of the manner in which we took our departure from the Court of the Grand Khan you have heard at the beginning of the book, in that Chapter where we told of the difficulties that Messer Maffeo and Messer Nicolo and Messer Marco had about getting the Grand Khan's leave to go; and in the same Chapter is

related the lucky chance that led to our departure. And you may be sure that but for that chance, we should never have got away in spite of all our trouble, and never to have got back to our country again. I believe it was God's pleasure that we should get back in order that the people might learn about the things that the world contains.

Thanks be to God! Amen! Amen!

This postscript has the ring of an end-note appended by some politically correct cleric, perhaps rather nervous of the magical, exotic and, in places, salacious manuscript he has just translated. Elements of Marco's story would probably have been regarded as heretical. Others would have found the manuscript morally dubious, if not downright profane. John Frampton's Elizabethan translation entitled *The Travels of Marco Polo* actually leaves out the twelve pages of text describing the seemingly never-ending wars between Genghis's descendants. Frampton chooses to close with the dramatic tale of the Tartar raids for rare furs into the Heart of Darkness in the frozen northland. (I have decided to include Marco's final notes on the troubled royal successions, but I must admit they are rather tedious.)

So, must we end this incredible tale on a note of anti-climax? Does Marco just run out of steam in spite of his dying protestations that he recounted only half of what he saw? Actually a sensational story does end the book. Both Marco and his co-author, Rustichello the romance-writer, for some reason only hint at an exciting end in their Introduction, but it very properly belongs here. It is the riveting tale of what happened when the Polos reached Venice and attempted to enter their old home.

On a dark and stormy night [in Venice] in the year 1295, a loud banging was heard on the front door of a tall house in the Corte Sabbionera. Fearful of burglars the inhabitants (distant relatives of Marco Polo) at first refused to open the door. But they had made the mistake of drawing the bolt and the intruders fought their way in.

The relatives found themselves confronting three ragamuffins dressed in tattered clothes of oriental design, bearded and speaking Italian in a guttural, halting style as if newly learned. They had huge packs and the three insisted that this was their house and that they were Nicolo, Maffeo and Marco Polo, who had long been given up for dead. A family conference was called, with other relatives coming from all over the city, and the Polos managed to convince their family that they were not impostors.

The story they told astounded the family and word quickly spread throughout Venice. Marco, much the youngest of the three whose life had been the most travelled and exciting, became famous overnight.

They staged an exotic party to finally confirm their claims. Before the grand dinner the travellers had presented themselves in cloaks of crimson satin – which they then removed and had the rich cloth cut into pieces for their guests! During the course of the meal, Nicolo, Maffeo and Marco disappeared again, returning this time in robes of silken velvet which were again cut up and passed around. The process was repeated three times in all, with the travellers explaining that this was all in strict accordance with Mongol custom.

The table was then cleared and the servants asked to leave the room. Marco Polo then produced the ragged street clothes the travellers had worn upon their arrival and, taking up a sharp knife, cut the seams and pleats. A shower of rubies, sapphires, diamonds, emeralds and other jewels, all chosen for their size and value, cascaded on to the dinner table and finally convinced the company that the men were indeed the long-lost Polos – and that they were very rich!

This splendid tale was told by the first print-editor of a Marco Polo manuscript, Giovanni Battista Ramusio, who in his *Collection of*

Voyages and Travels says he was told of it by Senator Haspara Malpieo, 'a gentleman of very great age and a Senator of great virtue and integrity, whose house was on the canal of San Marino . . . and he said he had heard it from his father and grandfather, and from other old men among the neighbours'. And why not?

Let us give the poet and Polian scholar, John Masefield, the final word:

It is difficult to read Marco Polo as one reads historical facts. One reads them as one reads romance. The East of which he writes is the East of romance.

In the East of romance there grows the 'tree of the sun', a sort of landmark or milestone at the end of the great desert. The apples of the sun and the moon grow on that tree. Darius and Alexander fought in its shade. These are the significant facts about the tree according to Marco Polo. We moderns who care little for any tree as soon as we can murmur its Latin name, have lost wonder in losing faith. Marco Polo, almost the first European to see the East, saw her in all her wonder, more fully than any man has seen her since.

Index

(TE) indicates part of Tartar empire

233

INDEX